# GITANJALI

## Tagore's other titles in Srishti

My Boyhood Days

Mashi & other stories

The Gardener

The Post Office

A Treasure of Tagore's Writings Vol. 1

The Home and the World

Four Chapters

Selected short stories

# GITANJALI

Rabindranath Tagore

Srishti
PUBLISHERS & DISTRIBUTORS

**Srishti Publishers & Distributors**
A unit of AJR Publishing LLP
212A, Peacock Lane
Shahpur Jat, New Delhi – 110 049
editorial@srishtipublishers.com

First published by
Srishti Publishers & Distributors in 2012



10 9 8 7



Printed and bound in India

# *Gitanjali*

Thou hast made me endless, such is thy pleasure. This frail vessel thou emptiest again and again, and fillest it ever with fresh life.

This little flute of a reed thou hast carried over hills and dales, and hast breathed through it melodies eternally new.

At the immortal touch of thy hands my little heart loses its limits in joy and gives birth to utterance ineffable.

Thy infinite gifts come to me only on these very small hands of mine. Ages pass, and still thou pourest, and still there is room to fill.

## II

When thou commandest me to sing, it seems that my heart would break with pride; and I look to thy face, and tears come to my eyes.

All that is harsh and dissonant in my life melts into

one sweet harmony—and my adoration spreads wings like a glad bird on its flight across the sea.

I know thou takest pleasure in my singing. I know that only as a singer I come before thy presence.

I touch by the edge of the far-spreading wing of my song thy feet which I could never aspire to reach.

Drunk with the joy of singing I forget myself and call thee friend who art my lord.

## III

I know not how thou singest, my master! I ever listen in silent amazement.

The light of thy music illumines the world. The life breath of thy music runs from sky to sky. The holy stream of thy music breaks through all stony obstacles and rushes on.

My heart longs to join in thy song, but vainly struggles for a voice. I would speak, but speech breaks not into song, and I cry out baffled. Ah, thou hast made my heart captive in the endless meshes of thy music, my master!

## IV

Life of my life, I shall ever try to keep my body

pure, knowing that thy living touch is upon all my limbs.

I shall ever try to keep all untruths out from my thoughts, knowing that thou art that truth which has kindled the light of reason in my mind.

I shall ever try to drive all evils away from my heart and keep my love in flower, knowing that thou hast thy seat in the inmost shrine of my heart.

And it shall be my endeavour to reveal thee in my actions, knowing it is thy power gives me strength to act.

## V

I ask for a moment's indulgence to sit by thy side. The works that I have in hand I will finish afterwards.

Away from the sight of thy face my heart knows no rest nor respite, and my work becomes an endless toil in a shoreless sea of toil.

Today the summer has come at my window with its sighs and murmurs; and the bees are plying their minstrelsy at the court of the flowering grove.

Now, it is time to sit quiet, face-to-face with thee, and to sing dedication of life in this silent and overflowing leisure.

## VI

Pluck this little flower and take it. Delay not! I fear lest it droop and drop into the dust.

It may not find a place in thy garland, but honour it with a touch of pain from thy hand and pluck it. I fear, lest the day end before I am aware, and the time of offering go by.

Though its colour be not deep and its smell be faint, use this flower in thy service and pluck it while there is time.

## VII

My song has put off her adornments. She has no pride of dress and decoration. Ornaments would mar our union; they would come between thee and me; their jingling would drown thy whispers.

My poet's vanity dies in shame before thy sight. O master poet, I have sat down at thy feet. Only let me make my life simple and straight, like a flute of reed for thee to fill with music.

## VIII

The child, who is decked with prince's robes and who

has jewelled chains round his neck loses all pleasure in his play; his dress hampers him at every step.

In fear that it may be frayed, or stained with dust he keeps himself from the world, and is afraid even to move.

Mother, it is no gain, thy bondage of finery, if it keep one shut off from the healthful dust of the earth, if it rob one of the right of entrance to the great fair of common human life.

## IX

O fool, to try to carry thyself upon thy own shoulders! O beggar, to come to beg at thy own door!

Leave all thy burdens on his hands who can bear all, and never look behind in regret.

Thy desire at once puts out the light from the lamp it touches with its breath. It is unholy—take not thy gifts through its unclean hands. Accept only what is offered by sacred love.

## X

Here is thy footstool and there rest thy feet where live the poorest, and lowliest, and lost.

When I try to bow to thee, my obeisance cannot

reach down to the depth where thy feet rest among the poorest, and lowliest, and lost.

Pride can never approach to where thou walkest in the clothes of the humble among the poorest, and lowliest, and lost.

My heart can never find its way to where thou keepest company with the companionless among the poorest, the lowliest, and the lost.

## XI

Leave this chanting and singing and telling of beads! Whom dost thou worship in this lonely dark corner of a temple with doors all shut? Open thine eyes and see thy God is not before thee!

He is there where the tiller is tilling the hard ground and where the pathmaker is breaking stones. He is with them in sun and in shower, and his garment is covered with dust. Put off thy holy mantle and even like him come down on the dusty soil!

Deliverance? Where is this deliverance to be found? Our master himself has joyfully taken upon him the bonds of creation; he is bound with us all for ever.

Come out of thy meditations and leave aside thy flowers and incense! What harm is there if thy clothes become tattered and stained? Meet him and stand by him in toil and in sweat of thy brow.

## XII

The time that my journey takes is long and the way of it long.

I came out on the chariot of the first gleam of light, and pursued my voyage through the wildernesses of worlds leaving my track on many a star and planet.

It is the most distant course that comes nearest to thyself, and that training is the most intricate which leads to the utter simplicity of a tune.

The traveller has to knock at every alien door to come to his own, and one has to wander through all the outer worlds to reach the innermost shrine at the end.

My eyes strayed far and wide before I shut them and said, "Here art thou!"

The question and the cry, "Oh, where?" melt into tears of a thousand streams and deluge the world with the flood of the assurance, "I am!"

## XIII

The song that I came to sing remains unsung to this day.

I have spent my days in stringing and in unstringing my instrument.

The time has not come true, the words have not been rightly set; only there is the agony of wishing in my heart.

The blossom has not opened; only the wind is sighing by.

I have not seen his face, nor have I listened to his voice; only I have heard his gentle footsteps from the road before my house.

The livelong day has passed in spreading his seat on the floor; but the lamp has not been lit and I cannot ask him into my house.

I live in the hope of meeting with him; but this meeting is not yet.

## XIV

My desires are many and my cry is pitiful, but ever didst thou save me by hard refusals; and this strong mercy has been wrought into my life through and through.

Day-by-day thou art making me worthy of the simple, great gifts that thou gavest to me unasked—this sky and the light, this body and the life and the mind—saving me from perils of overmuch desire.

There are times when I languidly linger and times when I awaken and hurry in search of my goal; but cruelly thou hidest thyself from before me.

Day-by-day thou art making me worthy of thy full acceptance by refusing me ever and anon, saving me from perils of weak, uncertain desire.

## XV

I am here to sing thee songs. In this hall of thine I have a corner seat.

In thy world I have no work to do; my useless life can only break out in tunes without a purpose.

When the hour strikes for thy silent worship at the dark temple of midnight, command me, my master, to stand before thee to sing.

When in the morning air the golden harp is tuned, honour me, commanding my presence.

## XVI

I have had my invitation to this world's festival, and thus my life has been blessed. My eyes have seen and my ears have heard.

It was my part at this feast to play upon my instrument, and I have done all I could.

Now, I ask, has the time come at last when I may go in and see thy face and offer thee my silent salutation?

## XVII

I am only waiting for love to give myself up at last into his hands. That is why it is so late and why I have been guilty of such omissions.

They come with their laws and their codes to bind me fast; but I evade them ever, for I am only waiting for love to give myself up at last into his hands.

People blame me and call me heedless; I doubt not they are right in their blame.

The market day is over and work is all done for the busy. Those who came to call me in vain have gone back in anger. I am only waiting for love to give myself up at last into his hands.

## XVIII

Clouds heap upon clouds and it darkens. Ah, love, why dost thou let me wait outside at the door all alone?

In the busy moments of the noontide work I am with the crowd, but on this dark lonely day it is only for thee that I hope.

If thou showest me not thy face, if thou leavest me wholly aside, I know not how I am to pass these long, rainy hours.

I keep gazing on the far-away gloom of the sky, and my heart wanders wailing with the restless wind.

## XIX

If thou speakest not I will fill my heart with thy silence and endure it. I will keep still and wait like the night with starry vigil and its head bent low with patience.

The morning will surely come, the darkness will vanish, and thy voice pour down in golden streams breaking through the sky.

Then thy words will take wing in songs from every one of my birds' nests, and thy melodies will break forth in flowers in all my forest groves.

## XX

On the day when the lotus bloomed, alas, my mind was straying, and I knew it not. My basket was empty and the flower remained unheeded.

Only now and again, a sadness fell upon me, and I started up from my dream and felt a sweet trace of a strange fragrance in the south wind.

That vague sweetness made my heart ache with longing and it seemed to me that it was the eager breath of the summer seeking for its completion.

I knew not then that it was so near, that it was mine, and that this perfect sweetness had blossomed in the depth of my own heart.

## XXI

I must launch out my boat. The languid hours pass by on the shore—Alas for me!

The spring has done its flowering and taken leave. And now with the burden of faded futile flowers I wait and linger.

The waves have become clamorous, and upon the bank in the shady lane the yellow leaves flutter and fall.

What emptiness do you gaze upon! Do you not feel a thrill passing through the air with the notes of the far-away song floating from the other shore?

## XXII

In the deep shadows of the rainy July, with secret steps, thou walkest, silent as night, eluding all watchers.

Today the morning has closed its eyes, heedless of the insistent calls of the loud east wind, and a thick veil has been drawn over the ever-wakeful blue sky.

The woodlands have hushed their songs, and doors are all shut at every house. Thou art the solitary wayfarer in this deserted street. Oh, my only friend, my best beloved, the gates are open in my house—do not pass by like a dream.

## XXIII

Art thou abroad on this stormy night on thy journey of love, my friend? The sky groans like one in despair.

I have no sleep tonight. Ever and again I open my door and look out on the darkness, my friend!

I can see nothing before me. I wonder where lies thy path!

By what dim shore of the ink-black river, by what far edge of the frowning forest, through what mazy depth of gloom art thou threading thy course to come to me, my friend?

## XXIV

If the day is done, if birds sing no more, if the wind has flagged tired, then draw the veil of darkness thick upon me, even as thou hast wrapt the earth with the coverlet of sleep and tenderly closed the petals of the drooping lotus at dusk.

From the traveller, whose sack of provisions is empty before the voyage is ended, whose garment is torn and dust-laden, whose strength is exhausted, remove shame and poverty, and renew his life like a flower under the cover of thy kindly night.

## XXV

In the night of weariness let me give myself up to sleep without struggle, resting my trust upon thee.

Let me not force my flagging spirit into a poor preparation for thy worship.

It is thou who drawest the veil of night upon the tired eyes of the day to renew its sight in a fresher gladness of awakening.

## XXVI

He came and sat by my side but I woke not. What a cursed sleep it was, O miserable me!

He came when the night was still; he had his harp in his hands, and my dreams became resonant with its melodies.

Alas, why are my nights all thus lost? Ah, why do I ever miss his sight whose breath touches my sleep?

## XXVII

Light, oh, where is the light? Kindle it with the burning fire of desire!

There is the lamp but never a flicker of a flame,—is such thy fate, my heart? Ah, death were better by far for thee!

Misery knocks at thy door, and her message is that thy lord is wakeful, and he calls thee to the love-tryst through the darkness of night.

The sky is overcast with clouds and the rain is ceaseless. I know not what this is that stirs in me,—I know not its meaning.

A moment's flash of lightning drags down a deeper gloom on my sight, and my heart gropes for the path to where the music of the night calls me.

Light, oh, where is the light? Kindle it with the burning fire of desire! It thunders and the wind rushes screaming through the void. The night is black as a black stone. Let not the hours pass by in the dark. Kindle the lamp of love with thy life.

## XXVIII

Obstinate are the trammels, but my heart aches when I try to break them.

Freedom is all I want, but to hope for it I feel ashamed.

I am certain that priceless wealth is in thee, and that thou art my best friend, but I have not the heart to sweep away the tinsel that fills my room.

The shroud that covers me is a shroud of dust and death; I hate it, yet hug it in love.

My debts are large, my failures great, my shame secret and heavy; yet when I come to ask for my good, I quake in fear, lest my prayer be granted.

## XXIX

He whom I enclose with my name is weeping in this dungeon. I am ever busy building this wall all around; and as this wall goes up into the sky day-by-day I lose sight of my true being in its dark shadow.

I take pride in this great wall, and I plaster it with dust and sand, lest a least hole should be left in this name; and for all the care I take I lose sight of my true being.

## XXX

I came out alone on my way to my tryst. But who is this that follows me in the silent dark?

I move aside to avoid his presence but I escape him not.

He makes the dust rise from the earth with his swagger; he adds his loud voice to every word that I utter.

He is my own little self, my lord, he knows no shame; but I am ashamed to come to thy door in his company.

## XXXI

"Prisoner, tell me, who was it that bound you?"

"It was my master," said the prisoner. "I thought I could outdo everybody in the world in wealth and power, and I amassed in my own treasure-house the money due to my king. When sleep overcame me I lay upon the bed that was for my lord, and on waking up I found I was a prisoner in my own treasure-house."

"Prisoner, tell me, who was it that wrought this unbreakable chain?"

"It was I," said the prisoner, "who forged this chain very carefully. I thought my invincible power would hold the world captive leaving me in a freedom undisturbed. Thus, night and day I worked at the chain with huge fires and cruel hard strokes. When at last the work was done and the links were complete and unbreakable, I found that it held me in its grip."

## XXXII

By all means they try to hold me secure who love me in this world. But it is otherwise with thy love which is greater than theirs, and thou keepest me free.

Lest I forget them they never venture to leave me alone. But day passes by after day and thou art not seen.

If I call not thee in my prayers, if I keep not thee in my heart, thy love for me still waits for my love.

## XXXIII

When it was day they came into my house and said, "We shall only take the smallest room here."

They said, "We shall help you in the worship of your God and humbly accept only our own share of his grace;" and then they took their seat in a corner and they sat quiet and meek.

But in the darkness of night I find they break into my sacred shrine, strong and turbulent, and snatch with unholy greed the offerings from God's altar.

## XXXIV

Let only that little be left of me whereby I may name thee my all.

Let only that little be left of my will whereby I may feel thee on every side, and come to thee in everything, and offer to thee my love every moment.

Let only that little be left of me whereby I may never hide thee.

Let only that little of my fetters be left whereby I am bound with thy will, and thy purpose is carried out in my life—and that is the fetter of thy love.

## XXXV

Where the mind is without fear and the head is held high;

Where knowledge is free;

Where the world has not been broken up into fragments by narrow domestic walls;

Where words come out from the depth of truth;

Where tireless striving stretches its arms towards perfection;

Where the clear stream of reason has not lost its way into the dreary desert sand of dead habit;

Where the mind is led forward by thee into ever-widening thought and action—

Into that heaven of freedom, my Father, let my country awake.

## XXXVI

This is my prayer to thee, my lord—strike, strike at the root of penury in my heart.

Give me the strength lightly to bear my joys and sorrows.

Give me the strength to make my love fruitful in service.

Give me the strength never to disown the poor or bend my knees before insolent might.

Give me the strength to raise my mind high above daily trifles.

And give me the strength to surrender my strength to thy will with love.

## XXXVII

I thought that my voyage had come to its end at the last limit of my power,—that the path before me was closed, that provisions were exhausted and the time come to take shelter in a silent obscurity.

But I find that thy will knows no end in me. And

when old words die out on the tongue, new melodies break forth from the heart; and where the old tracks are lost, new country is revealed with its wonders.

## XXXVIII

That I want thee, only thee—let my heart repeat without end. All desires that distract me, day and night, are false and empty to the core.

As the night keeps hidden in its gloom the petition for light, even thus in the depth of my unconsciousness rings the cry—"I want thee, only thee".

As the storm still seeks its end in peace when it strikes against peace with all its might, even thus my rebellion strikes against thy love and still its cry is—"I want thee, only thee".

## XXXIX

When the heart is hard and parched up, come upon me with a shower of mercy.

When grace is lost from life, come with a burst of song.

When tumultuous work raises its din on all sides shutting me out from beyond, come to me, my lord of silence, with thy peace and rest.

When my beggarly heart sits crouched, shut up in a corner, break open the door, my king, and come with the ceremony of a king.

When desire blinds the mind with delusion and dust, O thou holy one, thou wakeful, come with thy light and thy thunder.

## XL

The rain has held back for days and days, my God, in my arid heart. The horizon is fiercely naked—not the thinnest cover of a soft cloud, not the vaguest hint of a distant cool shower.

Send thy angry storm, dark with death, if it is thy wish, and with lashes of lightning startle the sky from end-to-end.

But call back, my lord, call back this pervading silent heat, still and keen and cruel, burning the heart with dire despair.

Let the cloud of grace bend low from above like the tearful look of the mother on the day of the father's wrath.

## XLI

Where dost thou stand behind them all, my lover,

hiding thyself in the shadows? They push thee and pass thee by on the dusty road, taking thee for naught. I wait here weary hours spreading my offerings for thee, while passers-by come and take my flowers, one-by-one, and my basket is nearly empty.

The morning time is past, and the noon. In the shade of evening my eyes are drowsy with sleep. Men going home glance at me and smile and fill me with shame. I sit like a beggar maid, drawing my skirt over my face, and when they ask me what it is I want, I drop my eyes and answer them not.

Oh, how, indeed, could I tell them that for thee I wait, and that thou hast promised to come? How could I utter for shame that I keep for my dowry this poverty? Ah, I hug this pride in the secret of my heart.

I sit on the grass and gaze upon the sky and dream of the sudden splendour of thy coming—all the lights ablaze, golden pennons flying over thy car, and they at the roadside standing agape, when they see thee come down from thy seat to raise me from the dust, and set at thy side this ragged beggar girl a-tremble with shame and pride, like a creeper in a summer breeze.

But time glides on and still no sound of the wheels of thy chariot. Many a procession passes by with noise and shouts and glamour of glory. Is it only thou who wouldst stand in the shadow silent and behind them all? And only I who would wait and weep and wear out my heart in vain longing?

## XLII

Early in the day it was whispered that we should sail in a boat, only thou and I, and never a soul in the world would know of this our pilgrimage to no country and to no end.

In that shoreless ocean, at thy silently listening smile my songs would swell in melodies, free as waves, free from all bondage of words.

Is the time not come yet? Are there works still to do? Lo, the evening has come down upon the shore and in the fading light the seabirds come flying to their nests.

Who knows when the chains will be off, and the boat, like the last glimmer of sunset, vanish into the night?

## XLIII

The day was when I did not keep myself in readiness for thee; and entering my heart unbidden even as one of the common crowd, unknown to me, my king, thou didst press the signet of eternity upon many a fleeting moment of my life.

And today when by chance I light upon them and see thy signature, I find they have lain scattered in the dust mixed with the memory of joys and sorrows of my trivial days forgotten.

Thou didst not turn in contempt from my childish play among dust, and the steps that I heard in my playroom are the same that are echoing from star to star.

## XLIV

This is my delight, thus to wait and watch at the wayside where shadow chases light and the rain comes in the wake of the summer.

Messengers, with tidings from unknown skies, greet me and speed along the road. My heart is glad within, and the breath of the passing breeze is sweet.

From dawn till dusk I sit here before my door, and I know that of a sudden the happy moment will arrive when I shall see.

In the meanwhile, I smile and I sing all alone. In the meanwhile, the air is filling with the perfume of promise.

## XLV

Have you not heard his silent steps? He comes, comes, ever comes.

Every moment and every age, every day and every night he comes, comes, ever comes. Many a song have I sung in many a mood of mind, but all their notes have always proclaimed, "He comes, comes, ever comes".

In the fragrant days of sunny April through the forest path he comes, comes, ever comes.

In the rainy gloom of July nights on the thundering chariot of clouds he comes, comes, ever comes.

In sorrow after sorrow it is his steps that press upon my heart, and it is the golden touch of his feet that makes my joy to shine.

## XLVI

I know not from what distant time thou art ever coming nearer to meet me. Thy sun and stars can never keep thee hidden from me for aye.

In many a morning and eve thy footsteps have been heard and thy messenger has come within my heart and called me in secret.

I know not why today my life is all astir, and a

feeling of tremulous joy is passing through my heart.

It is as if the time were come to wind up my work, and I feel in the air a faint smell of thy sweet presence.

## XLVII

The night is nearly spent waiting for him in vain. I fear, lest in the morning he suddenly come to my door when I have fallen asleep wearied out. Oh, friends, leave the way open to him—forbid him not.

If the sound of his steps does not wake me, do not try to rouse me, I pray. I wish not to be called from my sleep by the clamorous choir, of birds, by the riot of wind at the festival of morning light. Let me sleep undisturbed even if my lord comes of a sudden to my door.

Ah, my sleep, precious sleep, which only waits for his touch to vanish. Ah, my closed eyes that would open their lids only to the light of his smile when he stands before me like a dream emerging from darkness of sleep.

Let him appear before my sight as the first of all lights and all forms. The first thrill of joy to my awakened soul, let it come from his glance. And let my return to myself be immediate return to him.

## XLVIII

The morning sea of silence broke into ripples of bird songs; and the flowers were all merry by the roadside; and the wealth of gold was scattered through the rift of the clouds while we busily went on our way and paid no heed. We sang no glad songs nor played; we went not to the village for barter; we spoke not a word nor smiled; we lingered not on the way. We quickened our pace more and more as the time sped by.

The sun rose to the mid-sky and doves cooed in the shade. Withered leaves danced and whirled in the hot air of noon. The shepherd boy drowsed and dreamed in the shadow of the banyan tree, and I laid myself down by the water and stretched my tired limbs on the grass.

My companions laughed at me in scorn; they held their heads high and hurried on; they never looked back nor rested; they vanished in the distant blue haze. They crossed many meadows and hills, and passed through strange, far-away countries. All honour to you, heroic host of the interminable path! Mockery and reproach pricked me to rise, but found no response in me. I gave myself up for lost in the depth of a glad humiliation—in the shadow of a dim delight.

The repose of the sun-embroidered green gloom slowly spread over my heart. I forgot for what I had travelled, and I surrendered my mind without struggle to the maze of shadows and songs.

At last, when I woke from my slumber and opened my eyes, I saw thee standing by me, flooding my sleep with thy smile. How I had feared that the path was long and wearisome, and the struggle to reach thee was hard!

## XLIX

You came down from your throne and stood at my cottage door.

I was singing all alone in a corner, and the melody caught your ear. You came down and stood at my cottage door.

Masters are many in your hall, and songs are sung there at all hours. But the simple carol of this novice struck at your love. One plaintive little strain mingled with the great music of the world, and with a flower for a prize you came down and stopped at my cottage door.

## L

I had gone a-begging from door-to-door in the village

path, when thy golden chariot appeared in the distance like a gorgeous dream and I wondered who was this King of all kings!

My hopes rose high and methought my evil days were at an end, and I stood waiting for alms to be given unasked and for wealth scattered on all sides in the dust.

The chariot stopped where I stood. Thy glance fell on me and thou camest down with a smile. I felt that the luck of my life had come at last. Then, of a sudden thou didst hold out thy right hand and say, "What hast thou to give to me?"

Ah, what a kingly jest was it to open thy palm to a beggar to beg! I was confused and stood undecided, and then from my wallet I slowly cook out the least little grain of corn and gave it to thee.

But how great my surprise when at the day's end I emptied my bag on the floor to find a least little grain of gold among the poor heap! I bitterly wept and wished that I had had the heart to give thee my all.

## LI

The night darkened. Our day's works had been done. We thought that the last guest had arrived for the night and the doors in the village were all shut. Only some said the King was to come. We laughed and said, "No, it cannot be!"

It seemed there were knocks at the door and we said it was nothing but the wind. We put out the lamps and lay down to sleep. Only some said, "It is the messenger!" We laughed and said, "No, it must be the wind!"

There came a sound in the dead of the night. We sleepily thought it was the distant thunder. The earth shook, the walls rocked, and it troubled us in our sleep. Only some said it was the sound of wheels. We said in a drowsy murmur, "No, it must be the rumbling of clouds!"

The night was still dark when the drum sounded. The voice came, "Wake up! delay not!" We pressed our hands on our hearts and shuddered with fear. Some said, "Lo, there is the King's flag!" We stood up on our feet and cried "There is no time for delay!"

The King has come—but where are lights, where are wreaths? Where is the throne to seat him? Oh, shame! Oh utter shame! Where is the hall, the decorations? Someone has said, "Vain is this cry! Greet him with empty hands, lead him into thy rooms all bare!"

Open the doors, let the conch-shells be sounded! In the depth of the night has come the King of our dark, dreary house. The thunder roars in the sky. The darkness shudders with lightning. Bring out thy tattered piece of mat and spread it in the courtyard. With the storm has come of a sudden our King of the fearful night.

## LII

I thought I should ask of thee—but I dared not—the rose wreath thou hadst on thy neck. Thus, I waited for the morning, when thou didst depart, to find a few fragments on the bed. And like a beggar I searched in the dawn only for a stray petal or two.

Ah me, what is it I find? What token left of thy love? It is no flower, no spices, no vase of perfumed water. It is thy mighty sword, flashing as a flame, heavy as a bolt of thunder. The young light of morning comes through the window and spreads itself upon thy bed. The morning bird twitters and asks, "Woman, what hast thou got?" No, it is no flower, nor spices, nor vase of perfumed water—it is thy dreadful sword.

I sit and muse in wonder, what gift is this of thine. I can find no place where to hide it. I am ashamed to wear it, frail as I am, and it hurts me when I press it to my bosom. Yet, shall I bear in my heart this honour of the burden of pain, this gift of thine.

From now, there shall be no fear left for me in this world, and thou shalt be victorious in all my strife. Thou hast left death for my companion and I shall crown him with my life. Thy sword is with me to cut asunder my bonds, and there shall be no fear left for me in the world.

From now, I leave off all petty decorations. Lord of my heart, no more shall there be for me waiting and weeping in corners, no more coyness and sweetness of demeanour. Thou hast given me thy sword for adornment. No more doll's decorations for me!

## LIII

Beautiful is thy wristlet, decked with stars and cunningly wrought in myriad-coloured jewels. But more beautiful to me thy sword with its curve of lightning like the outspread wings of the divine bird of Vishnu, perfectly poised in the angry red light of the sunset.

It quivers like the one last response of life in ecstasy of pain at the final stroke of death; it shines like the pure flame of being burning up earthly sense with one fierce flash.

Beautiful is thy wristlet, decked with starry gems; but thy sword, O lord of thunder, is wrought with uttermost beauty, terrible to behold or to think of.

## LIV

I asked nothing from thee; I uttered not my name to thine ear. When thou took'st thy leave I stood silent. I was alone by the well where the shadow of the tree fell aslant, and the women had gone home with their brown earthen pitchers full to the brim. They called me and shouted, "Come with us, the morning is wearing on to noon." But I languidly lingered awhile lost in the midst of vague musings.

I heard nor thy steps as thou eamest. Thine eyes were sad when they fell on me; thy voice was tired as thou spokest low—"Ah, I am a thirsty traveller." I started up from my day-dreams and poured water from my jar on thy joined palms. The leaves rustled overhead; the cuckoo sang from the unseen dark, and perfume of *babla* flowers came from the bend of the road.

I stood speechless with shame when my name thou didst ask. Indeed, what had I done for thee to keep me in remembrance? But the memory that I could give water to thee to allay thy thirst will cling to my heart and enfold it in sweetness. The morning hour is late, the bird sings in weary notes, *neem* leaves rustle overhead and I sit and think and think.

## LV

Languors upon your heart and the slumber is still on your eyes.

Has not the word come to you that the flower is reigning in splendour among thorns? Wake, oh, awaken! Let not the time pass in vain!

At the end of the stony path, in the country of virgin solitude, my friend is sitting all alone. Deceive him not. Wake, oh, awaken!

What if the sky pants and trembles with the heat of the mid-day sun—what if the burning sand spreads its mantle of thirst—

Is there nc joy in the deep of your heart? At every footfall of yours, will not the harp of the road break out in sweet music of pain?

## LVI

Thus, it is that thy joy in me is so full. Thus, it is that thou hast come down to me. O thou Lord of all Heavens, where would be thy love if I were not?

Thou hast taken me as thy partner of all this wealth. In my heart is the endless play of thy delight. In my life thy will is ever taking shape.

And for this, thou who art the King of kings

hast decked thyself in beauty to captivate my heart. And for this thy love loses itself in the love of thy lover, and there art thou seen in the perfect union of two.

## LVII

Light, my light, the world-filling light, the eye-kissing light, heart-sweetening light!

Ah, the light dances, my darling, at the centre of my life; the light strikes, my darling, the chords of my love; the sky opens, the wind runs wild, laughter passes over the earth.

The butterflies spread their sails on the sea of light. Lilies and jasmines surge up on the crest of the waves of light.

The light is shattered into gold on every cloud, my darling, and it scatters gems in profusion.

Mirth spreads from leaf to leaf, my darling, and gladness without measure. The heaven's river has drowned its banks and the flood of joy is abroad.

## LVIII

Let all the strains of joy mingle in my last song—the joy that makes the earth flow over in the riotous excess of the grass, the joy that sets the twin brothers, life and death, dancing over the wide world, the joy that sweeps in with the tempest, shaking and waking all life with laughter, the joy that sits still with its tears on the open red lotus of pain, and the joy that throws everything it has upon the dust, and knows not a word.

## LIX

Yes, I know, this is nothing but thy love, O beloved of my heart—this golden light that dances upon the leaves, these idle clouds sailing across the sky, this passing breeze leaving its coolness upon my forehead. The morning light has flooded my. eyes—this is thy message to my heart. Thy face is bent from above, thy eyes look down on my eyes, and my heart has touched thy feet.

## LX

On the seashore of endless worlds children meet. The infinite sky is motionless overhead and the restless water is boisterous. On the seashore of endless worlds the children meet with shouts and dances.

They build their houses with sand and they play

with empty shells. With withered leaves they weave their boats and smilingly float them on the vast deep. Children have their play on the seashore of worlds.

They know not how to swim, they know not how to cast nets. Pearl fishers dive for pearls, merchants sail in their ships, while children gather pebbles and scatter them again. They seek not for hidden treasures, they know not how to cast nets.

The sea surges up with laughter and pale gleams the smile of the sea beach. Death-dealing waves sing meaningless ballads to the children, even like a mother while rocking her baby's cradle. The sea plays with children, and pale gleams the smile of the sea beach.

On the seashore of endless worlds children meet. Tempest roams in the pathless sky, ships get wrecked in the trackless water, death is abroad and children play. On the seashore of endless worlds is the great meeting of children.

## LXI

The sleep that flits on baby's eyes—does anybody know from where it comes? Yes, there is a rumour that it has its dwelling where, in the fairy village among shadows of the forest dimly lit with glow-worms, there hang two timid buds of enchantment.

From there it comes to kiss baby's eyes.

The smilc that flickers on baby's lips when he sleeps—does anybody know where it was born? Yes, there is a rumour that a young pale beam of a crescent moon touched the edge of a vanishing autumn cloud, and there the smile was first born in the dream of a dew-washed morning—the smile that flickers on baby's lips when he sleeps.

The sweet, soft freshness that blooms on baby's limbs—does anybody know where it was hidden so long? Yes, when the mother was a young girl it lay pervading her heart in tender and silent mystery of love,—the sweet, soft freshness that has bloomed on baby's limbs.

## LXII

When I bring to you coloured toys, my child, I understand why there is such a play of colours on clouds, on water, and why flowers are painted in tints—when I give coloured toys to you, my child.

When I sing to make you dance I truly know why there is music in leaves, and why waves send their chorus of voices to the heart of the listening earth—when I sing to make you dance.

When I Bring sweet things to your greedy hands

I know why there is honey in the cup of the flower and why fruits are secretly filled with sweet juice—when I bring sweet things to your greedy hands.

When I kiss your face to make you smile, my darling, I surely understand what the pleasure is that streams from the sky in morning light, and what delight that is which the summer breeze brings to my body—when I kiss you to make you smile.

## LXIII

Thou hast made me known to friends whom I knew not. Thou hast given me seats in homes not my own. Thou hast brought the distant near and made a brother of the stranger.

I am uneasy at heart when I have to leave my accustomed shelter; I forget that there abides the old in the new, and that there also thou abidest.

Through birth and death, in this world or in others, wherever thou leadest me it is thou, the same, the one companion of my endless life who ever linkest my heart with bonds of joy to the unfamiliar.

When one knows thee, then alien there is none, then no door is shut. Oh, grant me my prayer that I may never lose the bliss of the touch of the one in the play of the many.

## LXIV

On the slope of the desolate river among tall grasses I asked her, "Maiden, where do you go, shading your lamp with your mantle? My house is all dark and lonesome,—lend me your light!" She raised her dark eyes for a moment and looked at my face through the dusk. "I have come to the river," she said, "to float my lamp on the stream when the daylight wanes in the west." I stood alone among tall grasses and watched the timid flame of her lamp uselessly drifting in the tide.

In the silence of gathering night I asked her, "Maiden, your lights are all lit—then where do you go with your lamp? My house is all dark and lonesome,—lend me your light." She raised her dark eyes on my face and stood for a moment doubtful. "I have come," she said at last, "to dedicate my lamp to the sky." I stood and watched her light uselessly burning in the void.

In the moonless gloom of midnight I asked her, "Maiden, what is your quest, holding the lamp near your heart? My house is all dark and lonesome,—lend me your light." She stopped for a minute and thought and gazed at my face in the dark. "I have brought my light," she said, "to join the carnival of lamps." I stood and watched her little lamp uselessly lost among lights.

## LXV

What divine drink wouldst thou have, my God, from this overflowing cup of my life?

My poet, is it thy delight to see thy creation through my eyes and to stand at the portals of my ears silently to listen to thine own eternal harmony?

Thy world is weaving words in my mind and thy joy is adding music to them. Thou givest thyself to me in love and then feelest thine own entire sweetness in me.

## LXVI

She whoever had remained in the depth of my being, in the twilight of gleams and of glimpses; she who never opened her veils in the morning light, will be my last gift to thee, my God, folded in my final song.

Words have wooed yet failed to win her; persuasion has stretched to her its eager arms in vain.

I have roamed from country to country keeping her in the core of my heart, and around her have risen and fallen the growth and decay of my life.

Over my thoughts and actions, my slumbers and dreams, she reigned yet dwelled alone and apart.

Many a man knocked at my door and asked for her and turned away in despair.

There was none in the world whoever saw her face-to-face, and she remained in her loneliness waiting for thy recognition.

## LXVII

Thou art the sky and thou art the nest as well.

O thou beautiful, there in the nest it is thy love that encloses the soul with colours and sounds and odours.

There comes the morning with the golden basket in her right hand bearing the wreath of beauty, silently to crown the earth.

And there comes the evening over the lonely meadows deserted by herds, through trackless paths, carrying cool draughts of peace in her golden pitcher from the western ocean of rest.

But there, where spreads the infinite sky for the soul to take her flight in, reigns the stainless white radiance. There is no day nor night, nor form nor colour, and never, never a word.

## LXVIII

Thy sunbeam comes upon this earth of mine with arms outstretched and stands at my door the livelong day to carry back to thy feet clouds made of my tears and sighs and songs.

With fond delight thou wrappest about thy starry breast that mantle of misty cloud, turning it into numberless shapes and folds and colouring it with hues everchanging.

It is so light and so fleeting, tender and tearful and dark, that is why thou lovest it, O thou spotless and serene. And that is why it may cover thy awful white light with its pathetic shadows.

## LXIX

The same stream of life that runs through my veins night and day runs through the world and dances in rhythmic measures.

It is the same life that shoots in joy through the dust of the earth in numberless blades of grass and breaks into tumultuous waves of leaves and flowers.

It is the same life that is rocked in the ocean-cradle of birth and of death, in ebb and in flow.

I feel my limbs are made glorious by the touch of this world of life. And my pride is from the life-throb of ages dancing in my blood this moment.

## LXX

Is it beyond thee to be glad with the gladness of this rhythm? to be tossed and lost and broken in the whirl of this fearful joy?

All things rush on, they stop not, they look not behind, no power can hold them back, they rush on.

Keeping steps with that restless, rapid music, seasons come dancing and pass away—colours, tunes, and perfumes pour in endless cascades in the abounding joy that scatters and gives up and dies every moment.

## LXXI

That I should make much of myself and turn it on all sides, thus casting coloured shadows on thy radiance—such is thy *maya*. Thou settest a barrier in thine own being and then callest thy severed self in myriad notes. This thy self-separation has taken body in me.

The poignant song is echoed through all the sky in many-coloured tears and smiles, alarms and hopes;

waves rise up and sink again, dreams break and form. In me is thy own defeat of self.

This screen that thou hast raised is painted with innumerable figures with the brush of the night and the day. Behind it thy seat is woven in wondrous mysteries of curves, casting away all barren lines of straightness.

The great pageant of thee and me has overspread the sky. With the tune of thee and me all the air is vibrant, and all ages pass with the hiding and seeking of thee and me.

## LXXII

He it is, the innermost one, who awakens my being with his deep hidden touches.

He it is who puts his enchantment upon these eyes and joyfully plays on the chords of my heart in varied cadence of pleasure and pain.

He it is who weaves the web of this *maya* in evanescent hues of gold and silver, blue and green, and lets peep out through the folds his feet, at whose touch I forget myself.

Days come and ages pass, and it is ever he who moves my heart in many a name, in many a guise, in many a rapture of joy and of sorrow.

## LXXIII

Deliverance is not for me in renunciation. I feel the embrace of freedom in a thousand bonds of delight.

Thou ever pourest for me the fresh draught of thy wine of various colours ancl fragrance, filling this earthen vessel to the brim.

My world will light its hundred different lamps with thy flame and place them before the altar of thy temple.

No, I will never shut the doors of my senses. The delights of sight and hearing and touch will bear thy delight.

Yes, all my illusions will burn into illumination of joy, and all my desires ripen into fruits of love.

## LXXIV

The day is no more, the shadow is upon the earth. It is time that I go to the scream to fill my pitcher.

The evening air is eager with the sad music of the water. Ah, it calls me out into the dusk. In the lonely lane there is no passer-by, the wind is up, the ripples are rampant in the river.

I know not if I shall come back home. I know not whom I shall chance to meet. There at the fording in the little boat the unknown man plays upon his lute.

## LXXV

Thy gifts to us mortals fulfil all our needs and yet run back to thee undiminished.

The river has its everyday work to do and hastens through fields and hamlets; yet, its incessant stream winds towards the washing of thy feet.

The flower sweetens the air with its perfume; yet, its last service is to offer itself to thee.

Thy worship does not impoverish the world.

From the words of the poet men take what meanings please them; yet, their last meaning points to thee.

## LXXVI

Day after day, O lord of my life, shall I stand before thee face-to-face. With folded hands, O lord of all worlds, shall I stand before thee face-to-face.

Under thy great sky in solitude and silence, with humble heart shall I stand before thee face-to-face.

In this laborious world of thine, tumultuous with toil and with struggle, among hurrying crowds shall I stand before thee face-to-face.

And when my work shall be done in this world, O King of kings, alone and speechless shall I stand before thee face-to-face.

## LXXVII

I know thee as my God and stand apart—I do not know thee as my own and come closer. I know thee as my father and bow before thy feet—I do not grasp thy hand as my friend's.

I stand not where thou comest down and ownest thyself as mine, there to clasp thee to my heart and take thee as my comrade.

Thou art the Brother amongst my brothers, but I heed them not, I divide not my earnings with them, thus sharing my all with thee.

In pleasure and in pain I stand not by the side of men, and thus stand by thee. I shrink to give up my life, and thus do not plunge into the great waters of life.

## LXXVIII

When the creation was new and all the stars shone in their first splendour, the gods held their assembly in the sky and sang, "Oh, the picture of perfection! the joy unalloyed!"

But one cried of a sudden—"It seems that somewhere there is a break in the chain of light and one of the stars has been lost."

The golden string of their harp snapped, their song stopped, and they cried in dismay—"Yes, that lost star was the best, she was the glory of all heavens!"

From that day the search is unceasing for her, and the cry goes on from one to the other that in her the world has lost its one joy!

Only in the deepest silence of night the stars smile and whisper among themselves—"Vain is this seeking! Unbroken perfection is over all!"

## LXXIX

If it is not my portion to meet thee in this my life then let me ever feel that I have missed thy sight—let me not forget for a moment, let me carry the pangs of this sorrow in my dreams and in my wakeful hours.

As my days pass in the crowded market of this world and my hands grow full with the daily profits, let me ever feel that I have gained nothing—let me not forget for a moment, let me carry the pangs of this sorrow in my dreams and in my wakeful hours.

When I sit by the roadside, tired and panting, when I spread my bed low in the dust, let me ever feel that the long journey is still before me—let me not forget for a moment, let me carry the pangs of this sorrow in my dreams and in my wakeful hours.

When my rooms have been decked out and the flutes sound and the laughter there is loud, let me ever feel that I have not invited thee to my house—let me not forget for a moment, let me carry the pangs of this sorrow in my dreams and in my wakeful hours.

## LXXX

I am like a remnant of a cloud of autumn uselessly roaming in the sky, O my Sun ever-glorious! Thy touch has not yet melted my vapour, making me one with thy light, and thus I count months and years separated from thee.

If this be thy wish and if this be thy play, then take this fleeting emptiness of mine, paint it with colours, gild it with gold, float it on the wanton wind and spread it in varied wonders.

And again, when it shall be thy wish to end this play at night, I shall melt and vanish away in the dark, or it may be in a smile of the white morning, in a coolness of purity transparent.

## LXXXI

On many an idle day have I grieved over lost time. But it is never lost, my Lord. Thou hast taken every moment of my life in thine own hands.

Hidden in the heart of things thou art nourishing seeds into sprouts, buds into blossoms, and ripening flowers into fruitfulness.

I was tired and sleeping on my idle bed and imagined all work had ceased. In the morning I woke up and found my garden full with wonders of flowers.

## LXXXII

Time is endless in thy hands, my Lord. There is none to count thy minutes.

Days and nights pass and ages bloom and fade like flowers. Thou knowest how to wait.

Thy centuries follow each other perfecting a small wild flower.

We have no time to lose, and having no time we must scramble for our chances. We are too poor to be late.

And thus, it is that time goes by while I give it to every querulous man who claims it, and thine altar is empty of all offerings to the last.

At the end of the day I hasten in fear, lest thy gate be shut; but I find that yet there is time.

## LXXXIII

Mother, I shall weave a chain of pearls for thy neck with my tears of sorrow.

The stars have wrought their anklets of light to deck thy feet, but mine will hang upon thy breast.

Wealth and fame come from thee and it is for thee to give or to withhold them. But this my sorrow is absolutely mine own, and when I bring it to thee as my offering thou rewardest me with thy grace.

## LXXXIV

It is the pang of separation that spreads throughout the world and gives birth to shapes innumerable in the infinite sky.

It is this sorrow of separation that gazes in silence all night from star to star and becomes lyric among rustling leaves in rainy darkness of July.

It is this overspreading pain that deepens into loves and desires, into sufferings and joys in human homes; and this it is that ever melts and flows in songs through my poet's heart.

## LXXXV

When the warriors came out first from their master's hall, where had they hid their power? Where were their armour and their arms?

They looked poor and helpless, and the arrows were showered upon them on the day they came out from their master's hall.

When the warriors marched back again to their master's hall, where did they hide their power?

They had dropped the sword and dropped the bow and the arrow; peace was on their foreheads, and they had left the fruits of their life behind them on the day they marched back again to their master's hall.

## LXXXVI

Death, thy servant, is at my door. He has crossed the unknown sea and brought thy call to my home.

The night is dark and my heart is fearful—yet I will take up the lamp, open my gates and bow to him my welcome. It is thy messenger who stands at my door.

I will worship him with folded hands, and with tears. I will worship him placing at his feet the treasure of my heart.

He will go back with his errand done, leaving a dark shadow on my morning; and in my desolate home only my forlorn self will remain as my last offering to thee.

## LXXXVII

In desperate hope I go and search for her in all the corners of my room; I find her not.

My house is small and what once has gone from it can never be regained.

But infinite is thy mansion, my Lord, and seeking her I have come to thy door.

I stand under the golden canopy of thine evening sky and I lift my eager eyes to thy face.

I have come to the brink of eternity from which nothing can vanish—no hope, no happiness, no vision of a face seen through tears.

Oh, dip my emptied life into that ocean, plunge it into the deepest fullness. Let me for once feel that lost sweet touch in the allness of the universe.

## LXXXVIII

Deity of the ruined temple! The broken strings of *Veena* sing no more your praise. The bells in the evening proclaim not your time of worship. The air is still and silent about you.

In your desolate dwelling comes the vagrant spring breeze. It brings the tidings of flowers—the flowers that for your worship are offered no more.

Your worshipper of old wanders ever longing for favour still refused. In the eventide, when fires and shadows mingle with the gloom of dust, he wearily comes back to the ruined temple with hunger in his heart.

Many a festival day comes to you in silence, deity of the ruined temple. Many a night of worship goes away with lamp unlit.

Many new images are built by masters of cunning art and carried to the holy stream of oblivion when their time is come.

Only the deity of the ruined temple remains unworshipped in deathless neglect.

## LXXXIX

No more noisy, loud words from me—such is my master's will. Henceforth, I deal in whispers. The speech of my heart will be carried on in murmurings of a song.

Men hasten to the King's market. All the buyers

and sellers are there. But I have my untimely leave in the middle of the day, in the thick of work.

Let then the flowers come out in my garden, though it is not their time; and let the mid-day bees strike up their lazy hum.

Full many an hour have I spent in the strife of the good and the evil, but now it is the pleasure of my playmate of the empty days to draw my heart on to him; and I know not why is this sudden call to what useless inconsequence!

## XC

On the day when death will knock at thy door what wilt thou offer to him?

Oh, I will set before my guest the full vessel of my life—I will never let him go with empty hands.

All the sweet vintage of all my autumn days and summer nights, all the earnings and gleanings of my busy life will I place before him at the close of my days when death will knock at my door.

## XCI

O thou the last fulfilment of life, Death, my death, come and whisper to me!

Day after day have I kept watch for thee; for thee have I borne the joys and pangs of life.

All that I am, that I have, that I hope, and all my love have ever flowed towards thee in depth of secrecy. One final glance from thine eyes and my life will be ever thine own.

The flowers have been woven and the garland is ready for the bridegroom. After the wedding the bride shall leave her home and meet her Lord alone in the solitude of night.

## XCII

I know that the day will come when my sight of this earth shall be lost, and life will take its leave in silence, drawing the last curtain over my eyes.

Yet, stars will watch at night, and morning rise as before, and hours heave like sea waves casting up pleasures and pains.

When I think of this end of my moments, the barrier of the moments breaks and I see by the light of death thy world with its careless treasures. Rare is its lowliest seat, rare is its meanest of lives.

Things that I longed for in vain and things that I got—let them pass. Let me but truly possess the things that I ever spurned and overlooked.

## XCIII

I have got my leave. Bid me farewell, my brothers! I bow to you all and take my departure.

Here, I give back the keys of my door—and I give up all claims to my house. I only ask for last kind words from you.

We were neighbours for long, but I received more than I could give. Now, the day has dawned and the lamp that lit my dark corner is out. A summons has come and I am ready for my journey.

## XCIV

At this time of my parting, wish me good luck, my friends! The sky is flushed with the dawn and my path lies beautiful.

Ask not what I have with me to take there. I start on my journey with empty hands and expectant heart. I shall put on my wedding garland. Mine is not the red–brown dress of the traveller, and though there are dangers on the way I have no fear in my mind.

The evening star will come out when my voyage is done and the plaintive notes of the twilight melodies be struck up from the King's gateway.

## XCV

I was not aware of the moment when I first crossed the threshold of this life.

What was the power that made me open out into this vast mystery like a bud in the forest at—midnight?

When in the morning I looked upon the light I felt in a moment that I was no stranger in this world, that the inscrutable without name and form had taken me in her arms in the form of my own mother.

Even so, in death the same unknown will appear as ever known to me. And because I love this life, I know I shall love death as well.

The child cries out when from the right breast the mother takes it away, in the very next moment to find in the left one its consolation.

## XCVI

When I go from hence let this be my parting word, that what I have seen is unsurpassable.

I have tasted of the hidden honey of this lotus that expands on the ocean of light, and thus am I blessed—let this be my parting word.

In this playhouse of infinite forms I have had my play and here have I caught sight of him that is formless.

My whole body and my limbs have thrilled with his touch who is beyond touch; and if the end comes here, let it come—let this be my parting word.

## XCVII

When my play was with thee I never questioned who thou were. I knew nor shyness nor fear, my life was boisterous.

In the early morning thou wouldst call me from my sleep like my own comrade and lead me running from glade to glade.

On those days, I never cared to know the meaning of songs thou sangest to me. Only my voice took up the tunes, and my heart danced in their cadence.

Now, when the playtime is over, what is this sudden sight that is come upon me? The world with eyes bent upon thy feet stands in awe with all its silent stars.

## XCVIII

I will deck thee with trophies, garlands of my defeat. It is never in my power to escape unconquered.

I surely know my pride will go to the wall, my life will burst its bonds in exceeding pain, and my empty heart will sob out in music like a hollow reed, and the stone will melt in tears.

I surely know the hundred petals of a lotus will not remain closed forever and the secret recess of its honey will be bared.

From the blue sky an eye shall gaze upon me and summon me in silence. Nothing will be left for me, nothing whatever, and utter death shall I receive at thy feet.

## XCIX

When I give up the helm I know that the time has come for thee to take it. What there is to do will be instantly done. Vain is this struggle.

Then, take away your hands and silently put up with your defeat, my heart, and think it your good fortune to sit perfectly still where you are placed.

These my lamps are blown out at every little puff of wind, and trying to light them I forget all else again and again.

But I shall be wise this time and wait in the dark, spreading my mat on the floor; and whenever it is thy pleasure, my Lord, come silently and take thy seat here.

## C

I dive down into the depth of the ocean of forms, hoping to gain the perfect pearl of the formless.

No more sailing from harbour to harbour with this my weather-beaten boat. The days are long past when my sport was to be tossed on waves.

And now, I am eager to die into the deathless.

Into the audience hall by the fathomless abyss where swells up the music of toneless strings I shall take this harp of my life.

I shall tune it to the notes of forever, and, when it has sobbed out its last utterance, lay down my silent harp at the feet of the silent.

## CI

Ever in my life have I sought thee with my songs. It was they who led me from door-to-door, and with them have I felt about me, searching and touching my world.

It was my songs that taught me all the lessons I ever learnt; they showed me secret paths, they brought before my sight many a star on the horizon of my heart.

They guided me all the day long to the mysteries

of the country of pleasure and pain, and, at last, to what palace gate have they brought me in the evening at the end of my journey?

## CII

I boasted among men that I had known you. They see your pictures in all works of mine. They come and ask me, "Who is he?" I know not how to answer them. I say, "Indeed, I cannot tell." They blame me and they go away in scorn. And you sit there smiling.

I put my tales of you into lasting songs. The secret gushes out from my heart. They come and ask me "Tell me all your meanings." I know not how to answer them. I say, "Ah, who knows what they mean!" They smile and go away in utter scorn. And you sit there smiling.

## CIII

In one salutation to thee, my God, let all my sense spread out and touch this world at thy feet.

Like a rain-cloud of July hung low with its burden of unshed showers let all my mind bend down at thy door in one salutation to thee.

Let all my songs gather together their diverse

strains into a single current and flow to a sea of silence in one salutation to thee.

Like a flock of homesick cranes flying night and day back to their mountain nests let all my life take its voyage to its eternal home in one salutation to thee.

# The Nobel Prize Acceptance Speech

I am glad that I have been able to come at last to your country and that I may use this opportunity for expressing my gratitude to you for the honour you have done to me by acknowledging my work and rewarding me by giving me the Nobel Prize.

I remember the afternoon when I received the cablegram from my publisher in England that the prize had been awarded to me. I was staying then at the school Shantiniketan, about which I suppose you know. At that moment, we were taking a party over to a forest nearby the school, and when I was passing by the telegram office and the post office, a man came running to us and held up the telegraphic message. I had also an English visitor with me in the same carriage. I did not think that the message was of any importance, and I just put it into my pocket, thinking that I would read it, when I reached my destination. But my visitor supposed he knew the contents, and he urged me to read it, saying that it contained an important message.

And I opened and read the message, which I could hardly believe. I first thought that possibly the telegraphic language was not quite correct and that I might misread the meaning of it, but at last I felt certain about it. And you can well understand how rejoicing it was for my boys at the school and for the teachers. What touched me more deeply than anything else was that these boys who loved me and for whom I had the deepest love felt proud of the honour that had been awarded to him for whom they had feeling of reverence, and I realised that my countrymen would share with me the honour which had been awarded to myself.

The rest of the afternoon passed away in this manner, and when the night came I sat upon the terrace alone, and I asked myself the question what the reason could be of my poems being accepted and honoured by the West—in spite of my belonging to a different race, parted and separated by seas and mountains from the children of the West. And I can assure you that it was not with a feeling of exaltation but with a searching of the heart that I questioned myself, and I felt humble at that moment.

I remember how my life's work developed from the time when I was very young. When I was about 25 years I used to live in utmost seclusion in the solitude of an obscure Bengal village by the river Ganges in a boat-house. The wild ducks which came during the time of autumn from the Himalayan lakes were my only living companions, and in that solitude I seem to have drunk in the open space like wine overflowing with sunshine, and the murmur of the river used to speak to me and tell me the secrets of nature. And I passed my days in the solitude dreaming and giving shape to my dream in poems and studies and sending out my thoughts to the Calcutta public through the magazines and other papers. You can well understand that it was a life quite different from the life of the West. I do not know if any of your western poets or writers do pass the greatest part of their young days in such absolute seclusion. I am almost certain that it cannot be possible and that seclusion itself has no place in the western world.

And my life went on like this. I was an obscure individual—to most of my countrymen in those days. I mean that my name was hardly known outside my own province, but I was quite content with that obscurity, which protected me from the curiosity of the crowds.

And then came a time when my heart felt a longing to come out of that solitude and to do some work for my human fellow-beings, and not merely give shapes to my dreams and meditate deeply on the problems of life, but try to give expression to my ideas through some definite work, some definitive service for my fellow-beings.

And the one thing, the one work which came to my mind was to teach children. It was not because I was specially fitted for this work of teaching, for I have not had myself the full benefit of a regular education. For some time I hesitated to take upon myself this task, but I felt that as I had a deep love for nature I had naturally love for children also. My object in starting this institution was to give the children of men full freedom of joy, of life and of communion with nature. I myself had suffered when I was young through the impediments which were inflicted upon most boys while they attended school and I have had to go through the machine of education which crushes the joy and freedom of life for which children have such insatiable thirst. And my object was to give freedom and joy to children of men.

And so, I had a few boys around me, and I taught them, and I tried to make them happy. I was their playmate. I was their companion. I shared their life, and I felt that I was the biggest child of the party. And we all grew up together in this atmosphere of freedom. The vigour and the joy of the children, their chats and songs filled the air with a spirit of delight, which I drank every day I was there. And in the evening during the sun-set hour I often used to sit alone watching the trees of the shadowing avenue, and in the silence of the afternoon I could hear distinctly the voices of the children coming up in the air, and it seemed to me that these shouts and songs and glad voices were like those trees, which come out from the heart of the earth like fountains of life towards the bosom of the infinite sky. And it symbolised, it brought before my mind the whole cry of human life all expressions of joy and aspirations of men rising from the heart of Humanity up to this sky. I could see that, and I knew that we also, the grown-up children, send up our cries of aspiration to the Infinite. I felt it in my heart of hearts.

In this atmosphere and in this environment I used to write my poems Gitanjali, and I sang them to myself in the midnight under the glorious stars of the Indian sky. And in the early morning and in the afternoon glow of sun-set I used to write these songs till a day came when I felt impelled to come out once again and meet the heart of the large world.

I could see that my coming out from the seclusion of my life among these joyful children and doing my service to my fellow-creatures was only a prelude to my pilgrimage to a larger world. And I felt a great desire to come out and come into touch with the Humanity of the West, for I was conscious that the present age belongs to the western man with his superabundance of energy.

He has got the power of the whole world, and his life is overflowing all boundaries and is sending out its message to the great future. And I felt that I must before I die come to the West and meet the man of the secret shrine where the Divine presence has his dwelling, his temple. And I thought that the Divine man with all his powers and aspirations of life is dwelling in the West.

And so I came out. After my Gitanjali poems had been written in Bengali I translated those poems into English, without having any desire to have them published, being diffident of my mastery of that language, but I had—the manuscript with me when I came out to the West. And you know that the British public, when these poems were put before them, and those who had the opportunity of reading them in manuscript before, approved of them. I was accepted, and the heart of the West opened without delay.

And it was a miracle to me who had lived for fifty years far away from activity, far away from the West, that I should be almost in a moment accepted by the

West as one of its own poets. It was surprising to me, but I felt that possibly this had its deeper significance and that those years which I had spent in seclusion, separated from the life and the spirit of the West, had brought with them a deeper feeling of rest, serenity and feeling of the eternal, and that these were exactly the sentiments that were needed by the western people with their overactive life, who still in their heart of hearts have a thirst for the peace, for the infinite peace. My fitness was that training which my muse had from my young days in the absolute solitude of the beaches of the Ganges. The peace of those years had been stored in my nature so that I could bring it out and hold it up to the man of the West, and what I offered to him was accepted gratefully.

I know that I must not accept that praise as my individual share. It is the East in me which gave to the West. For is not the East the mother of spiritual Humanity and does not the West, do not the children of the West amidst their games and plays when they get hurt, when they get famished and hungry, turn their face to that serene mother, the East? Do they not expect their food to come from her, and their rest for the night when they are tired? And are they to be disappointed.

Fortunately for me I came in that very moment

when the West had turned her face again to the East and was seeking for some nourishment. Because I represented the East I got my reward from my eastern friends.

And I can assure you that the prize which you have awarded to me was not wasted upon myself. I as an individual had no right to accept it, and therefore, I have made use of it for others. I have dedicated it to our eastern children and students. But then, it is like a seed which is put into the earth and comes up again to those who have sown it, and for their benefit it is producing fruits. I have used this money which I got from you for establishing and maintaining the university which I started lately, and it seemed to me, that this university should be a place where western students might come and meet their eastern brethren and when they might work together in the pursuit of truth and try to find the treasures that have lain hidden in the East for centuries and work out the spiritual resources of the East, which are necessary for all Humanity.

I can remind you of a day when India had her great university in the glorious days of her civilisation. When a light is lighted it can not be held within a short range. It is for the whole world. And India had her civilisation with all its splendours and wisdom and wealth. It could not use it for its own children only. It had to open its gates in hospitality to all races of men. Chinese and Japanese and Persians and all different races of men, came, and they had their opportunity of gaining what was best in India, her best offering of all times and to all Humanity. And she offered it generously. You know the traditions of our country are never to accept any material fees from the students in return to the teaching, because we consider in India that he who has the knowledge has the responsibility to impart it to the students. It is not merely for the students to come and ask it from the master, but it is the master who must fulfil his mission of life by offering the best gift which he has to all who may need it. And thus, it was that need of self-expression, of giving what had been stored in India and offering the best thing that she has in herself that made it possible and was the cause and the origin of these universities that were started in the different provinces of India.

And I feel that what we suffer from in the present day is no other calamity but this calamity of obscurity, of seclusion, that we have missed our opportunity of offering hospitality to Humanity and asking the world to share the best things we have got. We lost our confidence in our own civilisation for over a century, when we came into contact with the western races with their material superiority over the eastern Humanity and eastern culture, and in the educational establishments no provision was made for our own culture. And for over a century our students have been brought up in utter ignorance of the worth of their own civilisation of the past. Thus, we did not only lose touch of the great which lay hidden in our own inheritance, but also the great honour of being able to contribute to the civilisation of Humanity, to have opportunity of giving what we have and not merely begging from others, not merely borrowing culture and living like eternal schoolboys.

But the time has come when we must not waste such our opportunities. We must try to do our best to bring out what we have, and not go from century to century, from land to land and display our poverty before others. We know what we have to be proud of, what we have inherited from our ancestors, and such opportunity of giving should not be lost—not only for the sake of our people, but for the sake of Humanity.

That is the reason, and that led me to the determination to establish an international institution where the western and eastern students could meet and share the common feast of spiritual food.

And thus, I am proud to say that your awarding me the prize has made some contribution to this great object which I had in my mind. This has made me come out once again to the West, and I have come to ask you, to invite you to the feast which is waiting for you in the far East. I hope that my invitation will not be rejected. I have visited different countries of Europe, and I have accepted from them an enthusiastic welcome. That welcome has its own meaning, that the West has need of the East, as the East has need of the West, and so the time has come when they should meet.

I am glad that I belong to this great time, this great age, and I am glad that I have done some work to give expression to this great age, when the East and the West are coming together. They are proceeding towards each other. They are coming to meet each other. They have got their invitation to meet each other and join hands in building up a new civilisation and the great culture of the future.

I feel certain that through my writing some such idea has reached you, even if obscurely through the translation, some idea which belongs both to the East and the West, some idea which proceeding from the East has been able to come to the West and claim its rest here, its dwelling, and to be able to receive its welcome, and has been accepted by the West. And if in my writings I have been fortunate enough to be able to interpret the voice of the need of the time I am deeply thankful to you for giving me this glorious opportunity. The acknowledgement I got from Sweden has brought me and my work before the western public, though I can assure you that it has also given me some trouble. It has broken through the seclusion which I have been accustomed to. It has brought me out before the great public to which I have never been accustomed. And the adjustment has not been yet made. I shrink in my heart when I stand before the great concourse of Humanity in the West. I have not yet been accustomed to accept the great gift of your praise and your admiration in the manner in which you have given it to me. And I feel ashamed and shy when standing before you—I do so now. But I will only say that I am thankful to God that he has given me this great opportunity, that I have been an instrument to bring together, to unite the hearts of the East and the West. And I must to the end of my life carry on that mission. I must do all that I can. The feeling of resentment between the East and the West must be pacified. I must do something, and with that one object I have started this institution.

I do not think that it is the spirit of India to reject

anything, reject any race, reject any culture. The spirit of India has always proclaimed the ideal of unity. This ideal of unity never rejects anything, any race, or any culture. It comprehends all, and it has been the highest aim of our spiritual exertion to be able to penetrate all things with one soul, to comprehend all things as they are, and not to keep out anything in the whole universe—to comprehend all things with sympathy and love. This is the spirit of India. Now, when in the present time of political unrest the children of the same great India cry for rejection of the West I feel hurt. I feel that it is a lesson which they have received from the West. Such is not our mission. India is there to unite all human races.

Because of that reason in India we have not been given the unity of races. Our problem is the race problem which is the problem of all Humanity. We have Dravidians, we have Mohammedans, we have Hindoos and all different sects and communities of men in India. Therefore, no superficial bond of political unity can appeal to us, can satisfy us, can ever be real to us. We must go deeper down. We must discover the most profound unity, the spiritual unity between the different races. We must go deeper down to the spirit of man and find out the great bond of unity, which is to be found in all human races. And for that we are well equipped. We have inherited the immortal works of our ancestors, those great writers who proclaimed the religion of unity and sympathy, in say: He who sees all beings as himself, who realizes all beings as himself, knows Truth. That has once again to be realised, not only by the children of the East but also by the children of the West. They also have to be reminded of these great immortal truths. Man is not to fight with other human races, other human individuals, but his work is to bring about reconciliation and Peace and to restore the bonds of friendship and love. We are not like fighting beasts. It is the life of self which is predominating in our life, the self which is creating the seclusion, giving rise to sufferings, to jealousy and hatred, to political and commercial competition. All these illusions will vanish, if we go down to the heart of the shrine, to the love and unity of all races.

For that great mission of India I have started this university. I ask you now, when I have this opportunity, I invite you to come to us and join hands with us and not to leave this institution merely to us, but let your own students and learned men come to us and help us to make this university to a common institution for the East and the West, may they give the contributions of their lives and may we all together make it living and representative of the undivided Humanity of the world.

For this I have come to you. I ask you this and I claim it of you in the name of the unity of men, and in the name of love, and in the name of God. I ask you to come. I invite you.

26 *May* 1921, *Stockholm*

# MY BOYHOOD DAYS

## Tagore's other titles in Srishti

Gitanjali

Mashi & other stories

The Gardener

The Post Office

A Treasure of Tagore's Writings Vol. 1

The Home and the World

Four Chapters

Selected short stories

# MY BOYHOOD DAYS

Rabindranath Tagore

Srishti
PUBLISHERS & DISTRIBUTORS

**SRISHTI PUBLISHERS & DISTRIBUTORS**
**Registered Office:** N-16, C. R. Park
New Delhi – 110 019
**Corporate Office:** 212A, Peacock Lane
Shahpur Jat, New Delhi – 110 049
editorial@srishtipublishers.com

First published by
Srishti Publishers & Distributors in 2012

10 9 8 7



Typeset by EGP at Srishti

Printed and bound in India

# I

The Calcutta where I was born was an altogether old-world place. Hackney carriages lumbered about the city raising clouds of dust, and the whips fell on the backs of skinny horses whose bones showed plainly below their hide. There were no trams then, no buses, no motors. Business was not the breathless rush that it is now, and the days went by in leisurely fashion. Clerks would take a good pull at the hookah before starting for office, and chew their betel as they went along. Some rode in palanquins, others joined in groups of four or five to hire a carriage in common, which was known as a "share-carriage". Wealthy men had monograms painted on their carriages, and a leather hood over the rear portion, like a half-drawn veil. The coachman sat on the box with his turban stylishly tilted to one side, and two grooms rode behind, girdles of yaks' tails round their waists, startling the pedestrians from their path with their shouts of "Hey-yo!"

Women used to go about in the stifling darkness of closed palanquins; they shrank from the idea of riding in carriages, and even to use an umbrella in sun or rain was considered unwomanly. Any woman who was so bold as to wear the new-fangled bodice, or shoes on her feet, was scornfully nicknamed "memsahib", that is to say, one who had cast off all sense of propriety or shame. If any woman unexpectedly encountered a stange man, one outside her family circle, her veil would promptly descend to the very tip of her nose, and she would at once turn her back on him. The palanquins in which women went out were shut as closely as their apartments in the house. An additional covering, a kind of thick tilt, completely enveloped the palanquin of a rich man's daughters and daighters-in-law, so that it looked like a moving tomb. By its side went the *durwan* carrying his brass-bound stick. His work was to sit in the entrance and watch the house, to tend his beard, safely to conduct the money to the bank and the women to their relatives' houses, and on festival days to dip the lady of the house into the Ganges, closed palanquin and all. Hawkers who came to the door with their array of wares would grease Shivnandan's palm to gain admission, and the drivers of hired carriages were also a source of profit to him. Sometimes, a man who was unwilling to fall in with this idea of going shares would create a great scene in front of the porch.

Our "jamadar" Sobha Ram, who was a wrestler, used to spend a good deal of time in practising his preparatory feints and approaches, and in brandishing his heavy clubs. Sometimes, he would sit and grind hemp for drink, and sometimes, he would be quietly eating his raw radishes, tender leaves and all, when we boys would creep upon him and yell "Radhakrishna!" in his ear. The more he waved his arms and protested the more we delighted in teasing him. And perhaps,—who knows?—his protests were merely a cunning device for hearing repeated the name of his favourite god.

There was no gas then in the city, and no electric light. When the kerosene lamp was introduced, its brilliance amazed us. In the evening the house-servant lit castor-oil lamps in every room. The one in our study-room had two wicks in a glass bowl.

By this dim light my master taught me from Peary Sarkar's First Book. First, I would begin to yawn, and then, growing more and more sleepy, rub my heavy eyes. At such times, I heard over and over again of the virtues of my master's other pupil Satin, a paragon of a boy with a wonderful head for study, who would rub snuff in his eyes to keep himself awake, so earnest was he. But as for me—the less said about that the better! Even the awful thought that I should probably remain the only dunce in the family could not keep me awake. When nine o'clock struck I was released, my eyes dazed and my mind drugged with sleep.

There was a narrow passage, enclosed by latticed walls, leading from the outer apartments to the interior of the house. A dimly burning lantern swung from the ceiling. As I went along this passage, my mind would be haunted by the idea that something was creeping upon me from behind. Little shivers ran up and down my back. In those days devils and spirits lurked in the recesses of every man's mind, and the air was full of ghost stories. One day it would be some servant girl falling in a dead faint because she had heard the nasal whine of Shañk-chunni. The female demon of that name was the most bad-tempered devil of all, and was said to be very greedy of fish. Another story was connected with the thick-leaved *bādām* tree at the western corner of the house. A mysterious Shape was said to stand with one foot in its branches and the other on the third-storey cornice of the house. Plenty of people declared that they had seen it, and there were not a few who believed them. A friend of my elder brother's laughingly made light of the story, and the servants looked upon him as lacking in all piety, and said that his neck would surely be wrung one day and his pretensions exposed. The very atmosphere was so enmeshed in ghostly terrors that I could not put my feet into the darkness under the table without them getting the creeps.

There were no water-pipes laid on in those days. In the spring months of *Māgh* and *Fālgoon* when the Ganges water was clear, our bearers would bring it up in brimming pots carried in a yoke across their shoulders. In the dark rooms of the ground floor stood rows of huge water jars filled with the whole year's supply of drinking water. All those musty, dingy, twilit rooms were the home of furtive "Things"—which of us did not know all about those "Things"? Great gaping mouths they had, eyes in their breasts, and ears like winnowing fans; and their feet turned backwards. Small wonder, that my heart would pound in my breast and my knees tremble when I went into the inner garden, with the vision of those devilish shapes before me.

At high tide the water of the Ganges would flow along a masonry channel at the side of the road. Since my grandfather's time an allowance of this water had been discharged into our tank. When the sluices were opened the water rushed in, gurgling and foaming like a waterfall. I used to watch it fascinated, holding on by the railings of the south verandah. But the days of our tank were numbered, and finally there came a day when cartload after cartload of rubbish was tipped into it. When the tank no longer reflected the garden, the last lingering illusion of rural life left it. That *bādām* tree is still standing near the third-storey cornice, but though his footholds remain, the ghostly shape that once bestrode them has disappeared for ever.

# II

The palanquin belonged to the days of my grandmother. It was of ample proportions and lordly appearance. It was big enough to have needed eight bearers for each pole. But when the former wealth and glory of the family had faded like the glowing clouds of sunset, the palanquin bearers, with their gold bracelets, their thick ear-rings, and their sleeveless red tunics, had disappeared along with it. The body of the palanquin had been decorated with coloured line drawings, some of which were now defaced. Its surface was stained and discoloured, and the coir stuffing was coming out of the upholstery. It lay in a corner of the counting-house verandah as though it were a piece of common-place lumber. I was seven or eight years old at that time.

I was not yet, therefore, of an age to put my hand to any serious work in the world, and the old palanquin on its part had been dismissed from all useful service. Perhaps, it was this fellow-feeling that so much attracted me towards it. It was to me an island in the midst of the ocean, and I on my holidays became Robinson Crusoe. There, I sat within its closed doors, completely lost to view, delightfully safe from prying eyes.

Outside my retreat, our house was full of people, innumerable relatives and other folk. From all parts of the house I could hear the shouts of the various servants at their work. Pari, the maid, is returning from the bazaar through the front courtyard with her vegetables in a basket on her hip. Dukhon, the bearer, is carrying in Ganges water in a yoke across his shoulder. The weaver woman has gone into the inner apartments to trade the newest style of saries. Dinu, the goldsmith, who receives a monthly wage, usually sits in the room next to the lane, blowing his bellows and carrying out the orders of the family; now he is coming to the counting house to present his bill to Kailash Mukherjee, who has a quill pen stuck over his ear. The carder sits in the courtyard cleaning the cotton mattress stuffing on his twanging bow. Mukundalal, the durwan, is rolling on the ground outside with the one-eyed wrestler, trying out a new wrestling fall. He slaps his thighs loudly, and repeats his "physical jerks" twenty or thirty times, dropping on all fours. There is a crowd of beggars sitting waiting for their regular dole.

The day wears on, the heat grows intense, the clock in the gate-house strikes the hour. But inside the palanquin the day does not acknowledge the authority of clocks. Our mid-day is that of former days, when the drum at the great door of the king's palace would be beaten for the breaking-up of the court, and the king would go to bathe in sandal-scented water. At mid-day on holidays those in charge of me have their meal and go to sleep. I sit on alone.

My palanquin, outwardly at rest, travels on its imaginary journeys. My bearers, sprung from "airy nothing" at my bidding, eating the salt of my imagination, carry me wherever my fancy leads. We pass through far, strange lands, and I give each country a name from the books I have read. My imagination has cut a road through a deep forest. Tigers' eyes blaze from the thickets, my flesh creeps and tingles. With me is Biswanath the hunter; his gun speaks—Crack! Crack!—and there, all is still. Sometimes, my palanquin becomes a peacock-boat, floating far out on the ocean till the shore is out of sight. The oars fall into the water with a gentle plash, the waves swing and swell around us. The sailors cry to us to beware, a storm is coming. By the tiller stands Abdul the sailor, with his pointed beard, shaven moustache and close-cropped head. I know him, he brings *hilsa* fish and turtle eggs from the Padma for my elder brother.

Abdul has a story for me. One day, at the end of *Chaitra*[1] he had gone out in a dinghy to catch fish when suddenly there arose a great *Vaisākh* gale[2]. It was a tremendous typhoon and the boat sank lower and lower. Abdul seized the tow-rope in his teeth, and jumping into the water swam to the shore, where he pulled his dinghy up after him by the rope. But the story comes to an end far

1. March‡April.
2. Nor-wester, a very common phenomenon in Bengal in the beginning of the hot weather.

too quickly for my taste, and besides, the boat is not lost, everything is saved—that isn't what I call a story! Again and again I demand, "What next?" "Well," says Abdul at last, "after that there were great doings. What should I see next but a panther with enormous whiskers. During the storm he had climbed up a *pākur* tree on the village ghat on the other side of the river. In the violent wind the tree broke and fell into the Padma. Brother Panther came floating down on the current, rolled over and over in the water and reached and climbed the bank on my side. As soon as I saw him I made a noose in my tow-rope. The wild beast drew near, his big eyes glaring. He had grown very hungry with swimming, and when he saw me saliva dribbled from his red, lolling tongue. But though he had known many other men, inside and out, he did not know Abdul. I shouted to him, "Come on old boy", and as soon as he raised his fore-feet for the attack I dropped my noose round his neck. The more he struggled to get free the tighter grew the noose, until his tongue began to loll out...." I am tremendously excited. "He didn't die, did he Abdul?" I ask. "Die?" says Abdul, "He couldn't die for the life of him! Well, the river was in spate, and I had to get back to Bahadurganj. I yoked my young panther to the dinghy and made him tow me fully forty miles. Oh, he might roar and snarl, but I goaded him on with my oar, and he carried me a ten or fifteen hours' journey in an hour and a half! Now, my little fellow, don't ask me what happened next, for you won't get an answer."

"All right," say I, "so much for the panther; now for the crocodile?" Says Abdul, "I have often seen the tip of his nose above the water. And, how wickedly he smiles as he lies basking in the sun, stretched at full length on the shelving sandbanks of the river. If I'd had a gun I should have made his acquaintance. But my license has expired....

"Still, I can tell you one good yarn. One day, Kanchi the gypsy woman was sitting on the bank of the river trimming bamboo with a bill-hook, with her young goat tethered nearby. All at once the crocodile appeared on the surface, seized the billy-goat by the leg and dragged it into the water. With one jump the gypsy woman landed astride on its back, and began sawing with her sickle at the throat of the "demon-lizard", over and over again. The beast let go of the goat and plunged into the water...."

"And then? And then?" comes my excited question. "Why," says Abdul, "the rest of the story went down to the bottom of the river with the crocodile. It will take some time to get it up again. Before I see you again I will send somebody to find out about it, and let you know." Abdul has never come again; perhaps he is still looking for news.

So much, then, for my travels in the palanquin. Outside the palanquin there were days when I assumed the role of teacher, and the railings of the verandah were my pupils. They were all afraid of me, and would cower before me in silence. Some of them were very naughty, and cared absolutely nothing for their books. I told them with dire threats that when they grew up they would be fit for nothing but casual labour. They bore the marks of my beatings from head to foot, yet they did not stop being naughty. For, it would not have done for them to stop, it would have made an end of my game.

There was another game, too, with my wooden lion. I heard stories of poojah sacrifices and decided that a lion sacrifice would be a magnificent thing. I rained blows on his back—with a frail little stick. There had to be a "mantra", of course, otherwise it would not have been a proper poojah:

"Liony, liony, off with your head,
Liony, liony, now you are dead.
Woofle the walnut goes clappety clap,
Snip, snop, SNAP!"

I had borrowed almost every word in this from other sources; only the word walnut was my own. I was very fond of walnuts. From the words "clappety clap" you can see that my sacrificial knife was made of wood. And, the word "snap" shows that it was not a strong one.

# III

The clouds have had no rest since yesterday evening. The rain is pouring incessantly. The trees stand huddled together in a seemingly foolish manner; the birds are silent. I call to mind the evenings of my boyhood.

We used then to spend our evening in the servants' quarters. At that time English spellings and meanings did not yet lie like a nightmare on my shoulders. My third brother used to say that I ought first to get a good foundation of Bengali and only afterwards to go on to the English superstructure. Consequently, while other schoolboys of my age were glibly reciting "I am up", "He is down", I had not even started on B, A, D, bad and M, A, D, mad.

In the speech of the *nabobs* the servants' quarters were then called "tosha-khana". Even though our house had fallen far below its former aristocratic state, these old high-sounding names, "tosha-khana", "daftar-khana", "baithak-khana", still clung to it.

On the southern side of this "tosha-khana", a castor oil lamp burned dimly on a glass stand in a big room; on the wall was a picture of Ganesh and a crude country painting of the goddess Kali, round which the wall lizards hunted their insect prey. There was no furniture in the room, merely a soiled mat spread on the floor.

You must understand that we lived like poor people, and were consequently saved the trouble of keeping a good stable. Away in a corner outside, in a thatched shed under a tamarind tree, was a shabby carriage and an old horse. We wore the very simplest and plainest clothes, and it was a long time before we even began to wear socks. It was luxury beyond our wildest dreams when our tiffin rations went beyond Brajeswar's inventory and included a loaf of bread, and butter wrapped in a banana leaf. We adapted ourselves easily to the broken wrecks of our former glory.

Brajeswar was the name of the servant who presided over our mat seat. His hair and beard were grizzled, the skin of his face dry and tight-drawn; he was a man of serious disposition, harsh voice, and deliberately mouthed speech. His former master had been a prosperous and well-known man, yet necessity had degraded him from that service to the work of looking after neglected children like us. I have heard that he used to be a master in a village school. To the end of his life he kept this school-masterly language and prim manner. Instead of saying "The gentlemen are waiting", he would say "They await you", and his masters smiled when they heard him. He was as finicky about caste matters as he was conceited. When bathing he would go down into the tank and push back the oily surface water five or six times with his hands before taking a plunge. When he came out of the tank after his bath Brajeswar would edge his way through the garden in so gingerly a way that one would think he could only keep caste by avoiding all contact with this unclean world that God has made. He would talk very emphatically about what was right and what was wrong in manners and behaviour. And besides, he held his head a little on one side, which made his words all the more impressive.

But with all this there was one flaw in his character as *guru*. He cherished secretly a suppressed greed for food. It was not his method to place a proper portion of food on our plates before the meal. Instead, when we sat down to eat he would take one *luchi*[1] at a time, and dangling it at a little distance ask, "Do you want any more?" We knew by the tone of his voice what answer he desired, and I usually said that I didn't want any. After that he never gave us an opportunity to change our minds. The milk bowls also had an irresistible attraction for him—an attraction which I never felt at all. In his room was a small wired foodsafe with shelves in it. In it was a big brass bowl of milk, and *luchis* and vegetables on a wooden platter. Outside the wire-netting the cat prowled longingly to and fro sniffing the air.

From my childhood upwards these short commons suited me very well. Small rations cannot be said to have made me weak. I was, if anything, stronger, certainly not

1. Fried pancake known in Hindusthani as *puri*.

weaker, than boys who had unlimited food. My constitution was so abominably sound that even when the most urgent need arose for avoiding school, I could never make myself ill by fair means or foul. I would get wet through shoes, stockings and all, but I could not catch cold. I would lie on the open roof in the heavy autumn dew; my hair and clothes would be soaked, but I never had the slightest suspicion of a cough. And, as for that sign of bad digestion known as stomach ache, my stomach was a complete stranger to it, though my tongue made use of its name with mother in time of need. Mother would smile to herself and not feel the least anxiety; she would merely call the servant and tell him to go and tell my teacher that he should not teach me that evening. Our old-fashioned mothers used to think it no great harm if the boys occasionally took a holiday from study. If we had fallen into the hands of these present-day mothers, we should certainly have been sent to the teacher, and had our ears tweaked into the bargain. Perhaps, with a knowing smile they would have dosed us with castor oil, and our pains would have been permanently cured. If by chance, I got a slight temperature no one ever called it fever, but "heated blood". I had never set eyes on a thermometer in those days. Dr Nilmadhav would come and place his hand on my body, and then prescribe as the first day's treatment castor oil and fasting. I was allowed very little water to drink, and what I had was hot, with a few sugar-coated cardamoms for flavouring. After this fast, the *mouralā fish* soup and soft-boiled rice which I got on the third day seemed a veritable food for the gods.

Serious fever I do not remember, and I never heard the name of malaria. I do not remember quinine—that castor oil was my most distasteful medicine. I never knew the slightest scratch of a surgeon's knife; and to this very day I do not know what measles and chicken-pox are. In short, my body remained obstinately healthy. If mothers want their children to be so healthy that they will be unable to escape from the school master, I recommended them to find a servant like Brajeswar. He would save not only food bills but doctor's bills also, especially in these days of mill flour and adulterated ghee and oil. You must remember that in those days chocolate was still unknown in the bazaar. There was a kind of rose lollipop to be had for a pice. I do not know whether modern boy's pockets are still made sticky by this sesamum-covered sugar-lump, with its faint scent of roses. It has certainly fled in shame from the houses of the respectable people of today. What has become of those cone-shaped packets of fried spices? And, those cheap sesamum sweetmeats? Do they still linger on? If not, it is no good trying to bring them back.

Day after day, in the evenings, I listened to Brajeswar reciting the seven cantos of Krittibas' *Rāmayanā*. Kishori Chatterjee used to drop in sometimes while the reading was going on. He had by heart *Pānçhāli*[2] versions of the whole *Rāmayanā,* tune and all. He took possession at once

2. A kind of folk-version very popular in Bengali.

of the seat of authority, and superseding Krittibas, would begin to recite his simple folk-stanzas in great style:

"Lakshman O hear me
Greatly I fear me
Dangers are near me."

There was a smile on his lips, his bald head gleamed, the song poured from his throat in a torrent of sound, the rhymes jingled and rang verse after verse, like the music of pebbles in a brook. At the same time he would be using his hands and feet in acting out the thought. It was Kishori Chatterjee's greatest grief that Dadabhai, as he called me, could not join a troupe of strolling players and turn such a voice to account. If I did that, he said, I should certainly make my name.

By and by it would grow late and the assembly on the mat would break up. We would go into the house, to Mother's room, haunted and oppressed on our way by the terror of devils. Mother would be playing cards with her aunt, the inlaid parquet floor gleamed like ivory, a coverlet was spread on the big divan. We would make such a disturbance that Mother would soon throw down her hand and say, "If they are going to be such a nuisance, auntie, you'd better go and tell them stories." We would wash our feet with water from the pot on the verandah outside, and climb on to the bed, pulling "Didima" with us. Then, it would begin—stories of the magical awakening of the princess and her rescue from the demon city. The princess might wake, but who could waken me? … In the early part of the night the jackals would begin to howl, for in those days they still haunted the basements of some of the old houses of Calcutta with their nightly wail.

# IV

When I was a little boy, Calcutta city was not so wakeful at night as it is now. Nowadays, as soon as the day of sunlight is over, the day of electric light begins. There is not much work done in it, but there is no rest, for the fire continues, as it were, to smoulder in the charcoal after the blazing wood has burnt itself out. The oil mills are still, the steamer sirens are silent, the labourers have left the factories, the buffaloes which pull the carts of jute bales are stabled in the tin-roofed sheds. But the nerves of the city are throbbing still with the fever of thought which has burned all day in her brain. Buying and selling go on as by day in the shops that line the streets, though the fire is a little choked with ash. Motors continue to run in all directions, emitting all kinds of raucous grunts and groans, though they no longer run with the zest of the morning. But in those old times which we knew, when the day was over whatever business remained undone wrapped itself up in the black blanket of the night and went to sleep in the darkened ground-floor premises of the city. Outside the house the evening sky rose quiet and mysterious. It was so still that we could hear, even in our own street, the shouts of the grooms from the carriages of those people of fashion who were returning from taking the air in Eden Gardens by the side of the Ganges.

In the hot season of *Chaitra* and *Vaishākh* the hawkers would go about the streets shouting "I-i-i-ce". In a big pot full of lumps of ice and salt water were little tin containers of what we called "kulpi" ice—nowadays, ousted by the more fashionable ices or "ice-cream". No one but myself knows how my mind thrilled to that cry as I stood on the verandah facing the street. Then there was another cry, "*Bela* flowers". Nowadays for some reason one hears little of the gardeners' baskets of spring flowers—I do not know why. But in those days the air was full of the scent of the thickly strung *bel* flowers which the women and girls wore in their hair knots. Before they went to bathe, the women would sit outside their rooms with a hand-mirror set up before them, and dress their hair. The knot would be skilfully bound with the black hair-braid into all sorts of different styles. They wore black-bordered Chandernagore sarees, skilfully crinkled before use by pleating and twisting after the fashion of those days. The barber's wife would come to scrub their feet with pumice and paint them with red lac. She and her like were the gossip mongers of the women's courts.

The crowds returning from office or from college did not then, as they do now, rush to the football fields, clinging in swarms to the foot-boards of the trams. Nor, did they crowd in front of cinema halls as they returned. There was some active interest shown in drama, but alas! I was only a child then.

Children of those times got no share in the pleasures of the grown-ups, even from a distance. If we were bold enough to go near, we should be told, "Off with you, go and play." But if we boys made the amount of noise appropriate for proper play, it would then be, "Be quiet, do." Not that the grown-ups themselves conducted their pleasures and conversation in silence, by any means; and now and again we would stand on the fringe of their far-flung jubilations, as though sprinkled by the spray of a waterfall. We would hang over the verandah on our side of the courtyard, staring across at the brilliantly lit reception-room on the other side. Big coaches would roll up to the portico one after another. Some of our elder brothers conducted the guests upstairs from the front door, sprinkling them with rose-water from the sprinkler, and giving each one a small buttonhole or nosegay of flowers. As the dramatic entertainment proceeded, we could hear the sobs of the "high-caste *kulin* heroine", but we could make out nothing of their meaning, and our longing to know grew intense. We discovered later that though the sobber was certainly highcaste, "she" was merely our own brother-in-law. But in those days grown-ups and children were kept apart as strictly as men and women with their separate apartments. The singing and dancing would go on in the blaze of the drawing-room chandeliers, the men would pull at the hookah, the women of the family would take their betel boxes and sit in the subdued light behind their screen, the visiting ladies would gather in these retired nooks, and there would be much whispering of intimate domestic gossip. But we children were in bed by this time, and lay listening as our maid-servants Piyari or Sankari told us stories—"In the moonlight, expanding like an opening flower..."

# V

A little before our day it was the fashion among wealthy householders to run *jātrās* or troupes of actors. There was a great demand for boys with shrill voices to join these troupes. One of my uncles was patron of such an amateur company. He had a gift for writing plays, and was very enthusiastic about training the boys. All over Bengal professional companies were the rage, just as the amateur companies were in aristocratic circles. Troupes of players sprang up like mushrooms on all sides, under the leadership of some well-known actor or other. Not that either patron or manager was necessarily of high family or good education. Their fame rested on their own merits. *Jātrā* performances used to take place in our house from time to time. But we children had no part in them, and I managed to see only the preliminaries. The verandah would be full of members of the company, the air full of tobacco smoke. There were the boys, long-haired, with dark rings of weariness under their eyes, and, young as they were, with the faces of grown men. Their lips were stained black with constant betel chewing. Their costumes and other paraphernalia were in painted tin boxes. The entrance door was open, people swarmed like ants into the courtyard, which, filled to the brim with the seething, buzzing mass, spilled over into the lane and beyond into the Chitpore Road. Then, nine o'clock would strike, and Shyam would swoop down on me like a hawk on a dove, grip my elbow with his rough, gnarled hand, and tell me that Mother was calling me, to go to bed. I would hang my head in confusion at being thus publicly dragged away, but would bow to superior force and go to my bedroom. Outside all was tumult and shouting, outside flared the lighted chandeliers, but in my room there was not a sound and a brass lamp burned low on its stand. Even in sleep I was dimly conscious of the crash of the cymbals marking the rhythm of the dance.

The grown-ups usually forbade everything on principle, but on one occasion for some reason or other they decided to be indulgent, and the order went forth that the children also might come to the play. It was a drama about Nala and Damayanti. Before it began we were sent to bed till half-past eleven. We were assured again and again that when the time came we should be roused, but we knew the ways of the grown-ups, and we had no faith at all in these promises—*they* were adults, and *we* were children!

That night, however, I did drag my unwilling body to bed. For one thing, Mother promised that she herself would come and wake me. For another thing, I always had to pinch myself to keep myself awake after nine o'clock.

When the time came I was awakened and brought outside, blinking and bewildered in the dazzling glare. Light streamed brightly from coloured chandeliers on the first and second storeys, and the white sheets spread in the courtyard made it seem much bigger than usual. On one side were seated the people of importance, senior members of the family, and their invited guests. The remaining space was filled with a motley crowed of all who cared to come. The performing company was led by a famous actor wearing a gold chain across his stomach, and old and young crowded together in the audience. The majority of the audience were what the respectable would call "riff-raff". The play itself had been written by men whose hands were trained only to the villager's reed pen, and who had never practised on the letters of an English copy book. Tunes, dances, and story had all sprung from the very heart of rural Bengal, and no pundit had polished their style.

We went and sat by our elder brothers in the audience, and they tied up small sums of money in kerchiefs and gave them to us. It was the custom to throw this money on to the stage at the points where applause was most deserved. By this means the actors gained some extra profit and the family a good reputation.

The night came to an end, but the play would not. I never knew whose arms gathered up my limp body, nor where they carried me. I was far too much ashamed to try to find out. I, a fellow who had been sitting like an equal among the grown-ups and doling out *baksheesh,* to be disgraced in this way before a whole courtyard full of people! When I woke up I was lying on the divan in my mother's room; it was very late, and already blazing hot. The sun had risen, but I had not risen!—Such a thing had never happened before.

Nowadays, the city's pleasures flow on in an unbroken stream. There is always a cinema show somewhere, and whoever pleases may see it for a trifling sum. But in those days entertainments were few and far between, like water holes dug in the sandy bed of a dried-up river, three or four miles apart. Like these too, they lasted only a few hours, and the wayfarers hastily gathered round, drinking from their cupped hands to quench their thirst.

The old days were like a king's son who, from time to time on festive occasions, or according to his whim, distributes rich and royal gifts to all within his jurisdiction. Modern days are like a merchant's son, sitting at the cross-roads on some great highway with many kinds of cheap and tawdry goods spread glittering before him, and drawing his customers by highway and byway from every side.

# VI

Brajeswar was the head-servant, and his second-in-command was called Shyam. He came from Jessore, and he was a real countryman, speaking in a dialect strange to Calcutta. He would say "tenārā" and "onārā" for "tārā" and "orā"; "jāti" and "khāti" for "jete" and "khete". He used to call us affectionately "Domani". He had a dark skin, big eyes, long hair glistening with oil, and a strong, well-built body. He was really good at heart, and affectionate and kind to children. He used to tell us stories of dacoits. Dacoity stories filled men's houses then as universally as the fear of ghosts filled their minds. Even today dacoity is not uncommon; murder, assault and looting still take place, and the police still do not catch the right man. But nowadays this is only a news-item, it has none of the fascination of romance. In those days dacoities were woven into stories, and passed from mouth to mouth for long periods. In my childhood men were still to be met with who in their prime had been members of dacoit gangs. They were all past-masters in the science of the *lathi,* and were surrounded by disciples eager to learn the art of single-stick. Men salaamed at the very mention of their names. Dacoity then was usually not a mere matter of rash, headstrong bloodshed. As bodily strength and skill played their part, so did a generous, gallant mind. Moreover, gentlemen's houses often contained an exercise-ground for the practice of *lathi*-fighting, and those who made a name on these grounds were acknowledged as masters even by dacoits, who gave them a wide berth. Many zemindars made a profession of dacoity. There was a story of a man of this class who had stationed his desperadoes at the mouth of a river. It was new moon, and poojah night, and when they returned, carrying a severed head to the temple in honour of Kali Kankali[1], the zemindar clapped his hands to his head and cried out, "What have you done? It's my son-in-law!"

We heard also about the exploits of the dacoits Raghu and Bishu. They used to give notice before they attacked, and there was nothing underhand in their dacoity. When their rallying-cry was heard in the distance, the blood of the villagers ran cold. But their code forbade them to lay hands on women. On one occasion, in fact, a woman even succeeded in "robbing the robbers", by appearing to them dressed as Kali, brandishing the goddess's heavy-curved blade, and claiming their devout offerings.

One day, there was a display of dacoits' wrestling feats in our house. They were all strong young fellows,

---

1. The destructive aspect of the goddess Kali, pictured with a necklace of skulls.

big-made, dark-skinned, and long-haired. One man tied a cloth round a heavy grain-pounder, seized the cloth in his teeth, and then flung the pounder upwards and backwards over his shoulder. Another got a man to grasp him by his shaggy hair, and then whirled him round and round by a mere turn of his head. Using a long pole as support and lever, they leaped up to the second storey. Then, one man stood with his hands clasped above his bent head, and others shot through the aperture like diving birds. They also showed how it was possible for them to manage a dacoity twenty or thirty miles away, and the same night be found sleeping peacefully in their beds like law-abiding citizens. They had a pair of very long poles with a piece of wood lashed cross-wise in the middle of each as a foot-rest. These poles were called *rang-pā* (stilts). When walking with the tops of the poles held in the hands, and the feet on these footholds, one stride had the value of ten ordinary steps, and a man could run faster than a horse. I used to encourage boys at Santiniketan to practise stilt-walking—though without any idea of committing dacoity! My imagination mingled such pictures of dacoity feats with Shyam's stories with gruesome effect, so that I have often spent the evening with my arms huddled against my pounding heart!

Sunday was a holiday. On the previous evening the crickets were chirping in the thickets outside in the south garden, and the story was about Raghu the highwayman. My heart went pit-a-pit in the dim light and flickering shadows of the room. The next day in my holiday leisure I climbed into the palanquin. It began to move unbidden, its destination unknown, and my mind, enthralled still by the magic of the previous night's romance, knew a thrill of delicious fear. In the silent darkness my pulses attuned themselves to the rhythmic shouts of the bearers, and my body grew numb with terrified anticipation.

On the boundless expanse of plain the air quivers in the heat, in the distance glistens the Kali tank; the sand sparkles, the wide-spreading *pākur* tree leans from the bank of the river over the cracked, ruined *ghāt*. My romance-fed terrors are concentrated on that thick clump of reeds, and in the shade of the tree on that unknown plain. Nearer and nearer we approach, quicker and quicker beats my heart. Above the reeds can be seen the tips of one or two stout bamboo staves. The bearers will stop there to change shoulders. They will drink, and wind wet towels round their heads. And then?…

Then, with a blood-curdling shout, the dacoits are upon us….

# VII

From morning till night the mills of learning went on grinding. To wind up this creaking machinery was the work of *Shejadādā*[1], Hemendranath. He was a stern taskmaster, but it is useless now to try to hide the fact that the greater part of the cargo with which he sought to load our minds was tipped out of the boat and sent to the bottom. My learning at any rate was a profit-less cargo. If one seeks to key an instrument to too high a pitch, the strings will snap beneath the strain.

*Shejadādā* made all arrangements for the education of his eldest daughter. When the time came he got her admitted into the Loreto Convent School, but even before that she had been given a foundation in Bengali. He also gave Protibha a thorough training in western music, which, however, did not cause her to lose her skill in Indian music. Among the gentlemen's families of that time she had no equal in Hindustani songs.

It is one merit of western music that its scales and exercises demand diligent practice, that it makes for a

1. Third elder brother.

sensitive ear, and that the discipline of the piano allows of no slackness in the matter of rhythm.

Meanwhile, she had learnt Indian music from her earliest years from our teacher Vishnu. In this school of music I also had to be entered. No present-day musician, whether famous or obscure, would have consented to touch the kind of songs with which Vishnu initiated us. They were the very commonest kind of Bengali folk songs. Let me give you a few examples:

"A gypsy lass is come to town
To paint tattoos, my sister.
The painting's nothing, so they tell,
Yet she on me has cast a spell,
And, makes me weep and mocks me well,
By her tattoos, my sister."

I remember also a few fragmentary lines, such as:

"The sun and moon have owned defeat,
the firefly's lamp lights up the stage;
the Moghul and the Pathan flag,
the weaver reads the Persian page."

and:

"Your daugher-in-law is the plantain tree,
Mother of Ganesh, let her be.
For if but one flower should blossom and grow
She will have so many children you won't
know what to do."

Lines too come back to me in which one can catch a glimpse of old forgotten histories:

"There was a jungle of thorn and burr,
  Fit for the dogs alone;
  There did he cut for himself a throne…"

The modern custom is first to practise scales—*sā-re-ga-ma,* etc., on the harmonium, and then to teach some simple Hindu songs. But the wise supervisor who was then in charge of our studies understood that boyhood has its own childish needs, and that these simple Bengali words would come much more easily to Bengali children than Hindi speech. Besides this, the rhythm of this folk music defied all accompaniment by *tabla*. It danced itself into our very pulses. The experiment thus made showed that just as a child learns his first enjoyment of literature from his mother's nursery rhymes, he learns his first enjoyment of music also from the same source.

The harmonium, that bane of Indian music, was not then in vogue. I practised my songs with my *tamburā* resting on my shoulder, I did not subject myself to the slavery of the keyboard.

It was no one's fault but my own, that nothing could keep me for many days together in the beaten track of learning. I strayed at will, filling my wallet with whatever gleanings of knowledge I chanced upon. If I had been disposed to give my mind to my studies, the musicians of these days would have had no cause to slight my work.

For I had plenty of opportunity. As long as my brother was in charge of my education, I repeated Brahmo songs with Vishnu in an absentminded fashion. When I felt so inclined I would sometimes hang about the doorway while *Shejadādā* was practising, and pick up the song that was going on. Once he was singing to the *Behāg* air, "O thou of slow and stately tread". Unobserved I listened and fixed the tune in my mind, and astounded my mother—an easy task—by singing it to her that evening. Our family friend Srikantha Babu was absorbed in music day and night. He would sit on the verandah, rubbing *chāmeli* oil on his body before his bath, his hookāh in his hand, and the fragrance of amber-scented tobacco rising into the air. He was always humming tunes, which attracted us boys around him. He never *taught* us songs, he simply sang them to us, and we picked them up almost without knowing it. When he could no longer restrain his enthusiasm, he would stand up and dance, accompanying himself on the *sitār.* His big expressive eyes shone with enjoyment, he burst into the song, *Mai chhōrō brajaki bāsari,* and would not rest content till I joined in, too.

In matters of hospitality, people kept open house in those days. There was no need for a man to be intimately known before he was received. There was a bed to be had at any time, and a plate of rice at the regular meal times for any who chanced to come. One day, for example, one such stranger guest, who carried his *tamburā* wrapped in a quilt on his shoulder, opened his bundle, sat down, and stretched his legs at ease on one side of our reception room, and Kanai the hookāh-tender offered him the customary courtesy of the hookāh.

*Pān,* like tobacco, played a great part in the reception of guests. In those days the morning occupation of the women in the inner apartments consisted in preparing piles of *pān* for the use of those who visited the outer reception room. Deftly they placed the lime on the leaf, smeared *catechu* on it with a small stick, and putting in the appropriate amount of spice folded and secured it with a clove. This prepared *pān* was then piled into a brass container, and a moist piece of cloth, stained with catechu, acted as cover. Meanwhile, in the room under the staircase outside, the stir and bustle of preparing tobacco would be going on. In a big earthenware tub were balls of charcoal covered with ash, the pipes of the hookāhs hung down like snakes of *Nāgaloka,* with the scent of rosewater in their veins. This amber scent of tobacco was the first welcome extended by the household to those who climbed the steps to visit the house. Such was the invariable custom then prescribed for the fitting reception of guests. That overflowing bowl of *pān* has long since been discarded, and the caste of hookāh-tenders have thrown off their liveries and taken to the sweetmeat shops, where they knead up three-day-old *sandesh* and re-fashion it for sale.

That unknown musician stayed for a few days, just as he chose. No one asked him any questions. At dawn I used to drag him from his mosquito curtains and make him sing to me. (Those who have no fancy for regular study revel in study that is irregular). The morning melody of *Bansi hāmāri re* ... would rise on the air.

After this, when I was a little older, a very great musician called Jadu Bhatta came and stayed in the house. He made one big mistake in being determined to teach me music, and consequently no teaching took place. Nevertheless, I did casually pick up from him a certain amount of stolen knowledge. I was very fond of the song *Ruma jhuma barakhē āju bādara¯ā* ... which was set to a *Kāfi* tune, and which remains to this day in my store of rainy season songs. But unfortunately just at this time another guest arrived without warning, who had a name as a tiger-killer. A Bengali tiger-killer was a real marvel in those days, and it followed that I remained captivated in his room for the greater part of the time. I realise clearly now what I never dreamed of then, that the tiger whose fell clutches he so thrillingly described could never have bitten him at all; perhaps, he got the idea from the snarling jaws of the stuffed Museum tigers. But in those days I busied myself eagerly in the liberal provision of *pān* and tobacco for this hero, while the distant strains of *kānārā* music fell faintly on my indifferent ears.

So much for music. In other studies the foundation provided by *Shejadādā* was equally generously laid. It was the fault of my own nature that no great matter came of it.

It was with people like me in view that Ramprosad Sen wrote, "O Mind, you do not understand the art of cultivation." With me, the work of cultivation never took place. But let me tell you of a few fields where the ploughing at least was done.

I got up while it was still dark and practised wrestling—on cold days I shivered and trembled with cold. In the city was a celebrated one-eyed wrestler, who gave me practice. On the north side of the outer room was an open space known as the "granary". The name clearly had survived from a time when the city had not yet completely crushed out all rural life, and a few open spaces still remained. When the life of the city was still young our granary had been filled with the whole year's store of grain, and the *ryots* who held their land on lease from us brought to it their appointed portion. It was here that the lean-to shed for wrestling was built against the compound wall. The ground had been prepared by digging and loosening the earth to a depth of about a cubit and pouring over it a maund of mustard oil. It was mere child's play for the wrestler to try a fall with me there, but I would manage to get well smeared with dust by the end of the lesson, when I put on my shirt and went indoors.

Mother did not like to see me come in every morning so covered with dust—she feared that the colour of her son's skin would be darkened and spoiled. As a result, she occupied herself on holidays in scrubbing me. (Fashionable housewives of today buy their toilet preparations in boxes from western shops; but then they used to make their unguent with their own hands. It contained almond paste, thickened cream, the rind of oranges and many other things which I forget. If only I had learnt and remembered the receipt, I might have set up a shop and sold it as "Begum Bilash" unguent, and made at least as much money as the *sandesh-wāllāhs*.) On Sunday mornings there was a great rubbing and scrubbing on the verandah, and I would begin to grow restless to get away. Incidentally, a story used to go about among our school fellows that in our house babies were bathed in wine as soon as they were born, and that was the reason for our fair European complexions.

When I came in from the wrestling ground I saw a Medical College student waiting to teach me the lore of bones. A whole skeleton hung on the wall. It used to hang at night on the wall of our bedroom, and the bones swayed in the wind and rattled together. But the fear I might otherwise have felt had been overcome by constantly handling it, and by learning by heart the long, difficult names of the bones.

The clock in the porch struck seven. Master Nilkamal was a stickler for punctuality, there was no chance of a moment's variation. He had a thin, shrunken body, but his health was as good as his pupil's, and never once, unluckily for us, was he afflicted even by a headache. Taking my book and slate I sat down before the table, and he began to write figures on the blackboard in chalk. Everything was in Bengali, arithmetic, algebra and geometry. In literature

I jumped at one bound from *Sitār Banabās*[2] to *Meghnādbadh Kābya*[3]. Along with this there was natural science. From time to time Sitanath Datta would come, and we acquired some superficial knowledge of science by experiments with familiar things. Once, Heramba Tattvaratna, the Sanskrit scholar, came; and I began to learn the Mugdhabodh Sanskrit grammar by heart, though without understanding a word of it.

In this way, all through the morning, studies of all kinds were heaped upon me, but as the burden grew greater, my mind contrived to get rid of fragments of it; making a hole in the enveloping net, my parrot-learning slipped through its meshes and escaped—and the opinion that Master Nilkamal expressed of his pupil's intelligence was not of the kind to be made public.

In another part of the verandah is the old tailor, his thick-lensed spectacles on his nose, sitting bent over his sewing, and ever and anon, at the prescribed hours, going through the ritual of his Namāz[4]. I watch him and think what a lucky fellow Niāmat is. Then, with my head in a whirl from doing sums, I shade my eyes with my slate, and looking down see in front of the entrance porch Chandrabhān the *durwan* combing his long beard with a wooden comb, dividing it in two and looping it round each

2. "Sita in the Forest," by Iswarchandra Vidyasagar.
3. An Epic on the death of Meghnād (son of Rāvana in *Rāmāyana*) by Michael Madhusudan Dutta.
4. Muslim devotional exercises.

ear. The assistant *durwan,* a slender boy, is sitting nearby, a bracelet on his arm, and cutting tobacco. Over there the horse has already finished his morning allowance of gram, and the crows are hopping round pecking at the scattered grains. Our dog Johnny's sense of duty is aroused and he drives them away barking.

I had planted a custard-apple seed in the dust which continual sweeping had collected in one corner of the verandah. All agog with excitement, I watched for the sprouting of the new leaves. As soon as Master Nilkamal had gone, I had to run and examine it, and water it. In the end my hopes went unfulfilled—the same broom that had gathered the dust together dispersed it again to the four winds.

Now the sun climbs higher, and the slanting shadows cover only half the courtyard. The clock strikes nine. Govinda, short and dark, with a dirty yellow towel slung over his shoulder, takes me off to bathe me. Promptly at half past nine comes our monotonous, unvarying meal—the daily ration of rice, *dāl* and fish curry—it was not much to my taste.

The clock strikes ten. From the main street is heard the hawker's cry of "Green Mangoes"—what wistful dreams it awakens! From further and further away resounds the clanging of the receding brass-peddler, striking his wares till they ring again. The lady of the neighbouring house in the lane is drying her hair on the roof, and her two little girls are playing with shells. They have plenty of leisure, for in those days girls were not obliged to go to school, and I used to think how fine it would have been to be born a girl. But as it is, the old horse draws me in the rickety carriage to my Andamans, in which from ten to four I am doomed to exile.

At half past four, I return from school. The gymnastic master has come, and for about an hour I exercise my body on the parallel bars. He has no sooner gone than the drawing master arrives.

Gradually, the rusty light of day fades away. The many blurred noises of the evening are heard as a dreamy hum resounding over the demon city of brick and mortar. In the study room an oil lamp is burning. Master Aghor has come and the English lesson begins. The black-covered reader is lying in wait for me on the table. The cover is loose; the pages are stained and a little torn; I have tried my hand at writing my name in English in it, in the wrong places, and all in capital letters. As I read I nod, then jerk myself awake again with a start, but miss far more than I read. When finally I tumble into bed I have at last a little time to call my own. And, there I listen to endless stories of the king's son travelling over an endless, trackless plain.

# VIII

When I see the roofs of modern houses, uninhabited by either men or ghosts, I realise vividly the change that has taken place between those times and these. I have already mentioned how the *brahma-daitya*[1] of the *bādām* tree has fled, unable to endure the modern atmosphere of excessive learning. On the cornice where rumour had it that he had rested his foot, the crows snatch and squabble over our discarded mango stones. And, men too restrict themselves nowadays to the confined, boxed-in rooms of the lower storeys, and pass their time within four walls.

My mind goes back to the parapet-surrounded roof of the inner apartments. It is evening, and Mother has spread her mat and seated herself, with her friends gossiping round her. Their talk has no need of authentic information, it is only a means of passing the time. There was then no regular supply of valuable and varied ingredients to fill the day, which was not, as now, a closely woven mesh, but like a net of loose texture, full of holes. And therefore, stories

---

1. A class of formidable ghosts believed to be the spirits of departed Brahmins.

and rumours, laughter and jokes, all in the lightest vein, filled both the social gatherings of the men and the women's assemblies. Among Mother's friends the first in importance was Braja Acharji's sister, who was called "Acharjini". She was the daily purveyor of news to the company. Almost every day she picked up, (or made up!) and brought with her, every item of fantastic, ominous news in the country. By this means expenditure on all ceremonies calculated to avert impending calamity or the evil eye, was greatly increased.

Into this assembly I imported from time to time my recently acquired book-learning. I informed them that the sun is nine crore of miles distant from the earth. From the second part of my *Ṛju-Pāth* I recited a portion of Valmiki's *Rāmāyana* in the original, complete with Sanskrit terminations. Mother was no judge of the accuracy of her son's pronunciation, but the range of his learning filled her with awe, and seemed to her far to outrun the nine-crore miles journey of light. Who would have thought that any except Naradmuni himself could recite all these *slōkas?*

This inner apartment roof was entirely the women's domain, and had a close connection with the store room. The sun's rays fell full upon it, so it was used for preparing lemons for pickle. The women used to sit there with brass vessels full of *kalāi* paste, and while their hair was drying they made pulse-balls with their deft, quick fingers. The maid-servants who had washed the soiled linen came here to spread it in the sun, for the *dhoby* had little work in those days. Green mangoes were cut in slices and dried into *āmsi.* The mango juice was poured layer after layer into black stone moulds of all sizes and all patterns[2]. A pickle of young jack-fruit stood there to season in sun-warmed mustard oil. Catechu, scented with the fragrant screw-pine, would be prepared with great care.

I had a special reason for remembering this item. When my school-master informed me that he had heard the fame of my family's screw-pine catechu, it was not difficult to understand his meaning. What he had heard of, he wished to become acquainted with. So, to preserve the good name of my family, I occasionally climbed secretly to the roof containing the screw-pine catechu, and—what shall I say? "Appropriated" a piece or two sounds better than "stole". For, even kings and emperors may make "appropriations" when need arises, or indeed even if it does not, but vulgar "stealing" is punished by prison or impaling.

In the pleasant sunlight of the cold weather it was the family tradition for the women to sit on the roof gossiping, driving off crows and passing the time of day. I was the only younger brother-in-law in the house, the guardian of my sister-in-law's "*āmsatta*", and her friend and ally in many other trival pursuits. I used to read to them from *Bangādhipa Parājaya*[3]. From time to time the duty of cutting up betel-nut would devolve on me. I could cut betel

2. This preparation is called *āmsatta.*
3. "The Defeat of the King of Bengal."

very finely. My sister-in-law would never admit that I had any other good quality, so much so that she even made me angry with God for giving me such a faulty appearance. But she found no difficulty in speaking in exaggerated fashion of my skill in cutting betel. Therefore, the work of betel-cutting used to go on at a fine pace. But for a long time now, for want of anyone to encourage me, the hand that was so killed in fine betel-cutting has perforce busied itself in other fine work.

Around all this women's work spread on the roof there lingered the aroma of village life. These occupations belonged to the days when there was a pounding-room in the house, when confectionery balls were made, when the maid-servants sat in the evening rolling on their thighs the cotton wicks for the oil lamps, when invitations came from neighbours' houses to the ceremonies of the eighth day after birth. Modern children do not hear fairy stories from their mothers' lips, they read them for themselves in printed books. Pickles and chutney are bought from the Newmarket by the bottleful, each bottle corked and sealed with wax.

Another relic of a bygone village life was the *chandimandap,* the outer verandah where the school was held. Not only the boys of the house, but those of the neighbourhood, also, made there their first attempt to search letters on palm-leaves. I suppose that I too must have traced out my first laborious letters on that verandah, but I have no clear memory of the child I then was, who seems as far removed as the farthest planet of the solar system, and I possess no telescope which can bring him into view.

The first thing I remember about reading after this is the terrible story of Ṣanḍāmārka Muni's school, and of the *avatār* Narasiṃha tearing the bowels of Hiraṇyakaśipu; I think also that there was a lead-plate engraving of it in the same book—and I remember also reading a few *slōkas* of Chānakya.

My chief holiday resort was the unfenced roof of the outer apartments. From my earliest childhood till I was grown up, many varied days were spent on that roof in many moods and thoughts. When my father was at home his room was on the second floor. How often I watched him at a distance, from my hiding place at the head of the staircase. The sun had not yet risen, and he sat on the roof silent as an image of white stone, his hands folded in his lap. From time to time he would leave home for long periods in the mountains, and then the journey to the roof held for me the joy of a voyage through the seven seas. Sitting on the familiar first floor verandah I had daily watched through the railings the people going about the street. But to climb to that roof was to be raised beyond the swarming habitations of men. When I went on to the roof my mind strode proudly over prostrate Calcutta to where the last blue of the sky mingled with the last green of the earth; my eye fell on the roofs of countless houses, of all shapes and sizes, high and low, with the shaggy tops of trees between.

I would go up secretly to this roof, usually at mid-day. The mid-day hours have always held a fascination for me. They are like the night of the daytime, the time when the *Sannyāsi* spirit in every boy makes him long to quit his familiar surroundings. I put my hand through the shutter and drew the bolt of the door. Right opposite the door was a sofa, and I sat there in perfect bliss of solitude. The servants who acted as my warders had eaten their fill and become drowsy, and yawning and stretching had betaken themselves to sleep on their mats. The afternoon sunlight deepened into gold, and the kite rose screaming into the sky. The bangle-seller went crying his wares down the opposite lane. His sudden cry would penetrate to where the housewife lay with her loosened hair falling over her pillow, a maidservant would bring him in, and the old bangle-seller dexterously kneaded the tender fingers as he fitted on the glass bangles that took her fancy. The hushed pause of that old-world mid-day is now no more, and the hawkers of the silent time are heard no longer. The girl who in those days had married status. nowadays has still not attained it, she is learning her lessons in the second class. Perhaps, the bangle-seller runs, pulling a rickshaw, down that very lane.

The roof was like what I imagined the deserts of my books to be, a sheer expanse of quivering haze. A hot wind ran panting across it, whirling up the dust, the blue of the sky paled above it. Moreover, in this roof desert there appeared an oasis. Nowadays, the pipe water does not reach the upper floors, but then it ran even up to the second floor rooms. Like some young Livingstone of Bengal, alone and unaided, I secretly sought and found a new Niagara, the private bathroom. I would turn on the tap, and the water would run all over my body. I then took a sheet from the bed and dried myself, looking the picture of innocence.

Gradually, the holiday drew towards its close, and four struck on the gateway clock. The face of the sky on Sunday evenings was always very ill-favoured. There fell across it the shadow of the coming Monday's gaping jaws, already swallowing it in dark eclipse. Below at last, a search had been instituted for the boy who had given his guards the slip, for now it was tiffin time. This part of the day was a red-letter time for Brajeswar. He was in charge of buying the tiffin. In those days the shop-keepers did not make thirty or forty per cent profit on the price of *ghee,* and in odour and flavour the tiffin was still unpoisoned. When we were lucky enough to get them, we lost no time in eating up our *kochuri, singārā,* or even *ālur dom*. But when the time came round and Brajeswar, with his neck still further twisted, called to us, "Look *babu,* what I have brought you today", what was usually to be found in his cone of paper was merely a handful of fried groundnuts. It was not that I did not like this, but its attractiveness lay in its price. I never made the least objection, not even on the days when only sesamum *gojā* came out of the palm-leaf wrapper.

The light of day begins to grow murky. Once more with a gloomy spirit, I make the round of the roof. I gaze down at the scene below, where a procession of geese has climbed out of the tank. People have begun to come and go again on the steps of the *ghāt*, the shadow of the banyan tree lengthens across half the tank, the driver of a carriage and pair is yelling at the pedestrians in the street.

# IX

In this way the days passed monotonously on. School grabbed the best part of the day, and only fragments of time in the morning and evening slipped through its clutching fingers. As soon as I entered the classroom, the benches and tables forced themselves rudely on my attention, elbowing and jostling their way into my mind. They were always the same—stiff, cramping, and dead. In the evening I went home, and the oil lamp in our study-room, like a stern signal, summoned me to the preparation of the next day's lessons. There is a kind of grass-hopper which takes the colour of the withered leaves among which it lurks unobserved. In like manner my spirit also shrank and faded among those faded, drab-coloured days.

Now and again, there came to our courtyard a man with a dancing bear, or a snake charmer playing with his snakes. Now and again, the visit of a juggler provided some little novelty. Today, the drums of the juggler and snake-charmer no longer beat in our Chitpore Road. From afar they have salaamed to the cinema, and fled before it from the city. Games were few and of very ordinary kinds. We had marbles, we had what is called "bat-ball," a very poor distant relation of cricket, and there were also top-spinning and kite-flying. All the games of the city children were of this same lazy kind. Football, with all its running and jumping about on a big field, was still in its overseas home. And so, I was fenced in by the deadly sameness of the days, as though by an imprisoning hedge of lifeless, withered twigs.

In the midst of this monotony there played one day the flutes of festivity. A new bride came to the house, slender gold bracelets on her delicate brown hands. In the twinkling of an eye the cramping fence was broken, and a new being came into view from the magic land beyond the bounds of the familiar. I circled around her at a safe distance, but I did not dare to go near. She was enthroned at the centre of affection, and I was only a neglected, insignificant child.

The house was then divided into two suites of rooms. The men lived in the outer, and the women in the inner apartments. The ways of the *nabobs* obtained there still. I remember how my elder sister was walking on the roof with the new bride at her side, and they were exchanging intimacies freely. As soon as I tried to go near, however, I brought reprimand on my head, for these quarters were outside the boundaries laid down for boys. I saw myself obliged to go back crest-fallen to my shabby retreat of former days.

The monsoon rain, rushing down suddenly from the distant mountains, undermines the ancient banks in a moment, and that is what happened now. The new mistress brought a new régime into the house. The quarters of the bride were in the room adjoining the roof of the inner suite. That roof was under her complete control. It was there that the leaf-plates were spread for the dolls' weddings. On such feast days, boy as I was, I became the guest of honour. My new sister-in-law could cook well, and enjoyed feeding people, and I was always ready to satisfy this craving for playing the hostess. As soon as I returned from school some delicacy made with her own hands stood ready for me. One day, she gave me shrimp curry with yesterday's soaked rice, and a dash of chillies for flavouring, and I felt that I had nothing left to wish for. Sometimes, when she went to stay with relatives and I did not see her slippers outside the door of her room, I would go in a temper and steal some valuable object from her room, and lay the foundation of a quarrel. When she returned and missed it, I had only to make such a remark as "Do you expect *me* to keep an eye on your room when you go away? Am I a watchman?" She would pretend to be angry and say, "You have no need to keep an eye on the room. Watch your own hands." Modern women will smile at the *naïveté* of their predecessors who knew how to entertain only their own brothers-in-law, and I daresay they are right. People today are much more grown-up in every way than they were then. Then, we were all children alike, both young and old.

# X

And so began a new chapter of my lonely Bedouin life on the roof, and human company and friendship entered it. Across the roof kingdom a new wind blew, and a new season began there. My brother Jyotidada played a large part in this change. At that time my father finally left our home at Jorasanko. Jyotidada settled himself into that outside second-floor room, and I claimed a little corner of it for my own.

No *purdah* was observed in my sister-in-law's apartments. That will strike no one as strange today, but it then sounded an unimaginable depth of novelty. A long time even before that, when I was a baby, my second brother had returned from England to enter the Civil Service. When he went to Bombay to take up his first post he astonished the neighbourhood by taking off his wife with him before their very eyes. And, as if it was not enough to take her away to a distant province, instead of leaving her in the family home, he made no provision for proper privacy on the journey. That was a terrible breach of propriety. Even the relatives felt as if the sky had fallen on their heads.

A style of dress suitable for going out was still not in vogue among women. It was this sister-in-law who first introduced the manner of wearing the sari and blouse which is now customary. Little girls had not then begun to wear frocks or let their hair hang in plaits—at least not in our family. The little ones used to wear the tight Rajput pyjamas instead of the traditional sari. When the Bethune School was first opened, my eldest sister was quite young. She was one of the pioneers who made the road to education easy for girls. She was very fair, uniquely so for this country. I have heard that once when she was going to school in her palanquin the police detained her, thinking her in her Rajput dress to be an English girl who had been kidnapped.

I said before that in those days there was no bridge of intimacy between adults and children. Into the tangle of these old customs Jyotidada brought a vigorously original mind. I was twelve years younger than he, and that I should come to his notice in spite of such a difference in age is in itself surprising. What was more surprising is that in my talks with him he never called me impudent or snubbed me. Thanks to this, I never lacked courage to think for myself. Today, I live with children, I try all kind of subjects of conversation, but I find them dumb. They hesitate to ask questions. They seem to me to belong to those old times when the grown-ups talked and the children remained silent. The self-confidence that doubts and questions is the mark of the children of the new age; those of the former age are known by a meek and docile acceptance of what they are told.

A piano appeared in the terrace room. There came also modern varnished furniture from Bowbazar. My breast swelled with pride, as the cheap grandeur of modern times was displayed before eyes inured to poverty. At this time the fountain of my song was unloosed. Jyotidada's hands would stray about the piano as he composed and rattled off tunes in various new styles, and he would keep me by his side as he did so. It was my work to fix the tunes which he composed so rapidly by setting words to them then and there.

At the end of the day a mat and pillow were spread on the terrace. Nearby was a thick garland of *bel* flowers on a silver plate, in a wet handkerchief, a glass of iced water on a saucer, and some *chhānchi pān* in a bowl. My sister-in-law would bathe, dress her hair and come and sit with us. Jyotidada would come out with a silk *chaddar* thrown over his shoulders, and draw the bow across his violin, and I would sing in my clear treble voice. For, providence had not yet taken away the gift of voice it had given me, and under the sunset sky my song rang out across the house-tops. The south wind came in great gusts from the distant sea, the sky filled with stars.

My sister-in-law turned the whole roof into a garden. She arranged rows of tall palms in barrels and beside and around them *chāmeli, gandharāj, rajanigandhā, karabi* and *dolan-champā*. She considered not at all the possible damage to the roof—we were all alike unpractical visionaries.

Akshay Chaudhuri used to come almost everyday. He himself knew that he had no voice, other people knew it even better. In spite of that nothing could stop the flow of his song. His special favourite was the *Behāg* mode. He sang with his eyes shut, so he did not see the expression on the faces of his hearers. As soon as anything capable of making a noise came to hand, he took it and turned it into a drum, beating it in happy absorption, biting his lips with his teeth in his earnestness. Even a book with a stiff binding would do very well. He was by nature a dreamy kind of man, one could see no difference between his working days and his holidays.

The evening party broke up, but I was a boy of nocturnal habits. All went to lie down, I alone would wander about all night with the *Brahma-daitya.* The whole district was steeped in silence. On moonlight nights the shadows of the lines of palm-trees on the terrace lay in dream-patterns on the floor. Beyond the terrace the top of the *sishu* tree swayed and tossed in the breeze, and its leaves gleamed as they caught the light. But for some reason, what caught my eye more than anything was a squat room with a sloping roof built over the staircase of the sleeping house on the opposite side of the lane. It stood like a finger pointing for ever towards I knew not what.

It may have been one or two in the morning, when in the main street in front a wailing chant arose—*Bolō-Hari Hari-bōl.*[1]

---

1. Funeral chant of the Hindus.

# XI

It was the fashion then in every house to keep caged birds. I hated this, and the worst thing of all to me was the call of a *koel* imprisoned in a cage in some house in the neighbourhood. *Bouthākrun*[1] had acquired a Chinese *shyama.* From under its covering of cloth its sweet whistling rose continuously, a fountain of song. Besides this, there were other birds of all kinds, and their cages hung in the west verandah. Every morning a bird-seed and insect hawker provided the birds' food. Grass-hoppers came from his basket, and gram-flour for the grain-eating birds.

Jyotidada gave me proper answers in my difficulties, but as much could not be expected from the women. Once, *Bouthākrun* took a fancy for keeping pet squirrels in cages. I said it wasn't right, and she told me not to set myself up to be her teacher. That could hardly be called a reasoned reply, and consequently, instead of wasting time in bickering, I privately set two of the little creatures free. After that too, I had to listen to a certain amount of scolding, but I made no retort.

---

1. Sister-in-law.

There was a permanent quarrel between us which was never made up, which was as follows.

There was a smart fellow called Umesh. He used to go the rounds of the English tailoring shops and buy up for an old song all their scraps, remnants and strips of many coloured silk, and make up women's garments from them with the addition of a bit of net and cheap lace. He would open his paper parcel and spread them carefully out before the eyes of the women, extolling them as "the very latest fashion". The women could not resist the attraction of such a *mantra,* but I disliked it all intensely. Again and again, unable to contain myself, I made known my objections, but all the answer I got was "Don't be cheeky". I used to tell *Bouthākrun* that the old-fashioned black-bordered white sarees, and the Dacca ones, were far better and more tasteful than these. I sometimes wonder, do modern brothers-in-law never open their mouths when they see their *Boudidis* robed in these modern georgette sarees, with their faces painted like dolls? Even *Bouthākrun* decked out in Umesh's handiwork was not as bad as they are. Ladies then were at least not so guilty of forgery in dress or complexion.

I was, however, always beaten by *Bouthākrun* in argument, because she would never deign to give a logical answer; and I was beaten too in chess, in which she was an expert.

As I have referred to Jyotidada I ought to give a little more information about him, to make him better known. To do that I must go back to rather earlier days.

He had to go very often to Shelidah to see after the business of the zemindari. Once, when he was travelling for this purpose he took me also with him. This was quite contrary to custom in those days, in fact it was what people would have called "altogether *too* much". He certainly considered that this travelling away from home was a kind of peripatetic schooling. He realised that my nature was attuned to ramblings in the open air, that in such surroundings it nourished itself spontaneously. A little later, when I was more mature, it was in Shelidah that my nature developed.

The old indigo factory was still standing, with the river Padma in the distance. The zemindari office was on the ground floor, and our living quarters on the upper floor. In front of them was a very large terrace. Beyond were tall casuarina trees, which had grown in stature with the growing prosperity of the indigo-trading *sahebs*. Today, the blustering shouts of the sahebs are completely silent. Where is now the indigo factory's steward, that "messenger of death"? Where the troop of bailiffs, loins girded up and *lāthis* on shoulder? Where is the dining hall with its long tables, where the sahebs rode back from their business in the town and turned night into day? The feasting reached its height, the dancing couples whirled round the room, the blood coursed madly through the veins in the swelling intoxication of champagne—and the authorities never heard the appealing cries of the wretched *ryots*, whose weary journey took them only to the District Jail. All traces of those days have vanished, save one record alone—the two graves of two of the sahebs. The high casuarina trees bend and sway in the wind, and sometimes at midnight the grandsons and grand-daughters of the former *ryots* see the ghosts of the sahebs wandering in the deserted waste of garden.

Here, I revelled in my solitude. I had a little corner room, and my days of ample leisure were spacious as the wide-spreading terrace. It was the leisure of a strange and unknown region, unfathomable as the dark waters of some ancient tank. The *bou-kathā-kao*[2] calls incessantly, my fancy unweariedly takes wing. Meantime, my note-book is gradually filled with verses. They were like the blossoms of the mango-tree's first flowering in the month of *Māgh,* destined like them to wither forgotten.

In those days if a young boy, or still more a young girl, laboriously counted out the fourteen syllables and wrote two lines of verse, the wise critics of the country used to hail it as a unique and unparalleled achievement.

I saw in the papers and magazines the names of these girl-poets, and their verses also were published. Nowadays these carefully constructed metres and crude rhyming platitudes have vanished along with the names of their authors, and the names of countless modern girls have appeared in their stead.

---

2. Also called "makwa-pāko", an Indian species of cuckoo. Both names are imitations of the call.

Boys are less bold and far more self-conscious than girls. I do not remember any young boy-poet writing verse in those days, except myself. My sister's son, who was older than I, explained to me one day that if one poured words into a fourteen-syllable mould, they would condense into verse. I soon tried this magic formula for myself. The lotus of poetry blossomed in no time in this fourteen-syllabled form and even the bees found a foothold on it. The gulf between me and the poets was bridged, and from that time on I have struggled to overtake them.

I remember how, when I was in the lowest class of the *chhātra britti*[3] our superintendent Govinda Babu heard a rumour that I wrote poetry. He thereupon ordered me to write, thinking that it would redound to the credit of the Normal School. There was nothing for it but to write, to read my work before my classmates, and to hear the verdict—"this verse is assuredly stolen goods". The cynics of that day did not know that when I increased in worldly wisdom I should grow shrewd in stealing, not words but thoughts. Yet, it is these stolen goods which are valuable.

I remember once composing a poem in the *Payār* and *Tripadi* metres, in which I lamented that as one swims to pluck the lotus it floats further and further away on the waves raised by one's own arms, and remains always out of reach. Akshay Babu took me round to the houses of his

3. This corresponds roughly to the modern transition from "primary" to "secondary" education.

relatives and made me recite it to them. "The boy has certainly a gift for writing", they said.

*Bouthākrun's* attitude was just the opposite. She would never admit that I should ever make a success of writing. She would say mockingly that I should never be able to write like Bihari Chakravarti. I used to think despondently that even if I were placed in a far lower class than he, she would then be prevented from so disregarding her little poet – brother-in-law's disapprobation of women's fashions.

Jyotidada was very fond of riding. He actually took even *Bouthākrun* riding along Chitpore Road to the Eden Gardens. In Shelidah he gave me a pony, a beast that was no mean runner. He sent me to give the pony a run on the open *rath-talā* field.[4] I did as I was bidden, in continual imminent danger of a fall on that uneven ground. That I did not fall was solely because he was so determined that I should *not* do so .Shortly afterwards Jyotidada sent me out riding on the roads of Calcutta also. Not on the pony, but on a high-spirited thoroughbred. One day, it galloped straight in through the porch, with me on its back, to the courtyard where it was accustomed to be fed. From that day on, I had nothing more to do with it.

I have referred elsewhere to the fact that Jyotidada was a practised shot. He was always eager for a tiger-hunt. One day, the *shikāri* Visvanath brought news that a tiger

---

4. The field reserved in a Bengali village for the celebration of the car-festival.

was living in the Shelidah jungle, and Jyotidada at once furbished up his gun and prepared for sport. Surprising to say, he took me with him. It never seemed to occur to him that there could be any danger.

Visvanath was indeed, an expert *shikāri.* He knew that there was nothing manly about hunting from a *māchān.* He would call the tiger out and shoot face-to-face, and he never missed his aim.

The jungle was dense, and in its lights and shadows the tiger refused to show himself. A rough kind of ladder was made by cutting footholds in a stout bamboo, and Jyotidada climbed up with his gun ready to hand. As for me, I was not even wearing slippers, I had not even that poor instrument with which to beat and humiliate the tiger. Visvanath signed to us to be on the alert, but for some time Jyotidada could not even see the tiger. After long straining of his bespectacled eyes he at last caught a glimpse of one of its markings in the thicket. He fired. By a lucky chance the shot pierced the animal's backbone, and it was unable to rise. It roared furiously, biting at all the sticks and twigs within reach, and lashing its tail. Thinking it over, I know that it is not in the nature of tigers to wait so long and patiently to be killed. I wonder if some-one had had the forethought to mix a little opium with its feed on the previous night? Otherwise, why such sound sleep?

There was another occasion when a tiger came to the jungles of Shelidah. My brother and I set out on elephants to look for him. My elephant lurched majestically on, uprooting cane from the sugar cane fields and munching as he went, so that it was like riding on an earthquake. The jungle lay ahead of us. He crushed the trees with his knees, pulled them up with his trunk and cast them to the ground. I had previously heard tales of terrible possibilities from Visvanath's brother Chamru, how sometimes the tiger leaps on to the elephant's back and clings there, digging in his claws. Then, the elephant trumpeting with pain, rushes madly through the forest, and whoever is on his back is dashed against the trees till arms, legs and head are crushed out of all recognition. That day, as I sat my elephant, the image of myself thus being pounded to a jelly filled my imagination from first to last. For very shame I concealed my fear, and glanced from side-to-side in nonchalant fashion, as though to say, "Let me but catch a glimpse of the tiger, and then!..." The elephant entered the densest part of the jungle, and coming to a certain place, suddenly stood stock-still. The māhout made no attempt to urge it forward. He had clearly more respect for the tiger's powers as a *shikāri* than for my brother's. His great anxiety was undoubtedly that Jyotidada should so wound the tiger as to drive it to desperation. Suddenly, the tiger leaped from the jungle, swift as the thunder-charged storm from the cloud. We are accustomed to the sight of a cat, dog, or jackal, but here were shoulders of terrific bulk and power, yet no sense of heaviness in that perfectly proportioned strength. It crossed the open fields at a canter in the full blaze of the mid-day sun. What loveliness, ease and speed of motion! The land was empty of crops; here, indeed, was a setting in which to feast one's eyes on the running tiger, this wide stretch of golden stubble drenched in the noonday sunlight.

There is one more story that may prove amusing. In Shelidah the gardener used to pluck flowers and arrange them in the vases. I took a fancy to write poetry with a pen dipped in the coloured essences of flowers. But the moisture that I could obtain by squeezing was not sufficient to wet the tip of my pen. I decided that it must be done by machinery. It would do, I thought, if I had a cup-shaped wooden sieve and a pestle revolving in it. It could be turned by an arrangement of ropes and pulleys. I made known my wants to Jyotidada. It may be that he smiled to himself, but he gave no outward sign. He issued instructions, and the carpenter brought wood. The machine was ready. I filled the wooden cup with flowers, but turn the ropes of the pestle as I would the flowers, merely turned to mud and not a drop of essence ran out. Jyotidada saw that the essence of flowers was incompatible with the grinding of machinery, yet he never laughed at me.

This was the only occasion in my life on which I tried my hand at engineering. It is said in the *sāstras* that there is a god who compasses the humiliation of those who ignore their own limitations. That god cast a mocking glance that day upon my engineering, and from that time I have not so much as laid hands on any kind of instrument, not even on a *sitār* or an *esrāj*.

I described in my *Reminiscences* how Jyotidada went bankrupt in his attempt to run a *swadeshi* steamer company on the rivers of Bengal in competition with the Flotilla Company. *Bouthākrun's* death had taken place before then. Jyotidada gave up his rooms on the third storey and finally built himself a house on a hill at Ranchi.

# XII

A new chapter in the life of the third-storey room now opened, as I took up my abode there. Up to that time it had been merely one of my gypsy haunts, like the palanquin and the granary, and I roamed from one to another. But when *Bouthākrun* came a garden appeared on the roof, and in the room a piano was established. Its flow of new tunes symbolised the changed tenor of my life.

Jyotidada used to arrange to have his coffee in the mornings in the shade of the staircase room on the eastern side of the terrace. At such times, he would read to us the first draft of some new play of his. From time to time, I also would be called upon to add a few lines with my unpractised hand. The sun's rays gradually invaded the shade, the crows cried hoarsely to each other as they sat on the roof keeping an eye upon the bread-crumbs. By ten o'clock the patch of shade had dwindled away and the terrace grew hot.

At mid-day Jyotidada used to go down to the office on the ground floor. *Bouthākrun* peeled and cut fruit and arranged it carefully on a silver plate, along with a few sweetmeats made with her own hands, and strewed a few rose petals over it. In a tumbler was coconut milk or fruit-juice or *tāl shāns* (fresh palmyra kernels), cooled in ice. Then, she covered it with a silk kerchief embroidered with flowers, put it on a Moradabad tray, and despatched it to the office at tiffin time, about one or two o'clock.

Just then *Bangadarśan*[1] was at the height of its fame, and *Suryamukhi* and *Kundanandini*[2] were familiar figures in every house. The whole country thought of nothing else but what had happened and what was gong to happen to the heroines.

When *Bangadarśan* came there was no mid-day nap for anyone in the neighbourhood. It was my good fortune not to have to snatch for it, for I had the gift of being an acceptable reader. *Bouthākrun* would rather listen to my reading aloud than read for herself. There were no electric fans then, but as I read I shared the benefits of *Bouthākrun's* hand fan.

1. A famous Bengali magazine edited by the well-known Bengali novelist, Bankim Chandra Chatterji.
2. Characters in Bankim Chandra's novel.

# XIII

Now and again, Jyotidada used to go for change of air to a garden house on the bank of the Ganges. The Ganges shores had then not yet lost caste at the defiling touch of English commerce. Both shores alike were still the undisturbed haunt of birds, and the mechanised dragons of industry did not darken the light of heaven with the black breath of their upreared snouts.

My earliest memory of our life by the Ganges is of a small two-storey house. The first rains had just fallen. Cloud shadows danced on the ripples of the stream, cloud shadows lay dark upon the jungles of the further shore. I had often composed songs of my own on such days, but that day I did not do so. The lines of Vidyapati came to my mind, *e bharā bādara māha bhādara śūnya mandira mōr.*[1] Moulding them to my own melody and stamping them with my own musical mood, I made them my own. The memory of that monsoon day, jewelled with that music on the Ganges shore, is still preserved in my treasury of rainy

1. Brimmed with rain is the month of Bhadra (August – September), empty my spirit's dwelling stands.

season songs. I see in memory the tree-tops struck ever and again by great gusts of wind, till their boughs and branches were tangled together in an ecstasy of play. The boats and dinghies raised their white sails and scudded before the gale, the waves leaped against the *ghāt* with sharp, slapping sounds. *Bouthākrun* came back and I sang my song to her. She listened in silence and said no word of praise. I must then have been sixteen or seventeen years old. We used to have arguments even then about various matters, but no longer in the old spirit of childish wrangling.

A little while after we removed to Moran's Garden. That was a regular palace. The rooms, of varying heights, had coloured glass in their windows, the floors were of marble, and steps led down from the long verandah to the very edge of the Ganges. Here, a fit of wakefulness by night came upon me, and I used to pace to and fro, as I did later on the banks of the Sabarmati. That garden is no longer in existence, the iron jaws of the Dundee Mills have crushed and swallowed it.

At the mention of Moran's Garden there comes back the memory of our occasional picnics under the *bakul* tree. The food owed its flavour not to spices but to the hands that prepared it. How I remember our sacred-thread ceremony, when we two boys were fed by *Bouthākrun* with the ceremonial rice and fresh *ghee*! For those three days we had our fill of tasty and savoury dishes.

It was a great annoyance to me that it was so difficult for me to fall ill. All the other boys in the house could manage it, and then they would enjoy *Bouthākrun's* personal care. Not only did they enjoy her care, but they took up all her time, and my own share of it was correspondingly diminished.

So came to an end that page of the history of the third storey, and with it *Bouthākrun* also passed away. After that the second floor became my own domain, but it was no longer as in the old days.

I have wandered in my story up to the very gateway of my young manhood. I must return to the territory of my boyhood once more.

Now, I must give some account of my sixteenth year. At its very entrance stands *Bhārati*.[2] Nowadays, the whole country seethes with the excitement of bringing out papers, and I can well understand the strength of that passion when I look back on my own madcap escapades. That a boy like me, with neither learning nor talents, should succeed in establishing himself in that *salon,* or at least in escaping reprimand there, shows what a youthful spirit was abroad everywhere. *Bangadarśan* was then the only magazine in the country controlled by a mature hand. As for ours, it was a medley of the mature and the crude. Baḍadada's contributions were as difficult to understand as they were to write; and side-by-side with them stood a story of mine,

2. Monthly magazine founded by Jyotidada (Jyotirindranath Tagore) and first edited by the Poet's eldest brother Dwijendranath Tagore, referred to here as Baḍadada. It ran for about half a century.

the raw verbosity of whose style I was too young to appraise, nor did others apparently possess the critical judegment to do so.

The time has come to say something of Baḍadada. Jyotidada held court in that third-storey room, and Baḍadada in our south verandah. At one time he plunged into the deepest problems of metaphysics, far outside the range of our comprehension. There were few to listen to what he wrote and thought, and he would not lightly let any man go who showed himself willing to be audience. Nor, would the man himself soon relinquish Baḍadada, but what he claimed from him was not alone the privilege of listening to metaphysics. One such man attached himself whose name I do not remember, but everyone called him "The Philosopher". My other brothers made great fun of him, not only about his love for mutton chops, but about his endless stream of varied and urgent necessities. Besides philosophy, Baḍadada then began to take great interest in the construction of mathematical problems. The verandah would be full of papers, covered with figures, flying about in the south wind. Baḍadada could not sing, but he used to play an English flute, not for the sake of the music, but in order to measure mathematically the notes of each scale. After that he occupied himself for a time in writing *Svapna-Prayāna.* To start with, he began to experiment in verse-making, weighing the sound-values of Sanskrit words in the scales of Bengali rhythm, and so creating new forms. Many of these attempts he retained, but many he threw away, and torn pages were scattered everywhere. After that he started to write his book of poems, but he rejected far more than he kept, for he was not easily satisfied with his work. We had not the sense to pick up and keep all these discarded lines. As he wrote he would read his work, and people would gather round him to listen. Our whole household was intoxicated with this wine of poetry. Sometimes, in the midst of his reading he would burst into a great shout of laughter. His laughter was ample and generous as the skies, but woe betide the man who sat within reach when the fit took him; he received slaps on the back to shake his very soul. The south verandah was the living fountain of the life of Jorasanko, but the fountain dried up when Baḍadada went to live at the Santiniketan *asrama.* I remember, however, times spent in the garden opposite that south verandah, when with mind made listless by the touch of the autumn sun I composed and sang a new song: "Today, in the autumn sun, in my dreams of dawn, a nameless yearning fills my soul." I remember also a song made in the quivering heat of one blazing noon: "In this listless abandon of spirit, I know not what games I kept on playing with my own self."

Another striking thing about Baḍadada was his swimming. He would swim backwards and forwards across our tank at least fifty times. When he lived at Panihati Garden he used to swim far out into the Ganges. With his example before us we also learned to swim as boys. We started to learn by ourselves. We would wet our pyjamas and then pull them up tight so as to fill them with air. In the water they swelled out round our waists like balloons, and we could not possibly sink. When I was older and stayed on the river-lands[3] of Shelidah, I once swam across the Padma. This was not as wonderful an achievement as it sounds. The Padma was full of alluvial islands which broke the force of its current, so that the feat was not worthy of any great respect. Still, it was certainly a story with which to impress others, and I have used it so many times. When I went as a boy to Dalhousie, my father never forbade me to wander about by myself. With an alpenstock in my hand I traversed the footpaths, climbing one hill after another. It was most amusing to scare myself with my own make-believe. Once, while going steeply downhill I stepped on a heap of withered leaves at the foot of a tree. My foot slipped a little and I saved myself with my stick. But perhaps, I might not have been able to stop myself! I wondered how long it would have taken to roll down the steep slope and fall into the waterfall far below. I described to Mother with picturesque inventiveness all that might have happened. Then, wandering in the deep pinewoods, I might suddenly have come upon a bear that also was certainly something worth talking about. As nothing ever really happened I stored up all these imaginary adventures in my mind. The story of my swimming across the Padma was much of a piece with this class of romances.

3. Tracts of rich alluvial land often found as islands in the great rivers (Beng. *Char*).

When I was seventeen I had to leave the editorial board of *Bhārati,* for it was then decided that I should go to England. Further, it was considered that before sailing I should live with *Mejadādā*[4] for a time to get some grounding in English manners. He was then a judge at Ahmedabad, and *Meja-Bouthākrun* and her children were in England, waiting for *Mejadādā* to get a furlough and join them.

I was torn up by the roots and transplanted from one soil to another, and had to get acclimatised to a new mental atmosphere. At first, my shyness was a stumbling-block at every turn. I wondered how I should keep my self-respect among all these new acquaintances. It was not easy to habituate myself to strange surroundings, yet there was no means of escape from them; in such a situation a boy of my temperament was bound to find his path a rough one.

My fancy, free to wander, conjured up pictures of the history of Ahmedabad in the Moghul period. The judge's quarters were in Shahibag, the former palace grounds of the Muslim kings. During the daytime *Mejadādā* was away at his work, the vast house seemed one cavernous emptiness, and I wandered about all day like one possessed. In front was a wide terrace, which commanded a view of the Sabarmati river, whose knee-deep waters meandered along through the sands. I felt as though the stone-built tanks, scattered here and there along the terrace, held

---

4. Second brother, Satyendranath Tagore.

locked in their masonry wonderful secrets of the luxurious bathing-halls of the Begums.

We are Calcutta people, and history nowhere gives us any evidence of its past grandeur there. Our vision had been confined to the narrow boundaries of these stunted times. In Ahmedabad I felt for the first time that history had paused, and was standing with her face turned towards the aristocratic past. Her former days were buried in the earth like the treasure of the *yakshas.*[5] My mind received the first suggestion for the story of *Hungry Stones.*

How many hundred years have passed since those times! Then, in the *nahabat-khānā,* the minstrel's gallery, an orchestra played day and night, choosing tunes appropriate to the eight periods of the day. The rhythmic beat of horses' hoofs echoed on the streets, and great parades were held of the mounted Turkish cavalry, the sun glittering on the points of their spears. In the court of the Pādshāh whispered conspiracies were ominously rife. Abyssinian eunuchs, with drawn swords, kept guard in the inner apartments. Rose-water fountains played in the *hamāms* of the Begums, the bangles tinkled on their arms. Today, Shahibag stands silent, like a forgotten tale; all its colour has faded, and its varied sounds have died away; the splendours of the day are withered and the nights have lost their savour.

Only the bare skeleton of those old days remained, its

5. Demons who guard treasure.

head a naked skull whose crown was gone. It was like a mummy in a museum, but it would bc too much to say that my mind was able fully to re-clothe those dry bones with flesh and blood and restore the original form. Both the first rough model, and the background against which it stood, were largely a creation of the fancy. Such patchwork is easy when little is known and the rest has been forgotten. After these eighty years even the picture of myself that comes before me does not correspond line for line with the reality, but is largely a product of the imagination.

After I had stayed there for some time *Mejadādā* decided that perhaps I should be less homesick if I could mix with women who could familiarise me with conditions abroad. It would also be an easy way to learn English. So, for a while I lived with a Bombay family. One of the daughters of the house was a modern educated girl who had just returned with all the polish of a visit to England. My own attainments were only ordinary, and she could not have been blamed if she had ignored me. But she did not do so. Not having any store of book-learning to offer her, I took the first opportunity to tell her that I could write poetry. This was the only capital I had with which to gain attention. When I told her of my poetical gift, she did not receive it in any carping or dubious spirit, but accepted it without question. She asked the poet to give her a special name, and I chose one for her which she thought very beautiful. I wanted that name to be entwined with the music of my verse, and I enshrined it in a poem which I made for her. She listened as I sang it in the *Bhairavi* mode of early dawn, and then said, "Poet, I think that even if I were on my death-bed your songs would call me back to life." There is an example of how well girls know how to show their appreciation by some pleasant exaggeration. They simply do it for the pleasure of pleasing. I remember that it was from her that I first heard praise of my personal appearance, —praise that was often very delicately given.

For example, she asked me once very particularly to remember one thing: "You must never wear a beard. Don't let anything hide the outline of your face." Everyone knows that I have not followed that advice. But she herself did not live to see my disobediece proclaimed upon my face.

In some years, birds strange to Calcutta used to come and build nests in that banyan tree of ours. They would be off again almost before I had learnt to recognize the dance of their wings, but they brought with them a strangely lovely music from their distant jungle homes. So, in the course of our life's journey, some angel from a strange and unexpected quarter may cross our path, speaking the language of our own soul, and enlarging the boundaries of the heart's possessions. She comes unbidden, and when at last we call for her she is no longer there. But as she goes, she leaves on the drab web of our lives a border of embroidered flowers, and for ever and ever the night and day are for us enriched.

# XIV

The Master-Workman, who made me, fashioned his first model from the native clay of Bengal. I have described this first model, which is what I call my boyhood, and in it there is little admixture of other elements. Most of its ingredients were gathered from within, though the atmosphere of the home and the home people counted for something, too. Very often, the work of moulding goes no further than this stage. Some people get hammered into shape in the book-learning factories, and these are considered in the market to be goods of a superior stamp.

It was my fortune to escape almost entirely the impress of these mills of learning. The masters and pundits who were charged with my education soon abandoned the thankless task. There was Jnanachandra Bhattacharya, the son of Anandachandra Vedāntabāgish, who was a B.A. He realised that this boy could never be driven along the beaten tract of learning. The teachers of those days, alas! were not so strongly convinced that boys should all be poured into the mould of degree-holding respectability. There was then no demand that rich and poor alike should all be confined within the fenced-off regions of college studies. Our family had no wealth then, but it had a reputation, so the old traditions held good, and they were indifferent to conventional academic success. From the lower classes of the Normal School we were transferred to De Cruz's Bengal Academy. It was the hope of my guardians that even if I got nothing else, I should get enough mastery of spoken English to save my face. In the Latin class I was deaf and dumb, and my exercise books of all kinds kept from beginning to end the unrelieved whiteness of a widow's cloth. Confronted by such unprecedented determination not to study, my class teacher complained to Mr De Cruz, who explained that we were not born for study, but for the purpose of paying our monthly fees. Jnana Babu was of a similar opinion, but found means of keeping me occupied nevertheless. He gave me the whole of *Kumārasambhava*[1] to learn by heart. He shut me in a room and gave me *Macbeth* to translate. Then, Pundit Ramsarbaswa read *Sakuntalā* with me. By setting me free in this way from the fixed curriculum, they reaped some reward for their labours. These then were the materials that formed my boyish mind, together with what other Bengali books I picked up at random.

I landed in England, and foreign workmanship began to play a part in the fashioning of my life. The result is what is known in chemistry as a compound. How capricious is Fortune!—I went to England for a regular course of study, and a desultory start was made, but it came to nothing. *Meja-Bouthān* was there, and her children, and my own family circle absorbed nearly all my interest. I hung about around the school-room, a master taught me at the house, but I did not give my mind to it.

However, gradually the atmosphere of England made its impression on my mind, and what little I brought back from that country was from the people I came in contact with. Mr Palit finally succeeded in getting me away from my own family. I went to live with a doctor's family, where they made me forget that I was in a foreign land. Mrs Scott lavished on me a genuine affection, and cared for me like a mother. I had then been admitted to London University, and Henry Morley was teaching English literature. His teaching was no dry-as-dust exposition of dead books. Literature came to life in his mind and in the sound of his voice, it reached to our inner being where the soul seeks its nourishment, and nothing of its essential nature was lost. With his guidance, I found the study of the Clarendon Press books at home to be an easy matter and I took upon myself to be my own teacher. For no reason at all Mrs Scott would sometimes fancy that I did not look well, and would become very worried about me. She did not know that the portals of sickness had been barred against me from childhood. I used to bathe every morning in ice-cold water—in fact, in the opinion of the doctors, it was almost a sacrilege that I should survive such flagrant disregard of the accepted rules!

---

1. A work of Kalidasa.

I was able to study in the University for three months only, but I obtained almost all my understanding of English culture from personal contacts. The Artist who fashions us takes every opportunity to mingle new elements in his creation. Three months of close intimacy with English hearts sufficed for this development. Mrs Scott made it my duty each evening till eleven o'clock to read aloud from poetic drama and history by turn. In this way I did a great deal of reading in a short space of time. It was not prescribed class study, and my understanding of human nature developed side-by-side with my knowledge of literature. I went to England but I did not become a barrister. I received no shock calculated to shatter the original framework of my life—rather East and West met in friendship in my own person. Thus, it has been given me to realise in my own life the meaning of my name.[2]

2. The poet's name *Rabi* means the sun, which does not distinguish between East and West.

# THE POST OFFICE

**Tagore's other titles in Srishti**

Gitanjali

My Boyhood Days

Mashi & other stories

The Gardener

A Treasure of Tagore's Writings Vol. 1

The Home and the World

Four Chapters

Selected short stories

# THE POST OFFICE

Rabindranath Tagore

Srishti
PUBLISHERS & DISTRIBUTORS

**Srishti Publishers & Distributors**
**Registered Office:** N-16, C. R. Park
New Delhi – 110 019
**Corporate Office:** 212A, Peacock Lane
Shahpur Jat, New Delhi – 110 049
editorial@srishtipublishers.com

First published by
Srishti Publishers & Distributors in 2012

10 9 8 7



Typeset by EGP at Srishti

Printed and bound in India

## The Characters

MADHAV

AMAL, his adopted child

SUDHA, a little flower-girl

THE DOCTOR

DAIRYMAN

WATCHMAN

GAFFER

VILLAGE HEADMAN, a bully

KING'S HERALD

ROYAL PHYSICIAN

# The Characters

# ACT I

## *(Madhav's House)*

*Madhav.* What a state I am in! Before he came, nothing mattered; I felt so free. But now that he has come, goodness knows from where, my heart is filled with his dear self, and my home will be no home to me when he leaves. Doctor, do you think he –

*Physician.* If there's life in his fate, then he will live long. But what the medical scriptures say, it seems –

*Madhav.* Great heavens, what?

*Physician.* The scriptures have it: "Bile or palsy, cold or gout spring all alike."

*Madhav.* Oh, get along, don't fling your scriptures at me; you only make me more anxious; tell me what I can do.

*Physician (taking snuff).* The patient needs the most scrupulous care.

*Madhav.* That's true; but tell me how.

*Physician.* I have already mentioned, on no account must he be let out of doors.

*Madhav.* Poor child, it is very hard to keep him indoors all day long.

*Physician.* What else can you do? The autumn sun and the damp are both very bad for the little fellow—for the scriptures have it:

"In wheezing, swooning, or in nervous fret,

In jaundice or leaden eyes—"

*Madhav.* Never mind the scriptures, please. Eh, then we must shut the poor thing up. Is there no other method?

*Physician.* None at all: for "In the wind and in the sun—"

*Madhav.* What will your "in this and in that" do for me now? Why don't you let them alone and come straight to the point? What's to be done, then? Your system is very, very hard for the poor boy; and he is so quiet too with all his pain and sickness. It tears my heart to see him wince, as he takes your medicine.

*Physician.* The more he winces, the surer is the effect. That's why the sage Chyabana observes: "In medicine as in good advice, the least palatable is the truest." Ah, well! I must be trotting now. *[Exit*

***(Gaffer enters)***

*Madhav.* Well, I'm jiggered, there's Gaffer now.

*Gaffer.* Why, why, I won't bite you.

*Madhav.* No, but you are a devil to send children off their heads.

*Gaffer.* But you aren't a child, and you've no child in

the house; why worry, then?

*Madhav.* Oh, but I have brought a child into the house.

*Gaffer.* Indeed, how so?

*Madhav.* You remember how my wife was dying to adopt a child?

*Gaffer.* Yes, but that's an old story; you didn't like the idea.

*Madhav.* You know, brother, how hard all this getting money in has been. That somebody else's child would sail in and waste all this money earned with so much trouble—Oh, I hated the idea. But this boy clings to my heart in such a queer sort of way—

*Gaffer.* So, that's the trouble! And your money goes all for him and feels jolly lucky it does go at all.

*Madhav.* Formerly, earning was a sort of passion with me; I simply couldn't help working for money. Now, I make money, and as I know it is all for this dear boy, earning becomes a joy to me.

*Gaffer.* Ah, well, and where did you pick him up?

*Madhav.* He is the son of a man who was a brother to my wife by village ties. He has had no mother since infancy; and now the other day he lost his father as well.

*Gaffer.* Poor thing: and so he needs me all the more.

*Madhav.* The doctor says all the organs of his little body are at loggerheads with each other, and there isn't much hope for his life. There is only one way to save him and that is to keep him out of this autumn wind and sun. But you are such a terror! What with this game of yours at your age, too, to get children out of doors!

*Gaffer*. God bless my soul! So, I'm already as bad as autumn wind and sun, eh! But, friend, I know something, too, of the game of keeping them indoors. When my day's work is over I am coming in to make friends with this child of yours. *[Exit*

***(Amal enters)***

*Amal.* Uncle, I say, Uncle!

*Madhav.* Hullo! Is that you, Amal?

*Amal.* Mayn't I be out of the courtyard at all?

*Madhav*. No, my dear, no.

*Amal.* See there, where Auntie grinds lentils in the quern, the squirrel is sitting with his tail up and with his wee hands he's picking up the broken grains of lentils and crunching them. Can't I run up there?

*Madhav.* No, my darling, no.

*Amal.* Wish I were a squirrel!–it would be lovely. Uncle, why won't you let me go about?

*Madhav*. Doctor says it's bad for you to be out.

*Amal.* How can the doctor know?

*Madhav*. What a thing to say! The doctor can't know and he reads such huge books!

*Amal.* Does his book-learning tell him everything?

*Madhav*. Of course, don't you know!

*Amal (with a sigh).* Ah, I am so stupid! I don't read books.

*Madhav.* Now, think of it; very, very learned people are all like you; they are never out of doors.

*Amal.* Aren't they really?

*Madhav.* No, how can they? Early and late they toil and moil at their books, and they've eyes for nothing else. Now, my little man, you are going to be learned when you grow up; and then you will stay at home and read such big books, and people will notice you and say, "He's a wonder."

*Amal.* No, no, Uncle; I beg of you, by your dear feet–I don't want to be learned; I won't.

*Madhav.* Dear, dear; it would have been my saving if I could have been learned.

*Amal.* No, I would rather go about and see everything that there is.

*Madhav.* Listen to that! See! What will you see, what is there so much to see?

*Amal.* See that far-away hill from our window–I often long to go beyond those hills and right away.

*Madhav.* Oh, you silly! As if there's nothing more to be done but just get up to the top of that hill and away! Eh! You don't talk sense, my boy. Now listen, since that hill stands there upright as a barrier, it means you can't get beyond it. Else, what was the use in heaping up so many large stones to make such a big affair of it, eh!

*Amal.* Uncle, do you think it is meant to prevent us crossing over? It seems to me because the earth can't speak it raises its hands into the sky and beckons. And, those who live far off and sit alone by their windows can see the signal. But I suppose the learned people–

*Madhav.* No, they don't have time for that sort of nonsense. They are not crazy like you.

*Amal.* Do you know, yesterday I met someone quite as crazy as I am.

*Madhav.* Gracious me, really, how so?

*Amal.* He had a bamboo staff on his shoulder with a small bundle at the top, and a brass pot in his left hand, and an old pair of shoes on; he was making for those hills straight across that meadow there. I called out to him and asked, "Where are you going?" He answered, "I don't know; anywhere!" I asked again, "Why are you going?" He said, "I'm going out to seek work." Say, Uncle, have you to seek work?

*Madhav.* Of course, I have to. There's many about looking for jobs.

*Amal.* How lovely! I'll go about like them too, finding things to do.

*Madhav.* Suppose you seek and don't find. Then–

*Amal.* Wouldn't that be jolly? Then I should go farther! I watched that man slowly walking on with his pair of worn-out shoes. And when he got to where the water flows under the fig tree, he stopped and washed his feet in the stream. Then he took out from his bundle some gram-flour, moistened it with water and began to eat. Then he tied up his bundle and shouldered it again; tucked up his cloth above his knees and crossed the stream. I've asked Auntie to let me go up to the stream, and eat my gram-flour just like him.

*Madhav.* And what did your Auntie say to that?

*Amal.* Auntie said, "Get well and then I'll take you over there." Please, Uncle, when shall I get well?

*Madhav.* It won't be long, dear.

*Amal.* Really, but then I shall go right away the moment I'm well again.

*Madhav.* And where will you go?

*Amal.* Oh, I will walk on, crossing so many streams, wading through water. Everybody will be asleep with their doors shut in the heat of the day and I will tramp on and on seeking work far, very far.

*Madhav.* I see! I think you had better be getting well first; then—

*Amal.* But then you won't want me to be learned, will you, Uncle?

*Madhav.* What would you rather be, then?

*Amal.* I can't think of anything just now; but I'll tell you later on.

*Madhav.* Very well. But mind you, you aren't to call out and talk to strangers again.

*Amal.* But I love to talk to strangers!

*Madhav.* Suppose they had kidnapped you?

*Amal.* That would have been splendid! But no one ever takes me away. They all want me to stay in here.

*Madhav.* I am off to my work–but, darling, you won't go out, will you?

*Amal.* No, I won't. But, Uncle, you'll let me be in this room by the roadside. *[Exit Madhav*

'*Dairyman.* Curds, curds, good nice curds.

*Amal.* Curdseller, I say, Curdseller.

*Dairyman.* Why do you call me? Will you buy some curds?

*Amal.* How can I buy? I have no money.

*Dairyman.* What a boy! Why call out then? Ugh! What a waste of time!

*Amal.* I would go with you if I could.

*Dairyman.* With me?

*Amal.* Yes, I seem to feel homesick when I hear you call from far down the road.

*Dairyman* (lowering his yoke-pole). Whatever are you doing here, my child?

*Amal.* The doctor says I'm not to be out, so I sit here all day long.

*Dairyman.* My poor child, whatever has happened to you?

*Amal.* I can't tell. You see, I am not learned, so I don't know what's the matter with me. Say, Dairyman, where do you come from?

*Dairyman.* From our village.

*Amal.* Your village? Is it very far?

*Dairyman.* Our village lies on the river Shamli at the foot of the Panch-mura hills.

*Amal.* Panch-mura hills! Shamli river! I wonder. I may have seen your village. I can't think when, though!

*Dairyman.* Have you seen it? Been to the foot of those hills?

*Amal.* Never. But I seem to remember having seen it. Your village is under some very old big trees, just by the side of the red road–isn't that so?

*Dairyman.* That's right, child.

*Amal.* And on the slope of the hill cattle grazing.

*Dairyman.* How wonderful! Cattle grazing in our village! Indeed there are!

*Amal.* And your women with red sarees fill their pitchers from the river and carry them on their heads.

*Dairyman.* Good, that's right! Women from our dairy village do come and draw their water from the river; but then it isn't everyone who has a red saree to put on. But, my dear child, surely you must have been there for a walk some time.

*Amal.* Really, Dairyman, never been there at all. But the first day doctor lets me go out, you are going to take me to your village.

*Dairyman.* I will, my child, with pleasure.

*Amal.* And you'll teach me to cry curds and shoulder the yoke like you and walk the long, long road?

*Dairyman.* Dear, dear, did you ever? Why should you sell curds? No, you will read big books and be learned.

*Amal.* No, I never want to be learned–I'll be like you and take my curds from the village by the red road near the old banyan tree, and I will hawk it from cottage to cottage. Oh, how do you cry–"Curds, curds, fine curds"? Teach me the tune, will you?

*Dairyman.* Dear, dear, teach you the tune; what a notion!

*Amal.* Please do. I love to hear it. I can't tell you how queer I feel when I hear you cry out from the bend of that road through the line of those trees! Do you know I feel like that when I hear the shrill cry of kites from almost the end of the sky?

*Dairyman.* Dear child, will you have some curds? Yes, do.

*Amal.* But I have no money.

*Dairyman.* No, no, no, don't talk of money! You'll make me so happy if you take some curds from me.

*Amal.* Say, have I kept you too long?

*Dairyman.* Not a bit; it has been no loss to me at all; you have taught me how to be happy selling curds.

*[Exit*

*Amal (intoning).* Curds, curds, fine curds–from the dairy village–from the country of the Panch-mura hills by the Shamli bank. Curds, good curds; in the early morning the women make the cows stand in a row under the trees and milk them, and in the evening they turn the milk into curds. Curds, good curds. Hello, there's the watchman on his rounds. Watchman, I say, come and have a word with me.

*Watchman.* What's all this row about? Aren't you afraid of the likes of me?

*Amal.* No, why should I be?

*Watchman.* Suppose I march you off, then?

*Amal.* Where will you take me to? Is it very far, right beyond the hills?

*Watchman.* Suppose I march you straight to the King?

*Amal.* To the King! Do, will you? But the doctor won't let me go out. No one can ever take me away. I've got to stay here all day long.

*Watchman.* Doctor won't let you, poor fellow! So I see! Your face is pale and there are dark rings round your eyes. Your veins stick out from your poor thin hands.

*Amal.* Won't you sound the gong, Watchman?

*Watchman.* Time has not yet come.

*Amal.* How curious! Some say time has not yet come, and some say time has gone by! But surely your time will come the moment you strike the gong!

*Watchman.* That's not possible; I strike up the gong only when it is time.

*Amal.* Yes, I love to hear your gong. When it is mid-day and our meal is over, Uncle goes off to his work and Auntie falls asleep reading her *Ramayana*, and in the courtyard under the shadow of the wall our doggie sleeps with his nose in his curled-up tail; then your gong strikes out, "Dong, dong, dong!" Tell me, why does your gong sound?

*Watchman.* My gong sounds to tell the people, Time waits for none, but goes on forever.

*Amal.* Where, to what land?

*Watchman.* That none knows.

*Amal.* Then I suppose no one has ever been there! Oh, I do wish to fly with the time to that land of which no one knows anything.

*Watchman.* All of us have to get there one day, my child.

*Amal.* Have I too?

*Watchman.* Yes, you too!

*Amal.* But doctor won't let me out.

*Watchman.* One day the doctor himself may take you there by the hand.

*Amal.* He won't; you don't know him. He only keeps me in.

*Watchman.* One greater than he comes and lets us free.

*Amal.* When will this great doctor come for me? I can't stick in here anymore.

*Watchman.* Shouldn't talk like that, my child.

*Amal.* No. I am here where they have left me—I never move a bit. But, when your gong goes off, dong, dong, dong, it goes to my heart. Say, Watchman?

*Watchman.* Yes, my dear.

*Amal.* Say, what's going on there in that big house on the other side, where there is a flag flying high up and the people are always going in and out?

*Watchman.* Oh, there? That's our new Post Office.

*Amal.* Post Office? Whose?

*Watchman.* Whose? Why, the King's, surely!

*Amal.* Do letters come from the King to his office here?

*Watchman.* Of course. One fine day there may be a letter for you in there.

*Amal.* A letter for me? But I am only a little boy.

*Watchman.* The King sends tiny notes to little boys.

*Amal.* Oh, how splendid! When shall I have my letter? How do you know he'll write to me?

*Watchman.* Otherwise why should he set his Post Office here right in front of your open window, with the golden flag flying?

*Amal.* But who will fetch me my King's letter when it comes?

*Watchman.* The King has many postmen. Don't you see them run about with round gilt badges on their chests?

*Amal.* Well, where do they go?

*Watchman.* Oh, from door to door, all through the country.

*Amal.* I'll be the King's postman when I grow up.

*Watchman.* Ha! ha! Postman, indeed! Rain or shine, rich or poor, from house to house delivering letters—that's very great work!

*Amal.* That's what I'd like best. What makes you smile so? Oh, yes, your work is great, too. When it is silent everywhere in the heat of the noonday, your gong sounds, Dong, dong, dong,–and sometimes when I wake up at night all of a sudden and find our lamp blown out, I can hear through the darkness your gong slowly sounding, Dong, dong, dong!

*Watchman.* There's the village headman! I must be off. If he catches me gossiping there'll be a great to-do.

*Amal.* The headman? Whereabouts is he?

*Watchman.* Right down the road there; see that huge palm-leaf umbrella hopping along? That's him!

*Amal.* I suppose the King's made him our headman here?

*Watchman.* Made him? Oh, no! A fussy busybody!

He knows so many ways of making himself unpleasant that everybody is afraid of him. It's just a game for the likes of him, making trouble for everybody. I must be off now! Mustn't keep work waiting, you know! I'll drop in again tomorrow morning and tell you all the news of the town.

*[Exit*

*Amal.* It would be splendid to have a letter from the King everyday. I'll read them at the window. But, oh! I can't read writing. Who'll read them out to me, I wonder! Auntie reads her *Ramayana*; she may know the King's writing. If no one will, then I must keep them carefully and read them when I'm grown up. But if the postman can't find me? Headman, Mr. Headman, may I have a word with you?

*Headman.* Who is yelling after me on the highway? Oh, it's you, is it, you wretched monkey?

*Amal.* You're the headman. Everybody minds you.

*Headman (looking pleased).* Yes, oh yes, they do! They must!

*Amal.* Do the King's postmen listen to you?

*Headman.* They've got to. By Jove, I'd like to see—

*Amal.* Will you tell the postman it's Amal who sits by the window here?

*Headman.* What's the good of that?

*Amal.* In case there's a letter for me.

*Headman.* A letter for you! Whoever's going to write to you?

*Amal.* If the King does.

*Headman.* Ha! ha! What an uncommon little fellow you are! Ha! ha! the King, indeed; aren't you his bosom friend, eh! You haven't met for a long while and the King is pining for you, I am sure. Wait till tomorrow and you'll have your letter.

*Amal.* Say, Headman, why do you speak to me in that tone of voice? Are you cross?

*Headman.* Upon my word! Cross, indeed! You write to the King! Madhav is a devilish swell nowadays. He's made a little pile; and so kings and padishahs are everyday talk with his people. Let me find him once and I'll make him dance. Oh, you,—you snipper-snapper! I'll get the King's letter sent to your house—indeed I will!

*Amal.* No, no, please don't trouble yourself about it.

*Headman.* And why not, pray! I'll tell the King about you and he won't be long. One of his footmen will come presently for news of you. Madhav's impudence staggers me. If the King hears of this, that'll take some of his nonsense out of him. *[Exit*

*Amal.* Who are you walking there? How your anklets tinkle! Do stop a while, won't you? (*A girl enters*)

*Girl.* I haven't a moment to spare; it is already late!

*Amal.* I see, you don't wish to stop; I don't care to stay on here either.

*Girl.* You make me think of some late star of the morning! Whatever's the matter with you?

*Amal.* I don't know; the doctor won't let me out.

*Girl.* Ah me! Don't go, then! Should listen to the doctor. People will be cross with you if you're naughty. I know, always looking out and watching must make you feel tired. Let me close the window a bit for you.

*Amal.* No, don't, only this one's open! All the others are shut. But will you tell me who you are? Don't seem to know you.

*Girl.* I am Sudha.

*Amal.* What Sudha?

*Sudha.* Don't you know? Daughter of the flower-seller here.

*Amal.* What do *you* do?

*Sudha.* I gather flowers in my basket.

*Amal.* Oh, flower-gathering! That is why your feet seem so glad and your anklets jingle so merrily as you walk. Wish I could be out too. Then I would pick some flowers for you from the very topmost branches right out of sight.

*Sudha.* Would you really? Do you know as much about flowers as I?

*Amal.* Yes, I do, quite as much. I know all about Champa of the fairy tale and his six brothers. If only they let me, I'll go right into the dense forest where you can't find your way. And where the honey-sipping humming-bird rocks himself on the end of the thinnest branch, I will blossom into a *champa*. Would you be my sister Parul?

*Sudha.* You are silly! How can I be sister Parul when I am Sudha and my mother is Sasi, the flower-seller? I have to weave so many garlands a day. It would be jolly if I could lounge here like you!

*Amal.* What would you do then, all the day long?

*Sudha.* I could have great times with my doll Benay the bride, and Meni the pussy-cat, and—but I say, it is getting late and I mustn't stop, or I won't find a single flower.

*Amal.* Oh, wait a little longer; I do like it so!

*Sudha.* Ah, well—now don't you be naughty. Be good and sit still, and on my way back home with the flowers I'll come and talk with you.

*Amal.* And you'll let me have a flower, then?

*Sudha.* No, how can I? It has to be paid for.

*Amal.* I'll pay when I grow up—before I leave to look for work out on the other side of that stream there.

*Sudha.* Very well, then.

*Amal.* And you'll come back when you have your flowers?

*Sudha.* I will.

*Amal.* You will, really?

*Sudha.* Yes, I will.

*Amal.* You won't forget me? I am Amal, remember that.

*Sudha.* I won't forget you, you'll see. *[Exit*

**(A *Troop of Boys enter*)**

*Amal.* Say, brothers, where are you all off to? Stop here a little.

*A Boy.* We're off to play.

*Amal.* What will you play at, brothers?

*A Boy.* We'll play at being ploughmen.

*Another Boy (showing a stick).* This is our ploughshare.

*Another Boy.* We two are the pair of oxen.

*Amal.* And you're going to play the whole day?

*A Boy.* Yes, all day long.

*Amal.* And you will come home in the evening by the road along the river bank?

*A Boy.* Yes.

*Amal.* Do you pass our house on your way home?

*A Boy.* Come out and play with us; yes, do.

*Amal.* Doctor won't let me out.

*A Boy.* Doctor! Do you mean to say you mind what the doctor says? Let's be off; it is getting late.

*Amal.* Don't go. Play on the road near this window. I could watch you, then.

*A Boy.* What can we play at here?

*Amal.* With all these toys of mine that are lying about. Here you are; have them. I can't play alone. They are getting dirty and are of no use to me.

*Boys.* How jolly! What fine toys! Look, here's a ship. There's old mother Jatai. Isn't this a gorgeous sepoy? And you'll let us have them all? You don't really mind?

*Amal.* No, not a bit; have them by all means.

*A Boy.* You don't want them back?

*Amal.* Oh, no, I shan't want them.

*A Boy.* Say, won't you get a scolding for this?

*Amal.* No one will scold me. But will you play with them in front of our door for a while every morning? I'll get you new ones when these are old.

*A Boy.* Oh, yes, we will. I say, put these sepoys into a line. We'll play at war; where can we get a musket? Oh, look here, this bit of reed will do nicely. Say, but you're off to sleep already.

*Amal.* I'm afraid I'm sleepy. I don't know, I feel like it at times. I have been sitting a long while and I'm tired; my back aches.

*A Boy*. It's hardly mid-day now. How is it you're sleepy? Listen! The gong's sounding the first watch.

*Amal*. Yes, Dong, dong, dong; it tolls me to sleep.

*A Boy*. We had better go, then. We'll come in again to-morrow morning.

*Amal*. I want to ask you something before you go. You are always out—do you know of the King's postmen?

*Boys*. Yes, quite well.

*Amal*. Who are they? Tell me their names.

*A Boy*. One's Badal.

*Another Boy*. Another's Sarat.

*Another Boy*. There's so many of them.

*Amal*. Do you think they will know me if there's a letter for me?

*A Boy*. Surely, if your name's on the letter they will find you out.

*Amal*. When you call in to-morrow morning, will you bring one of them along so that he'll know me?

*A Boy*. Yes, if you like.

**CURTAIN**

# ACT II

***(Amal in Bed)***

*Amal.* Can't I go near the window to-day, Uncle? Would the doctor mind that too?

*Madhav.* Yes, darling; you see you've made yourself worse squatting there day after day.

*Amal.* Oh, no, I don't know if it's made me more ill, but I always feel well when I'm there.

*Madhav.* No, you don't; you squat there and make friends with the whole lot of people round here, old and young, as if they are holding a fair right under my eaves—flesh and blood won't stand that strain. Just see—your face is quite pale.

*Amal.* Uncle, I fear my *fakir* 'll pass and not see me by the window.

*Madhav.* Your *fakir*; whoever's that?

*Amal.* He comes and chats to me of the many lands where he's been. I love to hear him.

*Madhav.* How's that? I don't know of any fakirs.

*Amal.* This is about the time he comes in. I beg of you, by your dear feet, ask him in for a moment to talk to me here.

***(Gaffer enters in a Fakir's guise)***

*Amal.* There you are. Come here, Fakir, by my bedside.

*Madhav.* Upon my word, but this is—

*Gaffer (winking hard).* I am the Fakir.

*Madhav.* It beats my reckoning what you're not.

*Amal.* Where have you been this time, Fakir?

*Gaffer.* To the Isle of Parrots. I am just back.

*Madhav.* The Parrots' Isle!

*Gaffer.* Is it so very astonishing? I am not like you. A journey doesn't cost a thing. I tramp just where I like.

*Amal (clapping).* How jolly for you! Remember your promise to take me with you as your follower when I'm well.

*Gaffer.* Of course, and I'll teach you so many travellers' secrets that nothing in sea or forest or mountain can bar your way.

*Madhav.* What's all this rigmarole?

*Gaffer.* Amal, my dear, I bow to nothing in sea or mountain; but if the doctor joins in with this uncle of yours, then I with all my magic must own myself beaten.

*Amal.* No. Uncle won't tell the doctor. And I promise to lie quiet; but the day I am well, off I go with the Fakir, and nothing in sea or mountain or torrent shall stand in my way.

*Madhav.* Fie, dear child, don't keep on harping upon going! It makes me so sad to hear you talk so.

*Amal.* Tell me, Fakir, what the Parrots' Isle is like.

*Gaffer.* It's a land of wonders; it's a haunt of birds. No men are there; and they neither speak nor walk, they simply sing and they fly.

*Amal.* How glorious! And it's by some sea?

*Gaffer.* Of course. It's on the sea.

*Amal.* And green hills are there?

*Gaffer.* Indeed, they live among the green hills; and in the time of the sunset when there is a red glow on the hillside, all the birds with their green wings go flocking to their nests.

*Amal.* And there are waterfalls!

*Gaffer.* Dear me, of course; you don't have a hill without its waterfalls. Oh, it's like molten diamonds; and, my dear, what dances they have! Don't they make the pebbles sing as they rush over them to the sea! No devil of a doctor can stop them for a moment. The birds looked upon me as nothing but a man, merely a trifling creature without wings–and they would have nothing to do with me. Were it not so I would build a small cabin for myself among their crowd of nests and pass my days counting the sea-waves.

*Amal.* How I wish I were a bird! Then–

*Gaffer.* But that would have been a bit of a job; I hear you've fixed up with the dairyman to be a hawker of curds when you grow up; I'm afraid such business won't flourish among birds; you might land yourself into serious loss.

*Madhav*. Really this is too much. Between you two I shall turn crazy. Now, I'm off.

*Amal*. Has the dairyman been, Uncle?

*Madhav*. And why shouldn't he? He won't bother his head running errands for your pet fakir, in and out among the nests in his Farrots' Isle. But he has left a jar of curds for you saying that he is busy with his niece's wedding in the village, and has to order a band at Kamlipara.

*Amal*. But he is going to marry me to his little niece.

*Gaffer*. Dear me, we are in a fix now.

*Amal*. He said she would be my lovely little bride with a pair of pearl drops in her ears and dressed in a lovely red saree; and in the morning she would milk with her own hands the black cow and feed me with warm milk with foam on it from a brand-new earthen cruse; and in the evenings she would carry the lamp round the cow-house, and then come and sit by me to tell me tales of Champa and his six brothers.

*Gaffer*. How charming! It would even tempt me, a hermit! But never mind, dear, about this wedding. Let it be. I tell you that when you marry there'll be no lack of nieces in his household.

*Madhav*. Shut up! This is more than I can stand.

*[Exit*

*Amal*. Fakir, now that Uncle's off, just tell me, has the King sent me a letter to the Post Office?

*Gaffer*. I gather that his letter has already started; it is on the way here.

*Amal.* On the way? Where is it? Is it on that road winding through the trees which you can follow to the end of the forest when the sky is quite clear after rain?

*Gaffer.* That is where it is. You know all about it already.

*Amal.* I do, everything.

*Gaffer.* So I see, but how?

*Amal.* I can't say; but it's quite clear to me. I fancy I've seen it often in days long gone by. How long ago I can't tell. Do you know when? I can see it all: there, the King's postman coming down the hillside alone, a lantern in his left hand and on his back a bag of letters; climbing down for ever so long, for days and nights, and where at the foot of the mountain the waterfall becomes a stream he takes to the footpath on the bank and walks on through the rye; then comes the sugarcane field and he disappears into the narrow lane cutting through the tall stems of sugarcanes; then he reaches the open meadow where the cricket chirps and where there is not a single man to be seen, only the snipe wagging their tails and poking at the mud with their bills. I can feel him coming nearer and nearer and my heart becomes glad.

*Gaffer.* My eyes are not young; but you make me see all the same.

*Amal.* Say, Fakir, do you know the King who has this Post Office?

*Gaffer.* I do; I go to him for my alms everyday.

*Amal.* Good! When I get well I must have my alms too from him, mayn't I?

*Gaffer.* You won't need to ask, my dear; he'll give it to you of his own accord.

*Amal.* No, I will go to his gate and cry, "Victory to thee, O King!" and dancing to the tabor's sound, ask for alms. Won't it be nice?

*Gaffer.* It will be splendid, and if you're with me I shall have my full share. But what will you ask?

*Amal.* I shall say, "Make me your postman, that I may go about, lantern in hand, delivering your letters from door to door. Don't let me stay at home all day!"

*Gaffer.* What is there to be sad for, my child, even were you to stay at home?

*Amal.* It isn't sad. When they shut me in here first I felt the day was so long. Since the King's Post Office was put there I like more and more being indoors, and as I think I shall get a letter one day, I feel quite happy and then I don't mind being quiet and alone. I wonder if I shall make out what'll be in the King's letter?

*Gaffer.* Even if you didn't wouldn't it be enough if it just bore your name?

***(Madhav enters)***

*Madhav.* Have you any idea of the trouble you've got me into, between you two?

*Gaffer.* What's the matter?

*Madhav.* I hear you've let it get rumoured about that

the King has planted his office here to send messages to both of you,

*Gaffer.* Well, what about it?

*Madhav.* Our headman Panchanan has had it told to the King anonymously,

*Gaffer.* Aren't we aware that everything reaches the King's ears?

*Madhav.* Then why don't you look out? Why take the King's name in vain? You'll bring me to ruin if you do.

*Amal.* Say, Fakir, will the King be cross?

*Gaffer.* Cross, nonsense! And with a child like you and a fakir such as I am? Let's see if the King be angry, and then won't I give him a piece of my mind!

*Amal.* Say, Fakir, I've been feeling a sort of darkness coming over my eyes since the morning. Everything seems like a dream. I long to be quiet. I don't feel like talking at all. Won't the King's letter come? Suppose this room melts away all of a sudden, suppose–

*Gaffer (fanning Amal).* The letter's sure to come today, my boy.

***(Doctor enters)***

*Doctor.* And how do you feel to-day?

*Amal.* Feel awfully well to-day, Doctor. All pain seems to have left me.

*Doctor (aside to Madhav).* Don't quite like the look of

that smile. Bad sign that, his feeling well! Chakradhan has observed—

*Madhav.* For goodness' sake, Doctor, leave Chakradhan alone. Tell me what's going to happen?

*Doctor.* Can t hold him in much longer, I fear! I warned you before—this looks like a fresh exposure.

*Madhav.* No, I've used the utmost care, never let him out of doors; and the windows have been shut almost all the time.

*Doctor.* There's a peculiar quality in the air to-day. As I came in I found a fearful draught through your front door. That's most hurtful. Better lock it at once. Would it matter if this kept your visitors off for two or three days? If someone happens to call unexpectedly—there's the back door. You had better shut this window as well, it's letting in the sunset rays only to keep the patient awake.

*Madhav.* Amal has shut his eyes. I expect he is sleeping. His face tells me—Oh, Doctor, I bring in a child who is a stranger and love him as my own, and now I suppose I must lose him!

*Doctor.* What's that? There's your headman sailing in!—What a bother! I must be going, brother. You had better stir about and see to the doors being properly fastened. I will send on a strong dose directly I get home. Try it on him—it may save him at last, if he can be saved at all.

*[Exeunt Madhav and Doctor*

*(The Headman enters)*

*Headman.* Hello, urchin!–

*Gaffer (rising hastily).* 'Sh, be quiet.

*Amal.* No, Fakir, did you think I was asleep? I wasn't. I can hear everything; yes, and voices far away. I feel that mother and father are sitting by my pillow and speaking to me.

*(Madhav enters)*

*Headman.* I say, Madhav, I hear you hobnob with bigwigs nowadays.

*Madhav.* Spare me your jokes, Headman; we are but common people.

*Headman.* But your child here is expecting a letter from the King.

*Madhav.* Don't you take any notice of him, a mere foolish boy!

*Headman.* Indeed, why not! It'll beat the King hard to find a better family! Don't you see why the King plants his new Post Office right before your window? Why, there's a letter for you from the King, urchin.

*Amal (starting up).* Indeed, really!

*Headman.* How can it be false? You're the King's chum. Here's your letter (*showing a blank slip of paper*). Ha, ha, ha! This is the letter.

*Amal.* Please don't mock me. Say, Fakir, is it so?

*Gaffer.* Yes, my dear. I as Fakir tell you it is his letter.

*Amal.* How is it I can't see? It all looks so blank to me. What is there in the letter, Mr. Headman?

*Headman.* The King says, "I am calling on you shortly; you had better have puffed rice for me.–Palace fare is quite tasteless to me now." Ha! ha! ha!

*Madhav (with folded palms).* I beseech you, Headman, don't you joke about these things–

*Gaffer.* Joking indeed! He would not dare.

*Madkav.* Are you out of your mind too, Gaffer?

*Gaffer.* Out of my mind; well then, I am; I can read plainly that the King writes he will come himself to see Amal, with the State Physician.

*Amal.* Fakir, Fakir, 'sh, his trumpet! Can't you hear?

*Headman.* Ha! ha! ha! I fear he won't until he's a bit more off his head.

*Amal.* Mr. Headman, I thought you were cross with me and didn't love me. I never could have believed you would fetch me the King's letter. Let me wipe the dust off your feet.

*Headman.* This little child does have an instinct of reverence. Though a little silly, he has a good heart.

*Amal.* It's hard on the fourth watch now, I suppose. Hark, the gong, "Dong, dong, ding–Dong, dong, ding." Is the evening star up? How is it I can't see–

*Gaffer.* Oh, the windows are all shut; I'll open them.

*(A knocking outside)*

*Madhav*. What's that?—Who is it?—What a bother!

*Voice (from outside)*. Open the door.

*Madhav*. Headman—I hope they're not robbers.

*Headman*. Who's there?—It is Panchanan, the headman, who calls.—Aren't you afraid to make that noise? Fancy! The noise has ceased! Panchanan's voice carries far.—Yes, show me the biggest robbers!—

*Madhav (peering out of the window)*. No wonder the noise has ceased. They've smashed the outer door. (*The King's Herald enters*)

*Herald*. Our Sovereign King comes to-night!

*Headman*. My God!

*Amal*. At what hour of the night, Herald?

*Herald*. On the second watch.

*Amal*. When my friend the watchman will strike his gong from the city gates, "Ding dong ding, ding dong ding"—then?

*Herald*. Yes, then. The King sends his greatest physician to attend on his young friend. (*State Physician enters*)

*State Physician*. What's this? How close it is here! Open wide all the doors and windows. (*Feeling Amal's body*.) How do you feel, my child?

*Amal*. I feel very well, Doctor, very well. All pain is gone. How fresh and open! I can see all the stars now twinkling from the other side of the dark.

*Physician.* Will you feel well enough to leave your bed when the King comes in the middle watches of the night?

*Amal.* Of course, I'm dying to be about for ever so long. I'll ask the King to find me the polar star.–I must have seen it often, but I don't know exactly which it is.

*Physician.* He will tell you everything. (*To Madhav.*) Arrange flowers through the room for the King's visit. (*Indicating the Headman.*) We can't have that person in here.

*Amal.* No, let him be, Doctor. He is a friend. It was he who brought me the King's letter.

*Physician.* Very well, my child. He may remain if he is a friend of yours.

*Madhav (whispering into Amal's ear).* My child, the King loves you. He is coming himself. Beg for a gift from him. You know our humble circumstances.

*Amal.* Don't you worry, Uncle.–I've made up my mind about it.

*Madhav.* What is it, my child?

*Amal.* I shall ask him to make me one of his postmen that I may wander far and wide, delivering his message from door to door.

*Madhav (slapping his forehead).* Alas, is that all?

*Amal.* What'll be our offerings to the King, Uncle, when he comes?

*Herald.* He has commanded puffed rice.

*Amal.* Puffed rice. Say, Headman, you're right. You said so. You knew all we didn't.

*Headman.* If you would send word to my house I could manage for the King's advent really nice—

*Physician.* No need at all. Now be quiet, all of you. Sleep is coming over him. I'll sit by his pillow; he's dropping asleep. Blow out the oil-lamp. Only let the star-light stream in. Hush, he sleeps.

*Madhav (addressing Gaffer).* What are you standing there for like a statue, folding your palms?—I am nervous.—Say, are there good omens? Why are they darkening the room? How will star-light help?

*Gaffer.* Silence, unbeliever!

***(Sudha enters)***

*Sudha.* Amal!

*Physician.* He's asleep.

*Sudha.* I have some flowers for him. Mayn't I give them into his own hand?

*Physician.* Yes, you may.

*Sudha.* When will he be awake?

*Physician.* Directly the King comes and calls him.

*Sudha.* Will you whisper a word for me in his ear?

*Physician.* What shall I say?

*Sudha.* Tell him Sudha has not forgotten him.

CURTAIN

# THE GARDENER

## Tagore's other titles in Srishti

Gitanjali

My Boyhood Days

Mashi & other stories

The Post Office

A Treasure of Tagore's Writings Vol. 1

The Home and the World

Four Chapters

Selected short stories

# THE GARDENER

Rabindranath Tagore

Srishti
PUBLISHERS & DISTRIBUTORS

**Srishti Publishers & Distributors**
**Registered Office:** N-16, C. R. Park
New Delhi – 110 019
**Corporate Office:** 212A, Peacock Lane
Shahpur Jat, New Delhi – 110 049
editorial@srishtipublishers.com

First published by
Srishti Publishers & Distributors in 2012

10 9 8 7



Typeset by EGP at Srishti

Printed and bound in India

# The Gardener

## 1

SERVANT: Have mercy upon your servant, my queen!

QUEEN: The assembly is over and my servants are all gone. Why do you come at this late hour?

SERVANT: When you have finished with others, that is my time.

I come to ask what remains for your last servant to do.

QUEEN: What can you expect when it is too late?

SERVANT: Make me the gardener of your flower garden.

QUEEN: What folly is this?

SERVANT: I will give up my other work.

I throw my swords and lances down in the dust. Do not send me to distant courts; do not bid me undertake new conquests. But make me the gardener of your flower garden.

QUEEN: What will your duties be?

SERVANT: The service of your idle days. I will keep fresh the grassy path where you walk in the morning, where your feet will be greeted with praise at every step by the flowers eager for death.

I will swing you in a swing among the branches of the *saptaparna*, where the early evening moon will struggle to kiss your skirt through the leaves.

I will replenish with scented oil the lamp that burns by your bedside, and decorate your footstool with sandal and saffron paste in wondrous designs.

QUEEN: What will you have for your reward?

SERVANT: To be allowed to hold your little fists like tender lotus-buds and slip flower chains over your wrists; to tinge the soles of your feet with the red juice of *ashoka* petals and kiss away the speck of dust that may chance to linger there.

QUEEN: Your prayers are granted, my servant, you will be the gardener of my flower garden.

## 2

'Ah, Poet, the evening draws near; your hair is turning grey.

'Do you in your lonely musing hear the message of the hereafter?'

'It is evening,' the poet said, 'and I am listening because some one may call from the village, late though it be.

'I watch if young straying hearts meet together, and two pairs of eager eyes beg for music to break their silence and speak for them.

'Who is there to weave their passionate songs, if I sit on the shore of life and contemplate death and the beyond?

'The early evening star disappears.
'The glow of a funcral pyre slowly dies by the silent river.
'Jackals cry in chorus from the courtyard of the deserted house in the light of the worn-out moon.
'If some wanderer, leaving home, come here to watch the night and with bowed head listens to the murmur of the darkness, who is there to whisper the secrets of life into his ears if I, shutting my doors, should try to free myself from mortal bonds?

'It is a trifle that my hair is turning grey.
'I am ever as young or as old as the youngest and the oldest of this village.
'Some have smiles, sweet and simple, and some a sly twinkle in their eyes.
'Some have tears that well up in the daylight, and others tears that are hidden in the gloom.
'They all have need for me, and I have no time to brood over the afterlife.
'I am of an age with each, what matter if my hair turns grey?'

## 3

In the morning I cast my net into the sea.
I dragged up from the dark abyss things of strange aspect and strange beauty—some shone like a smile, some glistened like tears, and some were flushed like the cheeks of a bride.

When with the day's burden I went home, my love was sitting in the garden idly tearing the leaves of a flower.
I hesitated for a moment, and then placed at her feet all that I had dragged up, and stood silent.
She glanced at them and said, 'What strange things are these? I know not of what use they are!'
I bowed my head in shame and thought, 'I have not fought for these, I did not buy them in the market; they are not fit gifts for her.'
Then the whole night through I flung them one by one into the street.
In the morning travellers came; they picked them up and carried them into far countries.

## 4

Ah me, why did they build my house by the road to the market town?
They moor their laden boats near my trees.
They come and go and wander at their will.
I sit and watch them; my time wears on.
Turn them away I cannot. And, thus my days pass by.

Night and day their steps sound by my door.
Vainly I cry, 'I do not know you.'
Some of them are known to my fingers, some to my nostrils, the blood in my veins seems to know them, and some are known to my dreams.

Turn them away I cannot. I call them and say, 'Come to my house whoever chooses. Ycs, come.'
In the morning the bell rings in the temple.
They come with their baskets in their hands.
Their feet are rosy red. The early light of dawn is on their faces.
Turn them away I cannot. I call them and I say, 'Come to my garden to gather flowers. Come hither.'
In the mid-day the gong sounds at the palace gate.
I know not why they leave their work and linger near my hedge.
The flowers in their hair are pale and faded; the notes are languid in their flutes.
Turn them away I cannot. I call them and say, 'The shade is cool under my trees. Come, friends.'

At night the crickets chirp in the woods.
Who is it that comes slowly to my door and gently knocks?
I vaguely see the face, not a word is spoken, the stillness of the sky is all around.
Turn away my silent guest I cannot. I look at the face through the dark, and hours of dreams pass by.

## 5

I am restless. I am athirst for faraway things.
My soul goes out in a longing to touch the skirt of the dim distance.

O Great Beyond, O the keen call of thy flute!
I forget, I ever forget, that I have no wings to fly, that I am bound in this spot evermore.
I am eager and wakeful, I am a stranger in a strange land.
Thy breath comes to me whispering an impossible hope.
Thy tongue is known to my heart as its very own.
O Far-to-seek, O the keen call of thy flute!
I forget, I ever forget, that I know not the way, that I have not the winged horse.
I am listless, I am a wanderer in my heart.
In the sunny haze of the languid hours, what vast vision of thine takes shape in the blue of the sky!
O Farthest End, O the keen call of thy flute!
I forget, I ever forget, that the gates are shut everywhere in the house where I dwell alone!

## 6

The tame bird was in a cage, the free bird was in the forest.
They met when the time came, it was a decree of fate.

The free bird cries, 'O my love, let us fly to the wood.'
The cage bird whispers, 'Come hither, let us both live in the cage.'
Says the free bird, 'Among bars, where is there room to spread one's wings?'
'Alas,' cries the cage bird, 'I should not know where to sit perched in the sky.'

The free bird cries, 'My darling, sing the songs of the woodlands.'
The cage bird says, 'Sit by my side, I'll teach you the speech of the learned.'
The forest bird cries, 'No, ah no! songs can never be taught.'
The cage bird says, 'Alas, for me, I know not the songs of the woodlands.'
Their love is intense with longing, but they never can fly wing to wing.
Through the bars of the cage they look, and vain is their wish to know each other.
They flutter their wings in yearning, and sing, 'Come closer, my love!'
The free bird cries, 'It cannot be, I fear the closed doors of the cage.'
The cage bird whispers. 'Alas, my wings are powerless and dead.'

## 7

O mother, the young Prince is to pass by our door,–how can I attend to my work this morning?
Show me how to braid up my hair; tell me what garment to put on.
Why do you look at me amazed, mother?
I know well he will not glance up once at my window; I know he will pass out of my sight in the twinkling

of an eye; only the vanishing strain of the flute will come sobbing to me from afar.

But the young Prince will pass by our door, and I will put on my best for the moment.

O mother, the young Prince did pass by our door, and the morning sun flashed from his chariot.

I swept aside the veil from my face, I tore the ruby chain from my neck and flung it in his path.

Why do you look at me amazed, mother?

I know well he did not pick up my chain; I know it was crushed under his wheels leaving a red stain upon the dust, and no one knows what my gift was nor to whom.

But the young Prince did pass by our door, and I flung the jewel from my breast before his path.

## 8

When the lamp went out by my bed I woke up with the early birds.

I sat at my open window with a fresh wreath on my loose hair.

The young traveller came along the road in the rosy mist of the morning.

A pearl chain was on his neck, and the sun's rays fell on his crown. He stopped before my door and asked me with an eager cry, 'Where is she?'

For shame I could not say, 'She is I, young traveller, she is I.'

It was dusk and the lamp was not lit.
I was listlessly braiding my hair.
The young traveller came on his chariot in the glow of the setting sun.
His horses were foaming at the mouth, and there was dust on his garment.
He alighted at my door and asked in a tired voice, 'Where is she?'
For shame I could not say, 'She is I, weary traveller, she is I.'

It is an April night. The lamp is burning in my room.
The breeze of the south comes gently. The noisy parrot sleeps in its cage.
My bodice is of the colour of the peacock's throat, and my mantle is green as young grass.
I sit upon the floor at the window watching the deserted street.
Through the dark night I keep humming, 'She is I, despairing traveller, she is I.'

## 9

When I go alone at night to my love-tryst, birds do not sing, the wind does not stir, the houses on both sides of the street stand silent.
It is my own anklets that grow loud at every step and I am ashamed.

When I sit on my balcony and listen for his footsteps, leaves do not rustle on the trees, and the water is still in the river like the sword on the knees of a sentry fallen asleep.

It is my own heart that beats wildly—I do not know how to quiet it.

When my love comes and sits by my side, when my body trembles and my eyelids droop, the night darkens, the wind blows out the lamp, and the clouds draw veils over the stars.

It is the jewel at my own breast that shines and gives light. I do not know how to hide it.

## 10

Let your work be, bride. Listen, the guest has come.

Do you hear, he is gently shaking the chain which fastens the door?

See that your anklets make no loud noise, and that your step is not over-hurried at meeting him.

Let your work be, bride, the guest has come in the evening.

No, it is not the ghostly wind, bride, do not be frightened.

It is the full moon on a night of April; shadows are pale in the courtyard; the sky overhead is bright.

Draw your veil over your face if you must, carry the lamp to the door if you fear.

No, it is not the ghostly wind, bride, do not be frightened.

Have no word with him if you are shy; stand aside by the door when you meet him.
If he asks you questions, and if you wish to, you can lower your eyes in silence.
Do not let your bracelets jingle when, lamp in hand, you lead him in.
Have no word with him if you are shy.

Have you not finished your work yet, bride? Listen, the guest has come.
Have you not lit the lamp in the cowshed?
Have you not got ready the offering basket for the evening service?
Have you not put the red lucky mark at the parting of your hair, and done your toilet for the night?
O bride, do you hear, the guest has come?
Let your work be!

## 11

Come as you are; do not loiter over your toilet.
If your braided hair has loosened, if the parting of your hair be not straight, if the ribbons of your bodice be not fastened, do not mind.
Come as you are; do not loiter over your toilet.

Come, with quick steps over the grass.
If the raddle comes from your feet because of the dew,

if the rings of bells upon your feet slacken, if pearls drop out of your chain, do not mind.
Come, with quick steps over the grass.

Do you see the clouds wrapping the sky?
Flocks of cranes fly up from the further river-bank and fitful gusts of wind rush over the heath.
The anxious cattle run to their stalls in the village.
Do you see the clouds wrapping the sky?

In vain you light your toilet lamp–it flickers and goes out in the wind.
Who can know that your eyelids have not been touched with lamp-black? For your eyes are darker than rain-clouds.
In vain you light your toilet lamp–it goes out.

Come as you are; do not loiter over your toilet.
If the wreath is not woven, who cares; if the wrist-chain has not been linked, let it be.
The sky is overcast with clouds–it is late.
Come as you are; do not loiter over your toilet.

## 12

If you would be busy and fill your pitcher, come, O come to my lake.
The water will cling round your feet and babble its secret.
The shadow of the coming rain is on the sands, and the

clouds hang low upon the blue lines of the trees like the heavy hair above your eyebrows.
I know well the rhythm of your steps, they are beating in my heart.
Come, O come to my lake, if you must fill your pitcher.
If you would be idle and sit listless and let your pitcher float on the water, come, O come to my lake.
The grassy slope is green, and the wild flowers beyond number.
Your thoughts will stray out of your dark eyes like birds from their nests.
Your veil will drop to your feet.
Come, O come to my lake if you must sit idle.

If you would leave off your play and dive in the water, come, O come to my lake.
Let your blue mantle lie on the shore; the blue water will cover you and hide you.

The waves will stand a-tiptoe to kiss your neck and whisper in your ears.
Come, O come to my lake, if you would dive in the water.
If you must be mad and leap to your death, come, O come to my lake.
It is cool and fathomlessly deep.
It is dark like a sleep that is dreamless.
There in its depths nights and days are one and songs are silence.

Come, O come to my lake, if you would plunge to your death.

## 13

I asked nothing, only stood at the edge of the wood behind the tree.
Languor was still upon the eyes of the dawn, and the dew in the air.
The lazy smell of the damp grass hung in the thin mist above the earth.
Under the banyan tree you were milking the cow with your hands, tender and fresh as butter.
And, I was standing still.

I did not say a word. It was the bird that sang unseen from the thicket.
The mango tree was shedding its flowers upon the village road, and the bees came humming one by one.
On the side of the pond the gate of Shiva's temple was opened and the worshipper had begun his chants.
With the vessel on your lap you were milking the cow.
I stood with my empty can.

I did not come near you.
The sky woke with the sound of the gong at the temple.
The dust was raised in the road from the hoofs of the driven cattle.

With the gurgling pitchers at their hips, women came
from the river.
Your bracelets were jingling, and foam brimming over
the jar.
The morning wore on and I did not come near you.

## 14

I was walking by the road, I do not know why, when the
noonday was past and bamboo branches rustled in
the wind.
The prone shadows with their outstretched arms clung
to the feet of the hurrying light.
The *koels* were weary of their songs.
I was walking by the road, I do not know why.

The hut by the side of the water is shaded by an
overhanging tree.
Someone was busy with her work, and her bangles made
music in the corner.
I stood before this hut, I know not why.
The narrow winding road crosses many a mustard field,
and many a mango forest.
It passes by the temple of the village and the market at
the river landing-place.
I stopped by this hut, I do not know why.

Years ago it was a day of breezy March when the murmur

of the spring was languorous, and mango blossoms were dropping on the dust.

The rippling water leapt and licked the brass vessel that stood on the landing-step.

I think of that day of breezy March, I do not know why.

Shadows are deepening and cattle returning to their folds.

The light is grey upon the lonely meadows, and the villagers are waiting for the ferry at the bank.

I slowly return upon my steps, I do not know why.

## 15

I run as a musk-deer runs in the shadow of the forest, mad with his own perfume.

The night is the night of mid-May, the breeze is the breeze of the south.

I lose my way and I wander, I seek what I cannot get, I get what I do not seek.

From my heart comes out and dances the image of my own desire.

The gleaming vision flits on.

I try to clasp it firmly, it eludes me and leads me astray.

I seek what I cannot get, I get what I do not seek.

## 16

Hands cling to hands and eyes linger on eyes: thus begins

the record of our hearts.
It is the moonlit night of March; the sweet smell of *henna* is in the air; my flute lies on the earth neglected and your garland of flowers is unfinished.
This love between you and me is simple as a song.
Your veil of the saffron colour makes my eyes drunk.
The jasmine wreath that you wove me thrills to my heart like praise.
It is a game of giving and with-holding, revealing and screening again; some smiles and some little shyness, and some sweet useless struggles.
This love between you and me is simple as a song.
No mystery beyond the present; no striving for the impossible; no shadow behind the charm; no groping in the depth of the dark.
This love between you and me is simple as a song.

We do not stray out of all words into the ever silent; we do not raise our hands to the void for things beyond hope.
It is enough what we give and we get.
We have not crushed the joy to the utmost to wring from it the wine of pain.
This love between you and me is simple as a song.

## 17

The yellow bird sings in its tree and makes my heart dance with gladness.

We both live in the same village, and that is our one piece of joy.
Her pair of pet lambs come to graze in the shade of our garden trees.
If they stray into our barley field, I take them up in my arms.
The name of our village is Khanjana, and Anjana they call our river.
My name is known to all the village, and her name is Ranjana.

Only one field lies between us.
Bees that have hived in our grove go to seek honey in theirs.
Flowers launched from their landing-stairs come floating by the stream where we bathe.
Baskets of dried *kusm* flowers come from their fields to our market.
The name of our village is Khanjana, and Anjana they call our river.
My name is known to all the village, and her name is Ranjana.

The lane that winds to their house is fragrant in the spring with mango flowers.
When their linseed is ripe for harvest, the hemp is in bloom in our field.
The stars that smile on their cottage send us the same twinkling look.

The rain that floods their tank makes glad our *kadam* forest.
The name of our village is Khanjana, and Anjana they call our river.
My name is known to all the village, and her name is Ranjana.

## 18

When the two sisters go to fetch water, they come to this spot and they smile.
They must be aware of somebody who stands behind the trees whenever they go to fetch water.
The two sisters whisper to each other when they pass this spot.
They must have guessed the secret of that somebody who stands behind the trees whenever they go to fetch water.
Their pitchers lurch suddenly, and water spills when they reach this spot.
They must have found out that somebody's heart is beating, who stands behind the tree whenever they go to fetch water.
The two sisters glance at each other when they come to this spot, and they smile.
There is a laughter in their swift-stepping feet, which makes confusion in somebody's mind who stands behind the trees whenever they go to fetch water.

## 19

You walked by the riverside path with the full pitcher upon your hip.

Why did you swiftly turn your face and peep at me through your fluttering veil?

That gleaming look from the dark came upon me like a breeze that sends a shiver through the rippling water and sweeps away to the shadowy shore.

It came to me like the bird of the evening that hurriedly flies across the lampless room from the one open window to the other, and disappears in the night.

You are hidden as a star behind the hills, and I am a passer-by upon the road.

But why did you stop for a moment and glance at my face through your veil while you walked by the riverside path with the full pitcher upon your hip?

## 20

Day after day he comes and goes away.

Go, and give him a flower from my hair, my friend.

If he asks who was it that sent it, I entreat you do not tell him my name—for he only comes and goes away.

He sits on the dust under the tree.

Spread there a seat with flowers and leaves, my friend.

His eyes are sad, and they bring sadness to my heart.

He does not speak what he has in mind; he only comes and goes away.

## 21

Why did he choose to come to my door, the wandering youth, when the day dawned?
As I come in and out I pass by him every time, and my eyes are caught by his face.
I know not if I should speak to him or keep silent. Why did he choose to come to my door?

The cloudy nights in July are dark; the sky is soft blue in the autumn; the spring days are restless with the south wind.
He weaves his songs with fresh tunes every time.
I turn from my work and my eyes fill with the mist. Why did he choose to come to my door?

## 22

When she passed by me with quick steps, the end of her skirt touched me.
From the unknown island of a heart came a sudden warm breath of spring.
A flutter of a flitting touch brushed me and vanished in a moment, like a torn flower petal blown in the breeze.

It fell upon my heart like a sigh of her body and whisper of her heart.

## 23

Why do you sit there and jingle your bracelets in mere idle sport?
Fill your pitcher. It is time for you to come home.

Why do you stir the water with your hands and fitfully glance at the road for someone in mere idle sport?
Fill your pitcher and come home.

The morning hours pass by–the dark water flows on.
The waves are laughing and whispering to each other in mere idle sport.

The wandering clouds have gathered at the edge of the sky on yonder rise of the land.
They linger and look at your face and smile in mere idle sport.
Fill your pitcher and come home.

## 24

Do not keep to yourself the secret of your heart, my friend!
Say it to me, only to me, in secret.

You who smile so gently, softly whisper, my heart will hear it, not my ears.
The night is deep, the house is silent, the birds' nests are shrouded with sleep.
Speak to me through hesitating tears, through faltering smiles, through sweet shame and pain, the secret of your heart!

## 25

'Come to us, youth, tell us truly why there is madness in your eyes.'
'I know not what wine of wild poppy I have drunk, that there is this madness in my eyes.'
'Ah, shame!'
'Well, some are wise and some foolish, some are watchful and some careless. There are eyes that smile and eyes that weep–and madness is in my eyes.'

'Youth, why do you stand so still under the shadow of the tree?'
'My feet are languid with the burden of my heart, and I stand still in the shadow.'
'Ah, shame!'
'Well, some march on their way and some linger, some are free and some are fettered–and my feet are languid with the burden of my heart.'

## 26

'What comes from your willing hands I take. I beg for nothing more.'

'Yes, yes, I know you, modest mendicant, you ask for all that one has.'

'If there be a stray flower for me, I will wear it in my heart.'

'But if there be thorns?'

'I will endure them.'

'Yes, yes, I know you, modest mendicant, you ask for all that one has.'

'If but once you should raise your loving eyes to my face, it would make my life sweet beyond death.'

'But if there be only cruel glances?'

'I will keep them piercing my heart.'

'Yes, yes, I know you, modest mendicant, you ask for all that one has.'

## 27

'Trust love even if it brings sorrow. Do not close up your heart.'

'Ah no, my friend, your words are dark, I cannot understand them.'

'The heart is only for giving away with a tear and a song,

my love.'
'Ah no, my friend, your words are dark, I cannot understand them.'
'Pleasure is frail like a dewdrop, while it laughs it dies. But sorrow is strong and abiding. Let sorrowful love wake in your eyes.'
'Ah no, my friend, your words are dark, I cannot understand them.'

'The lotus blooms in the sight of the sun, and loses all that it has. It would not remain in bud in the eternal winter mist.'
'Ah no, my friend, your words are dark, I cannot understand them.'

## 28

Your questioning eyes are sad. They seek to know my meaning as the moon would fathom the sea.
I have bared my life before your eyes from end to end, with nothing hidden or held back. That is why you know me not.
If it were only a gem, I could break it into a hundred pieces and string them into a chain to put on your neck.
If it were only a flower, round and small and sweet, I could pluck it from its stem to set it in your hair.
But it is a heart, my beloved. Where are its shores and its bottom?

You know not the limits of this kingdom, still you are its queen.
If it were only a moment of pleasure it would flower in an easy smile, and you could see it and read it in a moment.
If it were merely a pain it would melt in limpid tears, reflecting its inmost secret without a word.
But it is love, my beloved.
Its pleasure and pain are boundless, and endless its wants and wealth.
It is as near to you as your life, but you can never wholly know it.

## 29

Speak to me, my love! Tell me in words what you sang.
The night is dark. The stars are lost in clouds. The wind is sighing through the leaves.
I will let loose my hair. My blue cloak will cling round me like night. I will clasp your head to my bosom; and there in the sweet loneliness murmur on your heart. I will shut my eyes and listen. I will not look in your face.
When your words are ended, we will sit still and silent. Only the trees will whisper in the dark.
The night will pale. The day will dawn. We shall look at each other's eyes and go on our different paths.
Speak to me, my love! Tell me in words what you sang.

## 30

You are the evening cloud floating in the sky of my
dreams.
I paint you and fashion you ever with my love longings.
You are my own, my own, Dweller in my endless dreams!
Your feet are rosy-red with the glow of my heart's desire,
Gleaner of my sunset songs!
Your lips are bitter-sweet with the taste of my wine of
pain.
You are my own, my own, Dweller in my lonesome dreams!

With the shadow of my passion have I darkened your
eyes, Haunter of the depth of my gaze!
I have caught you and wrapt you, my love, in the net of
my music.
You are my own, my own, Dweller in my deathless dreams!

## 31

My heart, the bird of the wilderness, has found its sky
in your eyes.
They are the cradle of the morning, they are the kingdom
of the stars.
My songs are lost in their depths.
Let me but soar in that sky, in its lonely immensity.
Let me but cleave its clouds and spread wings in
its sunshine.

## 32

Tell me if this be all true, my love, tell me if this be true.
When these eyes flash their lightning the dark clouds in your breast make stormy answers.
Is it true that my lips are sweet like the opening bud of the first conscious love?
Do the memories of vanished months of May linger in my limbs?
Does the earth, like a harp, shiver into songs with the touch of my feet?
Is it then true that the dewdrops fall from the eyes of night when I am seen, and the morning light is glad when it wraps my body round?
Is it true, is it true, that your love travelled alone through ages and worlds in search of me?
That when you found me at last, your age-long desire found utter peace in my gentle speech and my eyes and lips and flowing hair?
Is it then true that the mystery of the Infinite is written on this little forehead of mine?
Tell me, my lover, if all this be true.

## 33

I love you, beloved. Forgive me my love.
Like a bird losing its way I am caught.
When my heart was shaken it lost its veil and was naked. Cover it with pity, beloved, and forgive me my love.

If you cannot love me, beloved, forgive me my pain.
Do not look askance at me from afar.
I will steal back to my corner and sit in the dark.
With both hands I will cover my naked shame.
Turn your face from me, beloved, and forgive me my pain.

If you love me, beloved, forgive me my joy.
When my heart is borne away by the flood of happiness, do not smile at my perilous abandonment.
When I sit on my throne and rule you with my tyranny of love, when like a goddess I grant you my favour, bear with my pride, beloved, and forgive me my joy.

## 34

Do not go, my love, without asking my leave.
I have watched all night, and now my eyes are heavy with sleep.
I fear lest I lose you when I am sleeping.
Do not go, my love, without asking my leave.
I start up and stretch my hands to touch you. I ask myself, 'Is it a dream?'
Could I but entangle your feet with my heart and hold them fast to my breast!
Do not go, my love, without asking my leave.

## 35

Lest I should know you too easily, you play with me.
You blind me with flashes of laughter to hide your tears.

I know, I know your art,
You never say the word you would.
Lest I should not prize you, you elude me in a thousand ways.
Lest I should confuse you with the crowd, you stand aside.
I know, I know your art,
You never walk the path you would.
Your claim is more than that of others, that is why you are silent.
With playful carelessness you avoid my gifts.
I know, I know your art,
You never will take what you would.

## 36

He whispered, 'My love, raise your eyes.'
I sharply chid him, and said 'Go!'; but he did not stir.
He stood before me and held both my hands. I said, 'Leave me!'; but he did not go.
He brought his face near my ear. I glanced at him and said, 'What a shame!'; but he did not move.
His lips touched my cheek. I trembled and said, 'You dare too much'; but he had no shame.
He put a flower in my hair. I said, 'It is useless!'; but he stood unmoved.
He took the garland from my neck and went away. I weep and ask my heart, 'Why does he not come back?'

## 37

Would you put your wreath of fresh flowers on my neck, fair one?
But you must know that the one wreath that I had woven is for the many, for those who are seen in glimpses, or dwell in lands unexplored, or live in poets' songs.

It is too late to ask my heart in return for yours.
There was a time when my life was like a bud, all its perfume was stored in its core.
Now, it is squandered far and wide.
Who knows the enchantment that can gather and shut it up again?
My heart is not mine to give to one only, it is given to the many.

## 38

My love, once upon a time your poet launched a great epic in his mind.
Alas, I was not careful, and it struck your ringing anklets and came to grief.
It broke up into scraps of songs and lay scattered at your feet.
All my cargo of the stories of old wars was tossed by the

laughing waves and soaked in tears and sank.
You must make this loss good to me, my love.
If my claims to immortal fame after death are shattered,
make me immortal while I live.
And, I will not mourn for my loss nor blame you.

## 39

I try to weave a wreath all morning, but the flowers slip
and they drop out.
You sit there watching me in secret through the corner
of your prying eyes.
Ask those eyes, darkly planning mischief, whose fault
it was.

I try to sing a song, but in vain.
A hidden smile trembles on your lips; ask of it the reason
of my failure.
Let your smiling lips say on oath how my voice lost itself
in silence like a drunken bee in the lotus.

It is evening, and the time for the flowers to close their
petals.
Give me leave to sit by your side, and bid my lips to do
the work that can be done in silence and in the dim
light of stars.

## 40

An unbelieving smile flits on your eyes when I come to

you to take my leave.

I have done it so often that you think I will soon return.
To tell you the truth I have the same doubt in my mind.
For the spring days come again time after time, the full moon takes leave and comes on another visit, the flowers come again and blush upon their branches year after year, and it is likely that I take my leave only to come to you again.
But keep the illusion awhile; do not send it away with ungentle haste.
When I say I leave you for all time, accept it as true, and let a mist of tears for one moment deepen the dark rim of your eyes.
Then smile as archly as you like when I come again.

## 41

I long to speak the deepest words I have to say to you; but I dare not, for fear you should laugh.
That is why I laugh at myself and shatter my secret in jest.
I make light of my pain, afraid you should do so.

I long to tell you the truest words I have to say to you; but I dare not being afraid that you would not believe them.
That is why I disguise them in untruth, saying the contrary of what I mean.

I make my pain appear absurd, afraid that you should do so.

I long to use the most precious words I have for you; butI dare not, fearing I should not be paid with like value.
That is why I give you hard names and boast of my callous strength.
I hurt you, for fear you should never know any pain.
I long to sit silent by you; but I dare not, lest my heart come out at my lips.
That is why I prattle and chatter lightly and hide my heart behind words.
I rudely handle my pain, for fear you should do so.

I long to go away from your side; but I dare not, for fear my cowardice should become known to you.
That is why I hold my head high and carelessly come into your presence.
Constant thrusts from your eyes keep my pain fresh forever.

## 42

O mad, superbly drunk;
If you kick open your doors and play the fool in public;
If you empty your bag in a night, and snap your fingers at prudence;
If you walk in curious paths and play with useless things;

Reck not rhyme or reason;
If unfurling your sails before the storm you snap the rudder in two,
Then, I will follow you, comrade, and be drunken and go to the dogs.

I have wasted my days and nights in the company of steady wise neighbours.
Much knowing has turned my hair grey, and much watching has made my sight dim.
For years, I have gathered and heaped up scraps and fragments of things.
Crush them and dance upon them, and scatter them all to the winds.
For I know 'tis the height of wisdom to be drunken and go to the dogs.
Let all crooked scruples vanish, let me hopelessly lose my way.
Let a gust of wild giddiness come and sweep me away from my anchors.
The world is peopled with worthies, and workers, useful and clever.
There are men who are easily first, and men who come decently after.
Let them be happy and prosper, and let me be foolishly futile.
For I know 'tis the end of all works to be drunken and go to the dogs.

I swear to surrender this moment all claims to the ranks of the decent.
I let go my pride of learning and judgement of right and of wrong.
I'll shatter memory's vessel, scattering the last drop of tears.
With the foam of the berry-red wine I will bathe and brighten my laughter.
The badge of the civil and staid I'll tear into shreds for the nonce.
I'll take the holy vow to be worthless, to be drunken and go to the dogs.

## 43

No, my friends, I shall never be an ascetic, whatever you may say.
I shall never be an ascetic if she does not take the vow with me.
It is my firm resolve that if I cannot find a shady shelter and a companion for my penance, I shall never turn ascetic.
No, my friends, I shall never leave my hearth and home, and retire into the forest solitude, if rings no merry laughter in its echoing shade and if the end of no saffron mantle flutters in the wind; if its silence is not deepened by soft whispers.
I shall never be an ascetic.

## 44

Reverend sir, forgive this pair of sinners. Spring winds to-day are blowing in wild eddies, driving dust and dead leaves away, and with them your lessons are all lost.

Do not say, father, that life is a vanity.

For, we have made truce with death for once, and only for a few fragrant hours we two have been made immortal.

Even if the king's army came and fiercely fell upon us we should sadly shake our heads and say, 'Brothers, you are disturbing us'. If you must have this noisy game, go and clatter your arms elsewhere. Since only for a few fleeting moments we have been made immortal.

If friendly people came and flocked around us, we should humbly bow to them and say, This extravagant good fortune is an embarrassment to us'. Room is scarce in the infinite sky where we dwell. For in the spring-time flowers come in crowds, and the busy wings of bees jostle with each other. Our little heaven, where dwell only we two immortals, is too absurdly narrow.

## 45

To the guests that must go bid God's speed and brush away all traces of their steps.

Take to your bosom with a smile what is easy and simple and near.
To-day is the festival of phantoms that know not when they die.
Let your laughter be but a meaningless mirth like twinkles of light on the ripples.
Let your life lightly dance on the edges of Time like dew on the tip of a leaf.
Strike in chords from your harp fitful momentary rhythms.

## 46

You left me and went on your way.
I thought I should mourn for you and set your solitary image in my heart wrought in a golden song.
But ah, my evil fortune, time is short.
Youth wanes year after year; the spring days are fugitive; the frail flowers die for nothing, and the wise man warns me that life is but a dewdrop on the lotus leaf.
Should I neglect all this to gaze after who has turned her back on me?
That would be rude and foolish, for time is short.

Then come, my rainy nights with pattering feet; smile, my golden autumn; come, careless April scattering your kisses abroad.
You come, and you, and you also!
My loves, you know we are mortals. Is it wise to break

one's heart for the one takes her heart away? For time is short.

It is sweet to sit in a corner to muse and write in rhymes that you are all my world.
It is heroic to hug one's sorrow and determine not to be consoled. But a fresh face peeps across my door and raises its eyes to my eyes. I cannot but wipe away my tears and change the tune of my song. For time short.

## 47

If you would have it so, I will end my singing.
If it sets your heart aflutter, I will take away my eyes from your face.
If it suddenly startles you in your walk, I will step aside and take another path.
If it confuses you in your flower-weaving, I will shun your lonely garden.
If it makes the water wanton and wild, I will not row my boat by your bank.

## 48

Free me from the bonds of your sweetness, my love! No more of this wine of kisses.
This mist of heavy incense stifles my heart.
Open the doors, make room for the morning light.
I am lost in you, wrapped in the folds of your caresses.

Free me from your spells, and give me back the manhood to offer you my freed heart.

## 49

I hold her hands and press her to my breast.

I try to fill my arms with her loveliness, to plunder her sweet smile with kisses, to drink her dark glances with my eyes.

Ah, but, where is it? Who can strain the blue from the sky?

I try to grasp the beauty; it eludes me, leaving only the body in my hands.

Baffled and weary I come back.

How can the body touch the flower which only the spirit may touch?

## 50

Love, my heart longs day and night for the meeting with you—for the meeting that is like all-devouring death.

Sweep me away like a storm; take everything I have; break open my sleep and plunder my dreams. Rob me of my world.

In that devastation, in the utter nakedness of spirit, let us become one in beauty.

Alas! for my vain desire! Where is this hope for union except in thee, my God?

## 51

Then finish the song and let us leave.
Forget this night when the night is no more.
Whom do I try to clasp in my arms? Dreams can never be made captive.
My eager hands press emptiness to my heart and it bruises my breast.

## 52

Why did the lamp go out?
I shaded it with my cloak to save it from the wind, that is why the lamp went out.

Why did the flower fade?
I pressed it to my heart with anxious love, that is why the flower faded.

Why did the stream dry up?
I put a dam across it to have it for my use, that is why the stream dried up.
Why did the harp-string break?
I tried to force a note that was beyond its power, that is why the harp-string is broken.

## 53

Why do you put me to shame with a look?
I have not come as a beggar.

Only for a passing hour I stood at the end of your courtyard outside the garden hedge.
Why do you put me to shame with a look?

Not a rose did I gather from your garden, not a fruit did I pluck.
I humbly took my shelter under the wayside shade where every strange traveller may stand.
Not a rose did I pluck.
Yes, my feet were tired, and the shower of rain came down.
The winds cried out among the swaying bamboo branches.
The clouds ran across the sky as though in the flight from defeat.
My feet were tired.

I know not what you thought of me or for whom you were waiting at your door.
Flashes of lightning dazzled your watching eyes.
How could I know that you could see me where I stood in the dark?
I know not what you thought of me.

The day is ended, and the rain has ceased for a moment.
I leave the shadow of the tree at the end of your garden and this seat on the grass.
It has darkened; shut your door; I go my way.
The day is ended.

## 54

Where do you hurry with your basket this late evening when the marketing is over?
They all have come home with their burdens; the moon peeps from above the village trees.
The echoes of the voices calling for the ferry run across the dark water to the distant swamp where wild ducks sleep.
Where do you hurry with your basket when the marketing is over?

Sleep has laid her fingers upon the eyes of the earth.
The nests of the crows have become silent, and the murmurs of the bamboo leaves are silent.
The labourers home from their fields spread their mats in the courtyards.
Where do you hurry with your basket when the marketing is over?

## 55

It was mid-day when you went away.
The sun was strong in the sky.
I had done my work and sat alone on my balcony when you went away.
Fitful gusts came winnowing through the smells of many distant fields.
The doves cooed tireless in the shade, and a bee strayed

in my room humming the news of many distant fields.

The village slept in the noonday heat. The road lay deserted.
In sudden fits the rustling of the leaves rose and died.
I gazed at the sky and wove in the blue the letters of a name I had known, while the village slept in the noonday heat.
I had forgotten to braid my hair. The languid breeze played with it upon my cheek.
The river ran unruffled under the shady bank.
The lazy white clouds did not move.
I had forgotten to braid my hair.

It was mid-day when you went away.
The dust of the road was hot and the fields panting.
The doves cooed among the dense leaves.
I was alone in my balcony when you went away.

## 56

I was one among many women busy with the obscure daily tasks of the household.
Why did you single me out and bring me away from the cool shelter of our common life?

Love unexpressed is sacred. It shines like gems in the gloom of the hidden heart. In the light of the curious day it looks pitifully dark.

Ah, you broke through the cover of my heart and dragged my trembling love into the open place, destroying for ever the shady corner where it hid its nest.

The other women are the same as ever.
No one has peeped into their inmost being, and they themselves know not their own secret.
Lightly they smile, and weep, chatter, and work. Daily they go to the temple, light their lamps, and fetch water from the river.

I hoped my love would be saved from the shivering shame of the shelterless, but you turn your face away.
Yes, your path lies open before you, but you have cut off my return, and left me stripped naked before the world with its lidless eyes staring night and day.

## 57

I plucked your flower, O world!
I pressed it to my heart and the thorn pricked.
When the day waned and it darkened, I found that the flower had faded, but the pain remained.

More flowers will come to you with perfume and pride, O world!
But my time for flower-gathering is over, and through the

dark night I have not my rose, only the pain remains.

## 58

One morning in the flower garden a blind girl came to offer me a flower chain in the cover of a lotus leaf.

I put it round my neck, and tears came to my eyes.

I kissed her and said, 'You are blind even as the flowers are.'

'You yourself know not how beautiful is your gift.'

## 59

O woman, you are not merely the handiwork of God, but also of men; these are ever endowing you with beauty from their hearts.

Poets are weaving for you a web with threads of golden imagery; painters are giving your form ever new immortality.

The sea gives its pearls, the mine their gold, the summer gardens their flowers to deck you, to cover you, to make you more precious.

The desire of men's hearts has shed its glory over your youth.

You are one half woman and one half dream.

## 60

Amidst the rush and roar of life, O Beauty, carved in

stone, you stand mute and still, alone and aloof.
Great Time sits enamoured at your feet and murmurs:
'Speak, speak to me, my love; speak, my bride!
But your speech is shut up in stone, O Immovable Beauty!

## 61

Peace, my heart, let the time for the parting be sweet.
Let it not be a death but completeness.
Let love melt into memory and pain into songs.
Let the flight through the sky end in the folding of the wings over the nest.
Let the last touch of your hands be gentle like the flower of the night.
Stand still, O Beautiful End, for a moment, and say your last words in silence.
I bow to you and hold up my lamp to light you on your way.

## 62

In the dusky path of a dream I went to seek the love who was mine in a former life.

Her house stood at the end of a desolate street.
In the evening breeze her pet peacock sat drowsing on its perch, and the pigeons were silent in their corner.

She set her lamp down by the portal and stood before me.

She raised her large eyes to my face and mutely asked, 'Are you well, my friend?'
I tried to answer, but our language had been lost and forgotten.
I thought and thought; our names would not come to my mind.
Tears shone in her eyes. She held up her right hand to me. I took it and stood silent.

Our lamp had flickered in the evening breeze and died.

## 63

Traveller, must you go?
The night is still and the darkness swoons upon the forest.
The lamps are bright in our balcony, the flowers all fresh, and the youthful eyes still awake.
Is the time for your parting come?
Traveller, must you go?

We have not bound your feet with our entreating arms.
Your doors are open. Your horse stands saddled at the gate.
If we have tried to bar your passage it was but with our songs.
Did we ever try to hold you back it was but with our eyes.
Traveller, we are helpless to keep you. We have only our tears.

What quenchless fire glows in your eyes?
What restless fever runs in your blood?
What call from the dark urges you?
What awful incantation have you read among the stars in the sky, that with a sealed secret message the night entered your heart, silent and strange?

If you do not care for merry meetings, if you must have peace, weary heart, we shall put our lamps out and silence our harps.
We shall sit still in the dark in the rustle of leaves, and the tired moon will shed pale rays on your window.
O traveller, what sleepless spirit has touched you from the heart of the midnight?

## 64

I spent my day on the scorching hot dust of the road.
Now, in the cool of the evening, I knock at the door of the inn. It is deserted and in ruins.
A grim *ashath* tree spreads its hungry clutching roots through the gaping fissures of the walls.

Days have been when wayfarers came here to wash their weary feet.
They spread their mats in the courtyard in the dim light of the early moon, and sat and talked of strange lands.

They woke refreshed in the morning when birds made them glad, and friendly flowers nodded their heads at them from the wayside.

But no lighted lamp awaited me when I came here.

The black smudges of smoke left by many a forgotten evening lamp stare, like blind eyes, from the wall.

Fireflies flit in the bush near the dried-up pond, and bamboo branches fling their shadows on the grass-grown path.

I am the guest of no one at the end of my day.

The long night is before me, and I am tired.

## 65

Is that your call again?

The evening has come. Weariness clings round me like the arms of entreating love.

Do you call me?

I had given all my day to you, cruel mistress, must you also rob me of my night?

Somewhere there is an end to everything, and the loneness of the dark is one's own.

Must your voice cut through it and smite me?

Has the evening no music of sleep at your gate?

Do the silent-winged stars never climb the sky above your pitiless tower?

Do the flowers never drop on the dust in soft death in your garden?

Must you call me, you unquiet one?
Then let the sad eyes of love vainly watch and weep.
Let the lamp burn in the lonely house.
Let the ferry-boat take the weary labourers to their home.
I leave behind my dreams and I hasten to your call.

## 66

A wandering madman was seeking the touchstone, with matted locks, tawny and dust-laden, and worn to a shadow, his lips tight-pressed, like the shut-up doors of his heart, his burning eyes like the lamp of a glow-worm seeking its mate.
Before him the endless ocean roared.
The garrulous waves ceaselessly talked of hidden treasures, mocking the ignorance that knew not their meaning.
Maybe, he now had no hope remaining, yet he would not rest, for the search had become his life,–
Just as the ocean for ever lifts its arms to the sky for the unattainable–
Just as the stars go in circles, yet seeking a goal that can never be reached–
Even so on the lonely shore the madman with dusty tawny locks still roamed in search of the touchstone.

One day, a village boy came up and asked, 'Tell me, where did you come at this golden chain about your waist?'

The madman started–the chain that once was iron was verily gold; it was not a dream, but he did not know when it had changed.

He struck his forehead wildly–where, O where had he without knowing it achieved success?

It had grown into a habit, to pick up pebbles and touch the chain, and to throw them away without looking to see if a change had come; thus the madman found and lost the touchstone.

The sun was sinking low in the west, the sky was of gold.

The madman returned on his footsteps to seek anew the lost treasure, with his strength gone, his body bent, and his heart in the dust, like a tree uprooted.

## 67

Though the evening comes with slow steps and has signalled for all songs to cease;

Though your companions have gone to their rest and you are tired;

Though fear broods in the dark and the face of the sky is veiled;

Yet, bird, O my bird, listen to me, do not close your wings.

That is not the gloom of the leaves of the forest, that is the sea swelling like a dark black snake.

That is not the dance of the flowering jasmine, that is flashing foam.
Ah, where is the sunny green shore, where is your nest?
Bird, O my bird, listen to me, do not close your wings.
The lone night lies along your path, the dawn sleeps behind the shadowy hills.
The stars hold their breath counting the hours, the feeble moon swims the deep night.
Bird, O my bird, listen to me, do not close your wings.

There is no hope, no fear for you.
There is no word, no whisper, no cry.
There is no home, no bed of rest.
There is only your own pair of wings and the pathless sky.
Bird, O my bird, listen to me, do not close your wings.

## 68

None lives for ever, brother, and nothing lasts for long. Keep that in mind and rejoice.
Our life is not the one old burden, our path is not the one long journey.
One sole poet has not to sing one aged song.
The flower fades and dies; but he who wears the flower has not to mourn for it for ever.
Brother, keep that in mind rejoice.

There must come a full pause to weave perfection

into music.
Life droops toward its sunset to be drowned in the golden shadows.
Love must be called from its play to drink sorrow and be borne to the heaven of tears.

Brother, keep that in mind and rejoice.
We hasten to gather our flowers lest they are plundered by the passing winds.
It quickens our blood and brightens our eyes to snatch kisses that would vanish if we delayed.
Our life is eager, our desires are keen, for time tolls the bell of parting.
Brother, keep that in mind and rejoice.
There is not time for us to clasp a thing and crush it and fling it away to the dust.
The hours trip rapidly away, hiding their dreams in their skirts. Our life is short; it yields but a few days for love.
Were it for work and drudgery it would be endlessly long.
Brother, keep that in mind and rejoice.

Beauty is sweet to us, because she dances to the same fleeting tune with our lives.
Knowledge is precious to us because we shall never have time to complete it.
All is done and finished in the eternal Heaven.
But earth's flowers of illusion are kept eternally fresh

by death.
Brother, keep that in mind and rejoice.

## 69

I hunt for the golden stag.
You may smile, my friends, but I pursue the vision that eludes me.
I run across hills and dales, I wander through nameless lands, because I am hunting for the golden stag.
You come and buy in the market and go back to your homes laden with goods, but the spell of the homeless winds has touched me I know not when and where.
I have no care in my heart; all my belongings I have left far behind me.
I run across hills and dales, I wander through nameless lands–because I am hunting for the golden stag.

## 70

I remember a day in my childhood I floated a paper boat in the ditch.
It was a wet day of July; I was alone and happy over my play.
I floated my paper boat in the ditch.

Suddenly the storm clouds thickened, winds came in gusts, and rain poured in torrents.

Rills of muddy water rushed and swelled the stream and sunk my boat.

Bitterly I thought in my mind that the storm came on purpose to spoil my happiness; all its malice was against me.

The cloudy day of July is long today, and I have been musing over all those games in life wherein I was loser.

I was blaming my fate for the many tricks it played on me, when suddenly I remembered the paper boat that sank in the ditch.

## 71

The day is not yet done, the fair is not over, the fair on the river-bank.

I had feared that my time had been squandered and my last penny lost.

But no, my brother, I have still something left. My fate has not cheated me of everything.

The selling and buying are over.

All the dues on both sides have been gathered in, and it is time for me to go home.

But, gatekeeper, do you ask for your toll?

Do not fear, I have still something left. My fate has not cheated me of everything.

The lull in the wind threatens storm, and the lowering clouds in the west bode no good.
The hushed water waits for the wind.
I hurry to cross the river before the night overtakes me.
O ferryman, you want your fee!
Yes, brother, I have still something left. My fate has not cheated me of everything.
In the wayside under the tree sits the beggar. Alas, he looks at my face with a timid hope!
He thinks I am rich with the day's profit.
Yes, brother, I have still something left. My fate has not cheated me of everything.
The night grows dark and the road lonely. Fireflies gleam among the leaves.
Who are you that follow me with stealthy silent steps?
Ah, I know, it is your desire to rob me of all my gains. I will not disappoint you!
For, I still have something left, and my fate has not cheated me of everything.
At midnight I reach home. My hands are empty.
You are waiting with anxious eyes at my door, sleepless and silent.
Like a timorous bird you fly to my breast with eager love.
Ay, ay, my God, much remains still. My fate has not cheated me of everything.

## 72

With days of hard travail I raised a temple. It had no

doors or windows, its walls were thickly built with massive stones.

I forgot all else, I shunned all the world, I gazed in rapt contemplation at the image I had set upon the altar.

It was always night inside, and lit by the lamps of perfumed oil.

The ceaseless smoke of incense wound my heart in its heavy coils.

Sleepless, I carved on the walls fantastic figures in mazy bewildering lines–winged horses, flowers with human faces, women with limbs like serpents.

No passage was left anywhere through which could enter the song of birds, the murmur of leaves, or hum of the busy village.

The only sound that echoed in its dark dome was that of incantations which I chanted.

My mind became keen and still like a pointed flame, my senses swooned in ecstasy.

I knew not how time passed till the thunderstorm had struck the temple, and a pain stung me through the heart.

The lamp looked pale and ashamed; the carvings on the walls, like chained dreams, stared meaningless in the light as they would fain hide themselves.

I looked at the image on the altar. I saw it smiling and alive with the living touch of God. The night I had imprisoned had spread its wings and vanished.

## 73

Infinite wealth is not yours, my patient and dusky mother dust!
You toil to fill the mouths of your children, but food is scarce.
The gift of gladness that you have for us is never perfect.
The toys that you make for your children are fragile.
You cannot satisfy all our hungry hopes, but should I desert you for that?
Your smile which is shadowed with pain is sweet to my eyes.
Your love which knows not fulfilment is dear to my heart.
From your breast you have fed us with life but not immortality, that is why your eyes are ever wakeful.
For ages you are working with colour and song, yet your heaven is not built, but only its sad suggestion.
Over your creations of beauty there is the mist of tears.
I will pour my songs into your mute heart, and my love into your love.
I will worship you with labour.
I have seen your tender face and I love your mournful dust, Mother Earth.

## 74

In the world's audience hall, the simple blade of grass sits on the same carpet with the sunbeam and the stars of midnight.

Thus, my songs share their seats in the heart of the world with the music of the clouds and forests.

But, you man of riches, your wealth has no part in the simple grandeur of the sun's glad gold and the mellow gleam of the musing moon.

The blessing of the all-embracing sky is not shed upon it.

And, when death appears, it pales and withers and crumbles into dust.

## 75

At midnight the would-be ascetic announced:

'This is the time to give up my home and seek for God. Ah, who has held me so long in delusion here?'

God whispered, 'I,' but the ears of the man were stopped.

With a baby asleep at her breast lay his wife, peacefully sleeping on one side of the bed.

The man said, 'Who are ye that have fooled me so long?

The voice said again, 'They are God,' but he heard it not.

The baby cried out in its dream, nestling close to its mother.

God commanded, 'Stop, fool, leave not thy home,' but still he heard not.

God sighed and complained, 'Why does my servant wander to seek me, forsaking me?'

## 76

The fair was on before the temple. It had rained from the early morning and the day came to its end.

Brighter than all the gladness of the crowd was the bright smile of a girl who bought for a farthing a whistle of palm leaf.

The shrill joy of that whistle floated above all laughter and noise.

An endless throng of people came and jostled together. The road was muddy, the river in flood, the field under water in ceaseless rain.

Greater than all the troubles of the crowd was a little boy's trouble–he had not a farthing to buy a painted stick.

His wistful eyes gazing at the shop made this whole meeting of men so pitiful.

## 77

The workman and his wife from the west country are busy digging to make bricks for the kiln.

Their little daughter goes to the landing-place by the river; there she has no end of scouring and scrubbing of pots and pans.

Her little brother, with shaven head and brown, naked mud-covered limbs, follows after her and waits patiently on the high bank at her bidding.

She goes back home with the full pitcher poised on her

head, the shining brass pot in her left hand, holding the child with her right–she the tiny servant of her mother, grave with the weight of the household cares.

One day, I saw this naked boy sitting with legs outstretched.

In the water his sister sat rubbing a drinking-pot with a handful of earth, turning it round and round.

Near, by a soft-haired lamb stood grazing along the bank.

It came close to where the boy sat and suddenly bleated aloud, and the child started up and screamed.

His sister left off cleaning her pot and ran up.

She took up her brother in one arm and the lamb in the other, and dividng her caresses between them bound in one bond of affection the offspring of beast and man.

## 78

It was in May. The sultry noon seemed endlessly long. The dry earth gaped with thirst in the heat.

When I heard from the riverside a voice calling, 'Come, my darling!'

I shut my book and opened the window to look out.

I saw a big buffalo with mud-stained hide standing near the river with placid, patient eyes; and a youth, knee-deep in water, calling it to its bath.

I smiled amused and felt a touch of sweetness in my heart.

## 79

I often wonder where lie hidden the boundaries of recognition between man and the beast whose heart knows no spoken language.
Through what primal paradise in a remote morning of creation ran the simple path by which their hearts visited each other.
Those marks of their constant tread have not been effaced though their kinship has been long forgotten.
Yet, suddenly in some wordless music the dim memory wakes up and the beast gazes into the man's face with a tender trust, and the man looks down into its eyes with amused affection.
It seems that the two friends meet masked, and vaguely know each other through the disguise.

## 80

With a glance of your eyes you could plunder all the wealth of songs struck from poets' harps, fair woman!
But for their praises you have no ear, therefore, I come to praise you.
You could humble at your feet the proudest heads in the world.
But it is your loved ones, unknown to fame, whom you choose to worship, therefore I worship you.
The perfection of your arms would add glory to kingly

splendour with their touch.
But you use them to sweep away the dust, and to make clean your humble home, therefore I am filled with awe.

## 81

Why do you whisper so faintly in my ears, O Death, my Death?
When the flowers droop in the evening and cattle come back to their stalls, you stealthily come to my side and speak words that I do not understand.
Is this how you must woo and win me with the opiate of drowsy murmur and cold kisses, O Death, my Death?

Will there be no proud ceremony for our wedding?
Will you not tie up with a wreath your tawny coiled locks?
Is there none to carry your banner before you, and will not the night be on fire with your red torch-lights, O Death, my Death?

Come with your conch-shells sounding, come in the sleepless night.
Dress me with a crimson mantle, grasp my hand and take me.
Let your chariot be ready at my door with your horses

neighing impatiently.
Raise my veil and look at my face proudly, O Death, my Death!

## 82

We are to play the game of death to-night, my bride and I.
The night is black, the clouds in the sky are capricious, and the waves are raving at sea.
We have left our bed of dreams, flung open the door and come out, my bride and I.
We sit upon a swing, and the storm winds give us a wild push from behind.
My bride starts up with fear and delight, she trembles and clings to my breast.
Long have I served her tenderly.
I made for her a bed of flowers and I closed the doors to shut out the rude light from her eyes.
I kissed her gently on her lips and whispered softly in her ears till she half-swooned in languor.
She was lost in the endless mist of vague sweetness.
She answered not to my touch, my songs failed to arouse her.
To-night has come to us the call of the storm from the wild.
My bride has shivered and stood up, she has clasped my hand and come out.

Her hair is flying in the wind, her veil is fluttering, her garland rustles over her breast.

The push of death has swung her into life.

We are face to face and heart to heart, my bride and I.

## 83

She dwelt on the hillside by the edge of a maize-field, near the spring that flows in laughing rills through the solemn shadows of ancient trees. The women came there to fill their jars, and travellers would sit there to rest and talk. She worked and dreamed daily to the tune of the bubbling stream.

One evening, the stranger came down from the cloud-hidden peak; his locks were tangled like drowsy snakes. We asked in wonder, 'Who are you?' He answered not but sat by the garrulous stream and silently gazed at the hut where she dwelt. Our hearts quaked in fear and we came back home when it was night.

Next morning, when the women came to fetch water at the spring by the *deodar* trees, they found the doors open in her hut, but her voice was gone and where was her smiling face? The empty jar lay on the floor and her lamp had burnt itself out in the corner. No one knew where she had fled to before it was morning–and the stranger had gone.

In the month of May the sun grew strong and the snow

melted, and we sat by the spring and wept. We wondered in our mind, 'Is there a spring in the land where she has gone and where she can fill her vessel in these hot thirsty days?' And, we asked each other in dismay, 'Is there a land beyond these hills where we live?'

It was a summer night; the breeze blew from the south; and I sat in her deserted room where the lamp stood still unlit, when suddenly from before my eyes the hills vanished like curtains drawn aside. 'Ah, it is she who comes. How are you, my child? Are you happy? But where can you shelter under this open sky? And, alas! our spring is not here to allay your thirst.'

'Here is the same sky,' she said, 'only free from the fencing hills,—this is the same stream grown into a river,—the same earth widened into a plain,' 'Everything is here,' I sighed, 'only we are not.' She smiled sadly and said, 'You are in my heart.' I woke up and heard the babbling of the stream and the rustling of the *deodars* at night.

## 84

Over the green and yellow rice-fields sweep the shadows of the autumn clouds followed by the swift-chasing sun.

The bees forget to sip their honey; drunken with light they foolishly hover and hum.

The ducks in the islands of the river clamour in joy for mere nothing.
Let none go back home, brothers, this morning, let none go to work.
Let us take the blue sky by storm and plunder space as we run.
Laughter floats in the air like foam on the flood.
Brothers, let us squander our morning in futile songs.

## 85

Who are you, reader, reading my poems a hundred years hence?
I cannot send you one single flower from this wealth of the spring, one single streak of gold from yonder clouds.
Open your doors and look abroad.
From your blossoming garden gather fragrant memories of the vanished flowers of a hundred years before.
In the joy of your heart may you feel the living joy that sang one spring morning, sending its glad voice across a hundred years.

# MASHI
# & Other Stories

## Tagore's other titles in Srishti

Gitanjali

My Boyhood Days

The Gardener

The Post Office

A Treasure of Tagore's Writings Vol. 1

The Home and the World

Four Chapters

Selected short stories

# MASHI
## & Other Stories

Rabindranath Tagore

Srishti
PUBLISHERS & DISTRIBUTORS

**Srishti Publishers & Distributors**
**Registered Office:** N-16, C. R. Park
New Delhi – 110 019
**Corporate Office:** 212A, Peacock Lane
Shahpur Jat, New Delhi – 110 049
editorial@srishtipublishers.com

First published by
Srishti Publishers & Distributors in 2012

10 9 8 7



Typeset by EGP at Srishti

Printed and bound in India

# Contents

# Mashi

## I

'Mashi!'[1]

'Try to sleep, Jotin, it is getting late.'

'Never mind if it is. I have not many days left. I was thinking that Mani should go to her father's house.—I forget where he is now.'

'Sitarampur.'

'Oh yes! Sitarampur. Send her there. She should not remain any longer near a sick man. She herself is not strong.'

'Just listen to him! How can she bear to leave you in this state?'

'Does she know what the doctors—?'

'But she can see for herself! The other day she cried her eyes out at the merest hint of having to go to her father's house.'

We must explain that in this statement there was a slight distortion of truth, to say the least of it. The actual talk with Mani was as follows:

---

1. The maternal aunt is addressed as Mashi.

'I suppose, my child, you have got some news from your father? I thought I saw your cousin Anath here.'

'Yes! Next Friday will be my little sister's *annaprasham*[2] ceremony. So I'm thinking—'

'Alright, my dear. Send her a gold necklace. It will please your mother.'

'I'm thinking of going myself. I've never seen my little sister, and I want to ever so much.'

'Whatever do you mean? You surely don't think of leaving Jotin alone? Haven't you heard what the doctor says about him?'

'But he said that just now there's no special cause for—'

'Even if he did, you can see his state.'

'This is the first girl after three brothers, and she's a great favourite.—I have heard that it's going to be a grand affair. If I don't go, mother will be very—'

'Yes, yes! I don't understand your mother. But I know very well that your father will be angry enough if you leave Jotin just now.'

'You'll have to write a line to him saying that there is no special cause for anxiety, and that even if I go, there will be no—'

'You're right there; it will certainly be no great loss if you do go. But remember, if I write to your father, I'll

---

2. The *annaprasham* ceremony takes place when a child is first given rice. Usually, it receives its name on that day.

tell him plainly what is in my mind.'

'Then you needn't write. I shall ask my husband, and he will surely—'

'Look here, child, I've borne a good deal from you, but if you do that, I won't stand it for a moment. Your father knows you too well for you to deceive him.'

When Mashi had left her, Mani lay down on her bed in a bad temper.

Her neighbour and friend came and asked what was the matter.

'Look here! What a shame it is! Here's my only sister's *annaprasham* coming, and they don't want to let me go to it!'

'Why! Surely you're never thinking of going, are you, with your husband so ill.'

'I don't do anything for him, and I couldn't if I tried. It's so deadly dull in this house, that I tell you frankly I can't bear it.'

'You are a strange woman!'

'But I can't pretend, as you people do, and look glum lest any one should think ill of me.'

'Well, tell me your plan.'

'I must go. Nobody can prevent me.'

'Isss! What an imperious young woman you are!'

## II

Hearing that Mani had wept at the mere thought of

going to her father's house, Jotin was so excited that he sat up in bed. Pulling his pillow towards him, he leaned back, and said: 'Mashi, open this window a little, and take that lamp away.'

The still night stood silently at the window like a pilgrim of eternity; and the stars gazed in, witnesses through untold ages of countless death-scenes.

Jotin saw his Mani's face traced on the background of the dark night, and saw those two big dark eyes brimming over with tears, as it were for all eternity.

Mashi felt relieved when she saw him so quiet, thinking he was asleep.

Suddenly he started up, and said: 'Mashi, you all thought that Mani was too frivolous ever to be happy in our house. But you see now—'

'Yes, I see now, my Baba,[3] I was mistaken—but trial tests a person.'

'Mashi!'

'Do try to sleep, dear!'

'Let me think a little, let me talk. Don't be vexed, Mashi!'

'Very well.'

'Once, when I used to think I could not win Mani's heart, I bore it silently. But you—'

'No, dear, I won't allow you to say that; I also bore it.'

---

3. Baba literally means Father, but is often used by elders as a term of endearment. In the same way 'Ma' is used.

'Our minds, you know, are not clods of earth which you can possess by merely picking up. I felt that Mani did not know her own mind, and that one day at some great shock—'

'Yes, Jotin, you are right.'

'Therefore, I never took much notice of her waywardness.'

Mashi remained silent, suppressing a sigh. Not once, but often she had seen Jotin spending the night on the verandah wet with the splashing rain, yet not caring to go into his bedroom. Many a day, he lay with a throbbing head, longing, she knew, that Mani would come and soothe his brow, while Mani was getting ready to go to the theatre. Yet, when Mashi went to fan him, he sent her away petulantly. She alone knew what pain lay hidden in that distress. Again and again she had wanted to say to Jotin: 'Don't pay so much attention to that silly child, my dear; let her learn to want,—to cry for things.' But these things cannot be said, and are apt to be misunderstood. Jotin had in his heart a shrine set up to the goddess Woman, and there Mani had her throne. It was hard for him to imagine that his own fate was to be denied his share of the wine of love poured out by that divinity. Therefore, the worship went on, the sacrifice was offered, and the hope of a boon never ceased.

Mashi imagined once more that Jotin was sleeping, when he cried out suddenly:

'I know you thought that I was not happy with Mani,

and therefore you were angry with her. But Mashi, happiness is like those stars. They don't cover all the darkness; there are gaps between. We make mistakes in life and we misunderstand, and yet there remain gaps through which truth shines. I do not know whence comes this gladness that fills my heart tonight.'

Mashi began gently to soothe Jotin's brow, her tears unseen in the dark.

'I was thinking, Mashi, she's so young! What will she do when I am—?'

'Young, Jotin? She's old enough. I too was young when I lost the idol of my life, only to find him in my heart for ever. Was that any loss, do you think? Besides, is happiness absolutely necessary?'

'Mashi, it seems as if just when Mani's heart shows signs of awakening I have to—'

'Don't you worry about that, Jotin. Isn't it enough if her heart awakes?'

Suddenly Jotin recollected the words of a village minstrel's song which he had heard long before:

> O *my heart! you woke not when the man of my heart came to my door.*
> *At the sound of his departing steps you woke up.*
> *Oh, you woke up in the dark!*

'Mashi, what is the time now?'

'About nine.'

'So early as that! Why, I thought it must be at least two or three o'clock. My midnight, you know, begins at sundown. But why did you want me to sleep, then?'

'Why, you know how late last night you kept awake talking; so today you must get to sleep early.'

'Is Mani asleep?'

'Oh no, she's busy making some soup for you.'

'You don't mean to say so, Mashi? Does she—?'

'Certainly! Why, she prepares all your food, the busy little woman.'

'I thought perhaps Mani could not—'

'It doesn't take long for a woman to learn such things. With the need it comes of itself.'

'The fish soup, that I had in the morning, had such a delicate flavour, I thought you had made it.'

'Dear me, no! Surely, you don't think Mani would let me do anything for you? Why, she does all your washing herself. She knows you can't bear anything dirty about you. If only you could see your sitting-room, how spick and span she keeps it! If I were to let her haunt your sick-room, she would wear herself out. But that's what she really wants to do.'

'Is Mani's health, then—?'

'The doctors think she should not be allowed to visit the sick-room too often. She's too tender-hearted.'

'But, Mashi, how do you prevent her from coming?'

'Because she obeys me implicitly. But still I have constantly to be giving her news of you.'

The stars glistened in the sky like tear-drops. Jotin bowed his head in gratitude to his life that was about to depart, and when Death stretched out his right hand towards him through the darkness, he took it in perfect trust.

Jotin sighed, and, with a slight gesture of impatience, said:

'Mashi, if Mani is still awake, then, could I—if only for a—?'

'Very well! I'll go and call her.'

'I won't keep her long, only for five minutes. I have something particular to tell her.'

Mashi, sighing, went out to call Mani. Meanwhile, Jotin's pulse began to beat fast. He knew too well that he had never been able to have an intimate talk with Mani. The two instruments were tuned differently and it was not easy to play them in unison. Again and again, Jotin had felt pangs of jealousy on hearing Mani chattering and laughing merrily with her girl companions. Jotin blamed only himself,—why couldn't he talk irrelevant trifles as they did? Not that he could not, for with his men friends he often chatted on all sorts of trivialities. But the small talk that suits men is not suitable for women. You can hold a philosophical discourse in monologue, ignoring your inattentive audience altogether, but small talk requires the co-operation of at least two. The bagpipes can be played singly, but there must be a pair of cymbals. How often in the evenings had Jotin, when sitting on the open verandah with Mani, made some strained attempts at conversation, only to feel the thread snap. And, the very silence of the evening felt ashamed. Jotin was certain that Mani longed to get away. He had even wished earnestly that a third person would come. For talking is easy with three, when it is hard for two.

He began to think what he should say when Mani came. But such manufactured talk would not satisfy him. Jotin felt afraid that this five minutes of tonight would be wasted. Yet, for him, there were but few moments left for intimate talk.

### III

'What's this, child, you're not going anywhere, are you?'

'Of course, I'm going to Sitarampur.'

'What do you mean? Who is going to take you?'

'Anath.'

'Not today, my child, some other day.'

'But the compartment has already been reserved.'

'What does that matter? That loss can easily be borne. Go tomorrow, early in the morning.'

'Mashi, I don't hold by your inauspicious days. What harm if I do go today?'

'Jotin wants to have a talk with you.'

'Alright! there's still some time. I'll just go and see him.'

'But you mustn't say that you are going.'

'Very well, I won't tell him, but I shan't be able to stay long. Tomorrow is my sister's *annaprasham*, and I must go today.'

'Oh, my child! I beg you to listen to me this once. Quiet your mind for a while and sit by him. Don't let him see your hurry.'

'What can I do? The train won't wait for me. Anath will be back in ten minutes. I can sit by him till then.'

'No, that won't do. I shall never let you go to him in that frame of mind.... Oh, you wretch! the man you are torturing is soon to leave this world; but I warn you, you will remember this day till the end of your days! That there is a God! that there is a God! you will some day understand!'

'Mashi, you mustn't curse me like that.'

'Oh, my darling boy! my darling! why do you go on living longer? There is no end to this sin, yet I cannot check it!'

Mashi after delaying a little returned to the sick-room, hoping by that time Jotin would be asleep. But Jotin moved in his bed when she entered. Mashi exclaimed:

'Just look what she has done!'

'What's happened? Hasn't Mani come? Why have you been so long, Mashi?'

'I found her weeping bitterly because she had allowed the milk for your soup to get burnt! I tried to console her, saying, "Why, there's more milk to be had!" But that she could be so careless about the preparation of *your* soup made her wild. With great trouble I managed to pacify her and put her to bed. So I haven't brought her today. Let her sleep it off.'

Though Jotin was pained when Mani didn't come, yet he felt a certain amount of relief. He had half-feared that Mani's bodily presence would do violence to his heart's image of her. Such things had happened before in his life. And, the gladness of the idea that Mani was miserable at burning his milk filled *his* heart to overflowing.

'Mashi!'

'What is it, Baba?

'I feel quite certain that my days are drawing to a close. But I have no regrets. Don't grieve for me.'

'No, dear, I won't grieve. I don't believe that only life is good and not death.'

'Mashi, I tell you truly that death seems sweet.'

Jotin, gazing at the dark sky, felt that it was Mani herself who was coming to him in Death's guise. She had immortal youth and the stars were flowers of blessing, showered upon her dark tresses by the hand of the World-Mother. It seemed as if once more he had his first sight of his bride under the veil of darkness.[4] The immense night became filled with the loving gaze of Mani's dark eyes. Mani, the bride of this house, the

---

4. The bride and the bridegroom see each other's face for the first time at the marriage ceremony under a veil thrown over their heads.

little girl, became transformed into a world-image, — her throne on the altar of the stars at the confluence of life and death. Jotin said to himself with clasped hands: 'At last the veil is raised, the covering is rent in this deep darkness. Ah, beautiful one! How often have you wrung my heart, but no longer shall you forsake me!'

## IV

'I'm suffering, Mashi, but nothing like you imagine. It seems to me as if my pain were, gradually separating itself from my life. Like a laden boat, it was so long being towed behind, but the rope has snapped, and now it floats away with all my burdens. Still I can see it, but it is no longer mine.... But, Mashi, I've not seen Mani even once for the last two days!'

'Jotin, let me give you another pillow.'

'It almost seems to me, Mashi, that Mani also has left me like that laden boat of sorrow which drifts away.'

'Just sip some pomegranate juice, dear! Your throat must be getting dry.'

'I wrote my will yesterday; did I show it to you? I can't recollect.'

'There's no need to show it to me, Jotin.'

'When mother died, I had nothing of my own. You fed me and brought me up. Therefore, I wassaying—'

'Nonsense, child! I had only this house and a little property. You earned the rest.'

'But this house—?'

'That's nothing. Why, you've added to it so much that it's difficult to find out where my house was!'

'I'm sure, Mani's love for you is really—'

'Yes, yes! I know that, Jotin. Now you try to sleep.'

'Though I have bequeathed all my property to Mani, it is practically yours, Mashi. She will never disobey you.'

'Why are you worrying so much about that, dear?'

'All I have I owe to you. When you see my will don't think for a moment that—'

'What do you mean, Jotin? Do you think I shall mind for a moment because you give to Mani what belongs to you? Surely, I'm not so mean as that?'

'But you also will have—'

'Look here, Jotin, I shall get angry with you. You want to console me with money!'

'Oh, Mashi, how I wish I could give you something better than money!'

'That you have done, Jotin!—more than enough. Haven't I had you to fill my lonely house? I must have won that great good-fortune in many previous births! You have given me so much that now, if my destiny's due is exhausted, I shall not complain. Yes, yes! Give away everything in Mani's name,—your house, your money, your carriage, and your land—such burdens are too heavy for me!'

'Of course, I know you have lost your taste for the

enjoyments of life, but Mani is so young that—'

'No! you mustn't say that. If you want to leave her your property, it is alright, but as for enjoyment—'

'What harm if she does enjoy herself, Mashi?'

'No, no, it will be impossible. Her throat will become parched, and it will be dust and ashes to her.'

Jotin remained silent. He could not decide whether it was true or not, and whether it was a matter of regret or otherwise, that the world, would become distasteful to Mani for want of him. The stars seemed to whisper in his heart:

'Indeed, it is true. We have been watching for thousands of years, and know that all these great preparations for enjoyment are but vanity.'

Jotin sighed and said: 'We cannot leave behind us what is really worth giving.'

'It's no trifle you are giving, dearest. I only pray she may have the power to know the value of what is given her.'

'Give me a little more of that pomegranate juice. Mashi, I'm thirsty. Did Mani come to me yesterday, I wonder?'

'Yes, she came, but you were asleep. She sat by your head, fanning you for a long time, and then went away to get your clothes washed.'

'How wonderful! I believe I was dreaming that very moment that Mani was trying to enter my room. The door was slightly open, and she was pushing against it, but it wouldn't open. But, Mashi, you're going too far,—you ought to let her see that I am dying; otherwise my death will be a terrible shock to her.'

'Baba, let me put this shawl over your feet; they are getting cold.'

'No, Mashi, I can't bear anything over me like that.'

'Do you know, Jotin, Mani made this shawl for you? When she ought to have been asleep, she was busy at it. It was finished only yesterday.'

Jotin took the shawl, and touched it tenderly with his hands. It seemed to him that the softness of the wool was Mani's own. Her loving thoughts had been woven night after night with its threads. It was not made merely of wool, but also of her touch. Therefore, when Mashi drew that shawl over his feet, it seemed as if, night after night, Mani had been caressing his tired limbs.

'But, Mashi, I thought Mani didn't know how to knit,—at any rate she never liked it.'

'It doesn't take long to learn a thing. Of course, I had to teach her. Then, there are a good many mistakes in it.'

'Let there be mistakes; we're not going to send it to the Paris Exhibition. It will keep my feet warm in spite of its mistakes.'

Jotin's mind began to picture Mani at her task, blundering and struggling, and yet patiently going on night after night. How sweetly pathetic it was! And again, he went over the shawl with his caressing fingers.

'Mashi, is the doctor downstairs?'

'Yes, he will stay here tonight.'

'But tell him it is useless for him to give me a sleeping draught. It doesn't bring me real rest and only adds to my pain. Let me remain properly awake. Do you know, Mashi, that my wedding took place on the night of the full moon in the month of *Baisakh*? Tomorrow will be that day, and the stars of that very night will be shining in the sky. Mani perhaps has forgotten. I want to remind her of it today; just call her to me for a minute or two.... Why do you keep silent? I suppose the doctor has told you I am so weak that any excitement will—but I tell you truly, Mashi, tonight, if I can have only a few minutes' talk with her, there will be no need for any sleeping draughts. Mashi, don't cry like that! I am quite well. Today my heart is full as it has never been in my life before. That's why I want to see Mani. No, no, Mashi, I can't bear to see you crying! You have been so quiet all these last days. Why are you so troubled tonight?'

'Oh, Jotin, I thought that I had exhausted all my tears, but I find there are plenty left. I can't bear it any longer.'

'Call Mani. I'll remind her of our wedding night, so that tomorrow she may—'

'I'm going, dear, Shombhu will wait at the door. If you want anything, call him.'

Mashi went to Mani's bedroom and sat down on the floor crying,—'Oh come, come once, you heartless wretch! Keep his last request who has given you his all!

Don't kill him who is already dying!'

Jotin hearing the sound of footsteps started up saying, 'Mani!'

'I am Shombhu. Did you call me?'

'Ask your mistress to come?'

'Ask whom?'

'Your mistress.'

'She has not yet returned.'

'Returned? From where?'

'From Sitarampur.'

'When did she go?'

'Three days ago.'

For a moment Jotin felt numb all over, and his head began to swim. He slipped down from the pillows, on which he was reclining, and kicked off the woollen shawl that was over his feet.

When Mashi came back after a long time, Jotin did not mention Mani's name, and Mashi thought he had forgotten all about her.

Suddenly Jotin cried out: 'Mashi, did I tell you about the dream I had the other night?'

'Which dream?'

'That in which Mani was pushing the door, and the door wouldn't open more than an inch. She stood outside unable to enter. Now I know that Mani has to stand outside my door till the last.'

Mashi kept silent. She realised that the heaven she had been building for Jotin out of falsehood had toppled down at last. If sorrow comes, it is best to acknowledge it.—When God strikes, we cannot avoid the blow.

'Mashi, the love I have got from you will last through all my births. I have filled this life with it to carry it with me. In the next birth, I am sure you will be born as my daughter, and I shall tend you with all my love.'

'What are you saying, Jotin? Do you mean to say I shall be born again as a woman? Why can't you pray that I should come to your arms as a son?'

'No, no, not a son! You will come to my house in that wonderful beauty which you had when you were young. I can even imagine how I shall dress you.'

'Don't talk so much, Jotin, but try to sleep.'

'I shall name you "Lakshmi." '

'But that is an old-fashioned name, Jotin!'

'Yes, but you are my old-fashioned Mashi. Come to my house again with those beautiful old-fashioned manners.'

'I can't wish that I should come and burden your home with the misfortune of a girl-child!'

'Mashi, you think me weak, and are wanting to save me all trouble.'

'My child, I am a woman, so I have my weakness. Therefore, I have tried all my life to save you from all sorts of trouble,—only to fail.'

'Mashi, I have not had time in this life to apply the

lessons I have learnt. But they will keep for my next birth. I shall show them what a man is able to do. I have learnt how false it is always to be looking after oneself.'

'Whatever you may say, darling, you have never grasped anything for yourself, but give everything to others.'

'Mashi, I can boast of one thing at any rate. I have never been a tyrant in my happiness, or tried to enforce my claims by violence. Because lies could not content me, I have had to wait long. Perhaps, truth will be kind to me at last.—Who is that, Mashi, who is that?'

'Where? There's no one there, Jotin!'

'Mashi, just go and see in the other room. I thought I—'

'No, dear! I don't see anybody.'

'But it seemed quite clear to me that—'

'No, Jotin, it's nothing. So keep quiet! The doctor is coming now.'

When the doctor entered, he said:

'Look here, you mustn't stay near the patient so much, you excite him. You go to bed, and my assistant will remain with him.'

'No, Mashi, I can't let you go.'

'Alright, Baba! I will sit quietly in that corner.'

'No, no! you must sit by my side. I can't let go your hand, not till the very end. I have been made by your hand, and only from your hand shall God take me.'

'Alright,' said the doctor, 'you can remain there. But, Jotin Babu, you must not talk to her. It's time for you to take your medicine.'

'Time for my medicine? Nonsense! The time for that is over. To give medicine now is merely to deceive; besides, I am not afraid to die. Mashi, Death is busy with his physic; why do you add another nuisance in the shape of a doctor? Send him away, send him away! It is you alone I need now! No one else, none whatever! No more falsehood!'

'I protest, as a doctor, this excitement is doing you harm.'

'Then go, doctor, don't excite me any more!–Mashi, has he gone?.... That's good! Now, come and take my head in your lap.'

'Alright, dear! Now, Baba, try to sleep!'

'No, Mashi, don't ask me to sleep. If I sleep, I shall never wake. I still need to keep awake a little longer. Don't you hear a sound? Somebody is coming.'

## V

'Jotin dear, just open your eyes a little. She has come. Look once and see!'

'Who has come? A dream?'

'Not a dream, darling! Mani has come with her father.'

'Who are you?'

'Can't you see? This is your Mani!'

'Mani? Has that door opened?'

'Yes, Baba, it is wide open.'

'No, Mashi, not that shawl! not *that* shawl! That shawl is a fraud!'

'It is not a shawl, Jotin! It is our Mani, who has flung herself on your feet. Put your hand on her head and bless her. Don't cry like that, Mani! There will be time enough for that. Keep quiet now for a little.'

# The Skeleton

In the room next to the one in which we boys used to sleep, there hung a human skeleton. In the night it would rattle in the breeze which played about its bones. In the day these bones were rattled by us. We were taking lessons in osteology from a student in the Campbell Medical School, for our guardians were determined to make us masters of all the sciences. How far they succeeded we need not tell those who know us; and it is better hidden from those who do not.

Many years have passed since then. In the meantime the skeleton has vanished from the room, and the science of osteology from our brains, leaving no trace behind.

The other day, our house was crowded with guests, and I had to pass the night in the same old room. In these now unfamiliar surroundings, sleep refused to come, and, as I tossed from side to side, I heard all the hours of the night chimed, one after another, by the church clock nearby. At length the lamp in the corner of the room, after some minutes of choking and spluttering, went out altogether. One or two bereavements had recently happened in the family, so the going out of the lamp naturally led me to thoughts of death. In the great arena of nature, I thought, the light of a lamp losing itself in eternal darkness, and the going out of the light of our little human lives, by day or by night, were much the same thing.

My train of thought recalled to my mind the skeleton. While I was trying to imagine what the body which had clothed it could have been like, it suddenly seemed to me that something was walking round and round my bed, groping along the walls of the room. I could hear its rapid breathing. It seemed as if it was searching for something which it could not find, and pacing round the room with ever-hastier steps. I felt quite sure that this was a mere fancy of my sleepless, excited brain; and that the throbbing of the veins in my temples was really the sound which seemed like running footsteps. Nevertheless, a cold shiver ran all over me. To help to get rid of this hallucination, I called out aloud: 'Who is there?' The footsteps seemed to stop at my bedside, and the reply came: 'It is I. I have come to look for that skeleton of mine.'

It seemed absurd to show any fear before the creature of my own imagination; so, clutching my pillow a little more tightly, I said in a casual sort of way: 'A nice business for this time of night! Of what use will that skeleton be to you now?'

The reply seemed to come almost from my mosquito-curtain itself. 'What a question! In that skeleton were the bones that encircled my heart; the youthful charm of my six-and-twenty years bloomed about it. Should I not desire to see it once more?'

'Of course,' said I, 'a perfectly reasonable desire. Well, go on with your search, while I try to get a little sleep.'

Said the voice: 'But I fancy you are lonely. Alright; I'll sit down a while, and we will have a little chat. Years ago I used to sit by men and talk to them. But during the last thirty-five years I have only moaned in the wind in the burning-places of the dead. I would talk once more with a man as in the old times.'

I felt that someone sat down just near my curtain. Resigning myself to the situation, I replied with as much cordiality as I could summon. 'That will be very nice, indeed. Let us talk of something cheerful.'

'The funniest thing I can think of is my own life-story. Let me tell you that.'

The church clock chimed the hour of two.

'When I was in the land of the living, and young, I feared one thing like death itself, and that was my husband. My feelings can be likened only to those of a fish caught with a hook. For it was as if a stranger had snatched me away with the sharpest of hooks from the peaceful calm of my childhood's home—and from him I had no means of escape. My husband died two months after my marriage, and my friends and relations moaned pathetically on my behalf. My husband's father, after scrutinising my face with great care, said to my mother-in-law: "Do you not see, she has the evil eye?"—Well, are you listening? I hope you are enjoying the story?'

'Very much, indeed!' said I. 'The beginning is extremely humorous.'

'Let me proceed then. I came back to my father's house in great glee. People tried to conceal it from me, but I know well that I was endowed with a rare and radiant beauty. What is your opinion?'

'Very likely,' I murmured. 'But you must remember that I never saw you.'

'What! Not seen me? What about that skeleton of mine? Ha! ha! ha! Never mind. I was only joking. How can I ever make you believe that those two cavernous hollows contained the brightest of dark, languishing eyes? And, that the smile which was revealed by those ruby lips had no resemblance whatever to the grinning teeth which you used to see? The mere attempt to convey to you some idea of the grace, the charm, the soft, firm, dimpled curves, which in the fulness of youth were growing and blossoming over those dry old bones makes me smile; it also makes me angry. The most eminent doctors of my time could not have dreamed of the bones of that body of mine as materials for teaching osteology. Do you know, one young doctor that I knew of, actually compared me to a golden *champak* blossom. It meant that to him the rest of human kind was fit only to illustrate the science of physiology, that I was a flower of beauty. Does any one think of the skeleton of a *champak* flower?

'When I walked, I felt that, like a diamond scattering splendour, my every movement set waves of beauty radiating on every side. I used to spend hours gazing on my hands—hands which could gracefully have reined the liveliest of male creatures.

'But that stark and staring old skeleton of mine has borne false-witness to you against me, while I was unable to refute the shameless libel. That is why of all men I hate you most! I feel I would like once for all to banish sleep from your eyes with a vision of that warm rosy loveliness of mine, to sweep out with it all the wretched osteological stuff of which your brain is full.'

'I could have sworn by your body,' cried I, 'if you had it still, that no vestige of osteology has remained in my head, and that the only thing that it is now full of is a radiant vision of perfect loveliness, glowing against the black background of night. I cannot say more than that.'

'I had no girl-companions,' went on the voice. 'My only brother had made up his mind not to marry. In the *zenana* I was alone. Alone I used to sit in the garden under the shade of the trees, and dream that the whole world was in love with me; that the stars with sleepless gaze were drinking in my beauty; that the wind was languishing in sighs as on some pretext or other it brushed past me; and that the lawn on which my feet rested, had it been

---

1. Widows are supposed to dress in white only, without ornaments or jewellery.

conscious, would have lost consciousness against their touch. It seemed to me that all the young men in the world were as blades of grass at my feet; and my heart, I know not why, used to grow sad.

'When my brother's friend, Shekhar, had passed out of the Medical College, he became our family doctor. I had already often seen him from behind a curtain. My brother was a strange man, and did not care to look on the world with open eyes. It was not empty enough for his taste; so he gradually moved away from it, until he was quiet lost in an obscure corner. Shekhar was his one friend, so he was the only young man I could ever get to see. And, when I held my evening court in my garden, then the host of imaginary young men whom I had at my feet were each one a Shekhar.—Are you listening? What are you thinking of?'

I sighed as I replied: 'I was wishing I was Shekhar!'

'Wait a bit. Hear the whole story first. One day, in the rains, I was feverish. The doctor came to see me. That was our first meeting. I was reclining opposite the window, so that the blush of the evening sky might temper the pallor of my complexion. When the doctor, coming in, looked up into my face, I put myself into his place, and gazed at myself in imagination. I saw in the glorious evening light that delicate wan face laid like a drooping flower against the soft white pillow, with the

2. See the previous note.

unrestrained curls playing over the forehead, and the bashfully lowered eyelids casting a pathetic shade over the whole countenance.

'The doctor, in a tone bashfully low, asked my brother: "Might I feel her pulse?"'

'I put out a tired, well-rounded wrist from beneath the coverlet. "Ah!" thought I, as I looked on it, "If only there had been a sapphire bracelet."[1] I have never before seen a doctor so awkward about feeling a patient's pulse. His fingers trembled as they felt my wrist. He measured the heat of my fever, I gauged the pulse of his heart.—Don't you believe me?'

'Very easily,' said I; 'the human heart-beat tells its tale.'

'After I had been taken ill and restored to health several times, I found that the number of the courtiers who attended my imaginary evening reception began to dwindle till they were reduced to only one! And at last, in my little world there remained only one doctor and one patient.

'In these evenings I used to dress myself[2] secretly in a canary-coloured *sari*; twine about the braided knot into which I did my hair a garland of white jasmine blossoms; and with a little mirror in my hand betake myself to my usual seat under the trees.

'Well! Are you perhaps thinking that the sight of one's own beauty would soon grow wearisome? Ah no! for I did not see myself with my own eyes. I was then one and also two. I used to see myself as though I were the doctor; I gazed, I was charmed, I fell madly in love. But, in spite of all the caresses I lavished on my self, a sigh would wander about my heart, moaning like the evening breeze.

'Anyhow, from that time I was never alone. When I walked I watched with downcast eyes the play of my dainty little toes on the earth, and wondered what the doctor would have felt had he been there to see. At mid-day the sky would be filled with the glare of the sun, without a sound, save now and then the distant cry of a passing kite. Outside our garden-walls the hawker would pass with his musical cry of "Bangles for sale, crystal bangles." And I, spreading a snow-white sheet on the lawn, would lie on it with my head on my arm. With studied carelessness the other arm would rest lightly on the soft sheet, and I would imagine to myself that someone had caught sight of the wonderful pose of my hand, that someone had clasped it in both of his and imprinted a kiss on its rosy palm, and was slowly walking away.—What if I ended the story here? How would it do?'

'Not half a bad ending,' I replied thoughtfully. 'It would no doubt remain a little incomplete, but I could easily spend the rest of the night putting in the finishing touches.'

'But that would make the story too serious. Where would the laugh come in? Where would be the skeleton with its grinning teeth?

'So let me go on. As soon as the doctor had got a little practice, he took a room on the ground floor of our house for a consulting-chamber. I used then sometimes to ask him jokingly about medicines and poisons, and how much of this drug or that would kill a man. The subject was congenial and he would wax eloquent. These talks familiarised me with the idea of death; and so love and death were the only two things that filled my little world. My story is now nearly ended—there is not much left.'

'Not much of the night is left either,' I muttered.

'After a time I noticed that the doctor had grown strangely absent-minded, and it seemed as if he were ashamed of something which he was trying to keep from me. One day he came in, somewhat smartly dressed, and borrowed my brother's carriage for the evening.

'My curiosity became too much for me, and I went up to my brother for information. After some talk beside the point, I at last asked him: "By the way, Dada,[3] where is the doctor going this evening in your carriage?"

'My brother briefly replied: "To his death."

"Oh, do tell me," I importuned. "Where is he really going?"

"To be married," he said, a little more explicitly.

"Oh, indeed!" said I, as I laughed long and loudly.

'I gradually learnt that the bride was an heiress, who would bring the doctor a large sum of money. But why

3. Elder brother.

did he insult me by hiding all this from me? Had I ever begged and prayed him not to marry. Because it would break my heart? Men are not to be trusted. I have known only one man in all my life, and in a moment I made this discovery.

'When the doctor came in after his work and was ready to start, I said to him, rippling with laughter the while: "Well, doctor, so you are to be married tonight?"

'My gaiety not only made the doctor lose countenance; it thoroughly irritated him.

' "How is it," I went on, "That there is no illumination, no band of music?"'

'With a sigh he replied: "Is marriage then such a joyful occasion?"'

'I burst out into renewed laughter. "No, no," said I, "this will never do. Who ever heard of a wedding without lights and music?"

I bothered my brother about it so much that he at once ordered all the trappings of a gay wedding.

'All the time I kept on gaily talking of the bride, of what would happen, of what I would do when the bride came home. "And, doctor," I asked, "will you still go on feeling pulses?" Ha! ha! ha! Though the inner workings of people's, especially men's, minds are not visible, still I can take my oath that these words were piercing the doctor's bosom like deadly darts.

'The marriage was to be celebrated late at night. Before starting, the doctor and my brother were having a glass of wine together on the terrace, as was their daily habit. The moon had just risen.

'I went up smiling, and said: "Have you forgotten your wedding, doctor? It is time to start."

'I must here tell you one little thing. I had meanwhile gone down to the dispensary and got a little powder, which at a convenient opportunity I had dropped unobserved into the doctor's glass.

'The doctor, draining his glass at a gulp, in a voice thick with emotion, and with a look that pierced me to the heart, said: "Then I must go."

'The music struck up. I went into my room and dressed myself in my bridal-robes of silk and gold. I took out my jewellery and ornaments from the safe and put them all on; I put the red mark of wifehood on the parting in my hair. And then, under the tree in the garden I prepared my bed.

'It was a beautiful night. The gentle south wind was kissing away the weariness of the world. The scent of jasmine and *bela* filled the garden with rejoicing.

'When the sound of the music began to grow fainter and fainter; the light of the moon to get dimmer and dimmer; the world with its lifelong associations of home and kin to fade away from my perceptions like some illusion:—then I closed my eyes, and smiled.

'I fancied that when people came and found me they would see that smile of mine lingering on my lips like a trace of rose-coloured wine, that when I thus slowly entered my eternal bridal-chamber I should carry with me this smile, illuminating my face. But alas for the bridal-chamber! Alas for the bridal-robes of silk and gold! When I woke at the sound of a rattling within me, I found three urchins learning osteology from my skeleton. Where in my bosom my joys and griefs used to throb, and the petals of youth to open one by one, there the master with his pointer was busy naming my bones. And, as to that last smile, which I had so carefully rehearsed, did you see any sign of that?

'Well, well, how did you like the story?'

'It has been delightful,' said I.

At this point the first crow began to caw. 'Are you there?' I asked. There was no reply.

The morning light entered the room.

# The Auspicious Vision

Kantichandra was young; yet after his wife's death he sought no second partner, and gave his mind to the hunting of beasts and birds. His body was long and slender, hard and agile; his sight keen; his aim unerring. He dressed like a countryman, and took with him Hira Singh the wrestler, Chakkanlal, Khan Saheb the musician, Mian Saheb, and many others. He had no lack of idle followers.

In the month of *Agrahayan* Kanti had gone out shooting near the swamp of Nydighi with a few sporting companions. They were in boats, and an army of servants, in boats also, filled the bathing-*ghats*. The village women found it well-nigh impossible to bathe or to draw water. All day long, land and water trembled to the firing of the guns; and every evening musicians killed the chance of sleep.

One morning as Kanti was seated in his boat cleaning a favourite gun, he suddenly started at what he thought was the cry of wild duck. Looking up, he saw a village maiden, coming to the water's edge, with two white ducklings clasped to her breast. The little stream was almost stagnant. Many weeds choked the current.

The girl put the birds into the water and watched them anxiously. Evidently, the presence of the sportsmen was the cause of her care and not the wildness of the ducks.

The girl's beauty had a rare freshness—as if she had just come from Vishwakarma's[1] workshop. It was difficult to guess her age. Her figure was almost a woman's, but her face was so childish that clearly the world had left no impression there. She seemed not to know herself that she had reached the threshold of youth.

Kanti's gun-cleaning stopped for a while. He was fascinated. He had not expected to see such a face in such a spot. And yet, its beauty suited its surroundings better than it would have suited a palace. A bud is lovelier on the bough than in a golden vase. That day the blossoming reeds glittered in the autumn dew and morning sun, and the fresh, simple face set in the midst was like a picture of festival to Kanti's enchanted mind. Kalidos has forgotten to sing how Siva's Mountain-Queen herself sometimes has come to the young Ganges, with just such ducklings in her breast. As he gazed, the maiden started in terror, and hurriedly took back the ducks into her bosom with a half-articulate cry of pain. In another moment, she had left the river-bank and disappeared into the bamboo thicket nearby. Looking round, Kanti saw one of his men pointing an unloaded gun at the ducks. He at once went up to him, wrenched away his gun, and bestowed on his cheek a

1. The divine craftsman in Hindu mythology.

prodigious slap. The astonished humourist finished his joke on the floor. Kanti went on cleaning his gun.

But curiosity drove Kanti to the thicket wherein he had seen the girl disappear. Pushing his way through, he found himself in the yard of a well-to-do householder. On one side was a row of conical thatched barns, on the other a clean cow-shed, at the end of which grew a *zizyph* bush. Under the bush was seated the girl he had seen that morning, sobbing over a wounded dove, into whose yellow beak she was trying to wring a little water from the moist corner of her garment. A grey cat, its fore-paws on her knee, was looking eagerly at the bird, and every now and then, when it got too forward, she kept it in its place by a warning tap on the nose.

This little picture, set in the peaceful mid-day surrounding of the householder's yard, instantly impressed itself on Kanti's sensitive heart. The checkered light and shade, flickering beneath the delicate foliage of the *zizyph*, played on the girl's lap. Not far off a cow was chewing the cud, and lazily keeping off the flies with slow movements of its head and tail. The north wind whispered softly in the rustling bamboo thickets. And, she who at dawn on the river-bank had looked like the Forest Queen, now in the silence of noon showed the eager pity of the Divine Housewife. Kanti, coming in upon her with his gun, had a sense of intrusion. He felt like a thief caught red-handed. He longed to explain that it was not he who had hurt the dove. As he wondered how he should begin, there came a call of 'Sudha!' from the house. The girl jumped up. 'Sudha!' came the voice again. She took up her dove, and ran within. 'Sudha,'[2] thought Kanti, 'what an appropriate name!'

Kanti returned to the boat, handed his gun to his men, and went over to the front door of the house. He found a middle-aged Brahmin, with a peaceful, clean-shaven face, seated on a bench outside, and reading a devotional book. Kanti saw in his kindly, thoughtful face something of the tenderness which shone in the face of the maiden.

Kanti saluted him, and said: 'May I ask for some water, sir? I am very thirsty.' The elder man welcomed him with eager hospitality, and, offering him a seat on the bench, went inside and fetched with his own hands a little brass plate of sugar wafers and a bell-metal vessel full of water.

After Kanti had eaten and drunk, the Brahmin begged him to introduce himself. Kanti gave his own name, his father's name, and the address of his home, and then said in the usual way: 'If I can be of any service, sir, I shall deem myself fortunate.'

'I require no service, my son,' said Nabin Banerji; 'I have only one care at present.'

'What is that, sir?' said Kanti.

'It is my daughter, Sudha, who is growing up' (Kanti

2. *Sudha* means nectar, ambrosia.

smiled as he thought of her babyish face), and for whom I have not yet been able to find a worthy bridegroom. If I could only see her well married, all my debt to this world would be paid. But there is no suitable bridegroom here, and I cannot leave my charge of Gopinath here, to search for a husband elsewhere.'

'If you would see me in my boat, sir, we would have a talk about the marriage of your daughter.' So saying, Kanti repeated his salute and went back. He then sent some of his men into the village to inquire, and in answer heard nothing but praise of the beauty and virtues of the Brahmin's daughter.

When next day the old man came to the boat on his promised visit, Kanti bent low in salutation, and begged the hand of his daughter for himself. The Brahmin was so much overcome by this undreamed-of piece of good fortune—for Kanti not only belonged to a well-known Brahmin family, but was also a landed proprietor of wealth and position—that at first he could hardly utter a word in reply. He thought there must have been some mistake, and at length mechanically repeated: 'You desire to marry my daughter?'

'If you will deign to give her to me,' said Kanti.

'You mean Sudha?' he asked again.

'Yes,' was the reply.

'But will you not first see and speak to her—?'

Kanti, pretending he had not seen her already, said: 'Oh, that we shall do at the moment of the Auspicious

Vision.'[3]

In a voice husky with emotion the old man said: 'My Sudha is indeed a good girl, well skilled in all the household arts. As you are so generously taking her on trust, may she never cause you a moment's regret. This is my blessing!'

The brick-built mansion of the Mazumdars had been borrowed for the wedding ceremony, which was fixed for next *Magh*, as Kanti did not wish to delay. In due time the bridegroom arrived on his elephant, with drums and music and with a torchlight procession, and the ceremony began.

When the bridal couple were covered with the scarlet screen for the rite of the Auspicious Vision, Kanti looked up at his bride. In that bashful, downcast face, crowned with the wedding coronet and bedecked with sandal paste, he could scarcely recognise the village maiden of his fancy, and in the fullness of his emotion a mist seemed to becloud his eyes.

At the gathering of women in the bridal chamber, after the wedding ceremony was over, an old village dame insisted that Kanti himself should take off his wife's bridal veil. As he did so he started back. It was not the same girl.

Something rose from within his breast and pierced

---

3. After betrothal the prospective bride and bridegroom are not supposed to see each other again till that part of the wedding ceremony which is called *The Auspicious Vision*.

into his brain. The light of the lamps seemed to grow dim, and darkness to tarnish the face of the bride herself.

At first he felt angry with his father-in-law. The old scoundrel had shown him one girl, and married him to another. But on calmer reflection he remembered that the old man had not shown him any daughter at all—that it was all his own fault. He thought it best not to show his arrant folly to the world, and took his place again with apparent calmness.

He could swallow the powder; he could not get rid of its taste. He could not bear the merry-makings of the festive throng. He was in a blaze of anger with himself as well as with everybody else.

Suddenly he felt the bride, seated by his side, give a little start and a suppressed scream; a leveret, scampering into the room, had brushed across her feet. Close upon it followed the girl he had seen before. She caught up the leveret into her arms, and began to caress it with an affectionate murmuring. 'Oh, the mad girl!' cried the women as they made signs to her to leave the room. She heeded them not, however, but came and unconcernedly sat in front of the wedded pair, looking into their faces with a childish curiosity. When a maidservant came and took her by the arm to lead her away, Kanti hurriedly interposed, saying, 'Let her be.'

'What is your name?' he then went on to ask her.

The girl swayed backwards and forwards but gave no reply. All the women in the room began to titter.

Kanti put another question: 'Have those ducklings of yours grown up?'

The girl stared at him as unconcernedly as before.

The bewildered Kanti screwed up courage for another effort, and asked tenderly after the wounded dove, but with no avail. The increasing laughter in the room betokened an amusing joke.

At last, Kanti learned that the girl was deaf and dumb, the companion of all the animals and birds of the locality. It was but by chance that she rose the other day when the name of Sudha was called.

Kanti now received a second shock. A black screen lifted from before his eyes. With a sigh of intense relief, as of escape from calamity, he looked once more into the face of his bride. Then came the true Auspicious Vision. The light from his heart and from the smokeless lamps fell on her gracious face; and he saw it in its true radiance, knowing that Nabin's blessing would find fulfilment.

# The Supreme Night

I used to go to the same dame's school with Surabala and play at marriage with her. When I paid visits to her house, her mother would pet me, and setting us side by side would say to herself: 'What a lovely pair!'

I was a child then, but I could understand her meaning well enough. The idea became rooted in my mind that I had a special right to Surabala above that of people in general. So it happened that, in the pride of ownership, at times I punished and tormented her; and she, too, fagged for me and bore all my punishments without complaint. The village was wont to praise her beauty; but in the eyes of a young barbarian like me that beauty had no glory;—I knew only that Surabala had been born in her father's house solely to bear my yoke, and that therefore she was the particular object of my neglect.

My father was the land-steward of the Chaudhuris, a family of *zemindars*. It was his plan, as soon as I had learnt to write a good hand, to train me in the work of estate management and secure a rent collectorship for me somewhere. But in my heart I disliked the proposal.

Nilratan of our village had run away to Calcutta, had learnt English there, and finally became the *Nazir*[1] of the District Magistrate; *that* was my life's ideal: I was secretly determined to be the Head Clerk of the Judge's Court, even if I could not become the Magistrate's *Nazir*.

I saw that my father always treated these court officers with the greatest respect. I knew from my childhood that they had to be propitiated with gifts of fish, vegetables, and even money. For this reason I had given a seat of high honour in my heart to the court underlings, even to the bailiffs. These are the gods worshipped in our Bengal,—a modern miniature edition of the 330 millions of deities of the Hindu pantheon. For gaining material success, people have more genuine faith in *them* than in the good Ganesh, the giver of success; hence the people now offer to these officers everything that was formerly Ganesh's due.

Fired by the example of Nilratan, I too seized a suitable opportunity and ran away to Calcutta. There I first put up in the house of a village acquaintance, and afterwards got some funds from my father for my education. Thus, I carried on my studies regularly.

In addition, I joined political and benevolent societies. I had no doubt whatever that it was urgently necessary for me to give my life suddenly for my country. But I knew not how such a hard task could be carried out. Also, no one showed me the way.

---

1. Superintendent of bailiffs.

But, nevertheless, my enthusiasm did not abate at all. We country lads had not learnt to sneer at everything like the precocious boys of Calcutta, and hence our faith was very strong. The 'leaders' of our associations delivered speeches, and we went begging for subscriptions from door to door in the hot blaze of noon without breaking our fast; or we stood by the roadside distributing hand-bills, or arranged the chairs and benches in the lecture-hall, and, if anybody whispered a word against our leader, we got ready to fight him. For these things the city boys used to laugh at us as provincials.

I had come to Calcutta to be a *Nazir* or a Head Clerk, but I was preparing to become a Mazzini or a Garibaldi.

At this time, Surabala's father and my father laid their heads together to unite us in marriage. I had come to Calcutta at the age of fifteen; Surabala was eight years old then. I was now eighteen, and in my father's opinion I was almost past the age of marriage. But it was my secret vow to remain unmarried all my life and to die for my country; so I told my father that I would not marry before I had finished my education.

In two or three months I learnt that Surabala had been married to a pleader named Ram Lochan. I was then busy collecting subscriptions for raising fallen India, and this news did not seem worth my thought.

I had matriculated, and was about to appear at the Intermediate Examination, when my father died. I was not alone in the world, but had to maintain my mother and two sisters. I had, therefore, to leave college and look out for employment. After a good deal of exertion I secured the post of second master in the matriculation school of a small town in the Noakhali District.

I thought, here is just the work for me! By my advice and inspiration I shall train up every one of my pupils as a general for future India.

I began to work, and then found that the impending examination was a more pressing affair than the future of India. The headmaster got angry whenever I talked of anything outside grammar or algebra. And, in a few months my enthusiasm, too, flagged.

I am no genius. In the quiet of the home I may form vast plans; but when I enter the field of work, I have to bear the yoke of the plough on my neck like the Indian bullock, get my tail twisted by my master, break clods all day, patiently and with bowed head, and then at sunset have to be satisfied if I can get any cud to chew. Such a creature has not the spirit to prance and caper.

One of the teachers lived in the school-house, to guard against fires. As I was a bachelor, this work was thrown on me. I lodged in a thatched shed close to the large cottage in which the school sat.

The school-house stood at some distance from the inhabited portion of the town, and beside a big tank. Around it were betel-nut, cocoa-nut, and *madar* trees, and very near to the school building two large ancient *nim* trees grew close together, and cast a cool shade around.

One thing I have forgotten to mention, and indeed,

I had not so long considered it worth mentioning. The local Government pleader, Ram Lochan Ray, lived near our school. I also knew that his wife—my early playmate, Surabala—lived with him.

I got acquainted with Ram Lochan Babu. I cannot say whether he knew that I had known Surabala in childhood. I did not think fit to mention the fact at my first introduction to him. Indeed, I did not clearly remember that Surabala had been ever linked with my life in any way.

One holiday I paid a visit to Ram Lochan Babu. The subject of our conversation has gone out of my mind; probably it was the unhappy condition of present-day India. Not that he was very much concerned or heart-broken over the matter; but the subject was such that one could freely pour forth one's sentimental sorrow over it for an hour or two while puffing at one's *hooka*.

While thus engaged, I heard in a side-room the softest possible jingle of bracelets, crackle of dress, and footfall; and I felt certain that two curious eyes were watching me through a small opening of the window.

All at once there flashed upon my memory a pair of eyes,—a pair of large eyes, beaming with trust, simplicity, and girlhood's love,—black pupils—thick dark eyelashes,—a calm fixed gaze. Suddenly some unseen force squeezed my heart in an iron grip, and it throbbed with intense pain.

I returned to my house, but the pain clung to me. Whether I read, wrote, or did any other work, I could not shake that weight off my heart; a heavy load seemed to be always swinging from my heart-strings.

In the evening, calming myself a little, I began to reflect: 'What ails me?' From within came the question: 'Where is *your* Surabala now?' I replied: 'I gave her up of my free will. Surely, I did not expect her to wait for me for ever.'

But something kept saying: '*Then*, you could have got her merely for the asking. *Now* you have not the right to look at her even once, do what you will. That Surabala of your boyhood may come very close to you; you may hear the jingle of her bracelets; you may breathe the air embalmed by the essence of her hair,—but there will always be a wall between you two.'

I answered: 'Be it so. What is Surabala to me?'

My heart rejoined: 'Today Surabala is nobody to you. But what might she not have been to you?'

Ah! that's true. *What* might she not have been to me? Dearest to me of all things, closer to me than the world besides, the sharer of all my life's joys and sorrows, she might have been. And now, she is so distant, so much of a stranger, that to look on her is forbidden, to talk with her is improper, and to think of her is a sin!—while this Ram Lochan, coming suddenly from nowhere, has muttered a few set religious texts, and in one swoop has carried off Surabala from the rest of mankind!

I have not come to preach a new ethical code, or to revolutionise society; I have no wish to tear asunder domestic ties. I am only expressing the exact working of my mind, though it may not be reasonable. I could not by any means banish from my mind the sense that Surabala, reigning there within shelter of Ram Lochan's home, was mine far more than his. The thought was, I admit, unreasonable and improper,—but it was not unnatural.

Thereafter I could not set my mind to any kind of work. At noon when the boys in my class hummed, when Nature outside simmered in the sun, when the sweet scent of the *nim* blossoms entered the room on the tepid breeze, I then wished,—I know not what I wished for; but this I can say, that I did not wish to pass all my life in correcting the grammar exercises of those future hopes of India.

When school was over, I could not bear to live in my large lonely house; and yet, if anyone paid me a visit, it bored me. In the gloaming as I sat by the tank and listened to the meaningless breeze sighing through the betel-and cocoa-nut palms, I used to muse that human society is a web of mistakes; nobody has the sense to do the right thing at the right time, and when the chance is gone we break our hearts over vain longings.

I could have married Surabala and lived happily. But I must be a Garibaldi,—and I ended by becoming the second master of a village school! And, pleader Ram Lochan Ray, who had no special call to be Surabala's husband,—to whom, before his marriage, Surabala was no wise different from a hundred other maidens,—has very quietly married her, and is earning lots of money as

Government pleader; when his dinner is badly cooked he scolds Surabala, and when he is in good humour he gives her a bangle! He is sleek and fat, tidily dressed, free from every kind of worry; *he* never passes his evenings by the tank gazing at the stars and sighing.

Ram Lochan was called away from our town for a few days by a big case elsewhere. Surabala in her house was as lonely as I was in my school building.

I remember it was a Monday. The sky was overcast with clouds from the morning. It began to drizzle at ten o'clock. At the aspect of the heavens our headmaster closed the school early. All day, the black detached clouds began to run about in the sky as if making ready for some grand display. Next day, towards afternoon, the rain descended in torrents, accompanied by storm. As the night advanced the fury of wind and water increased. At first the wind was easterly; gradually it veered, and blew towards the south and south-west.

It was idle to try to sleep on such a night. I remembered that in this terrible weather Surabala was alone in her house. Our school was much more strongly built than her bungalow. Often, and often did I plan to invite her to the school-house, while I meant to pass the night alone by the tank. But I could not summon up courage for it.

When it was half-past one in the morning, the roar of the tidal wave was suddenly heard,—the sea was rushing on us! I left my room and ran towards Surabala's house. In the way stood one embankment of our tank, and as

I was wading to it the flood already reached my knees. When I mounted the bank, a second wave broke on it. The highest part of the bank was more than seventeen feet above the plain.

As I climbed up the bank, another person reached it from the opposite side. Who she was, every fibre of my body knew at once, and my whole soul was thrilled with the consciousness. I had no doubt that she too, had recognised me.

On an island some three yards in area stood we two; all else was covered with water.

It was a time of cataclysm; the stars had been blotted out of the sky; all the lights of the earth had been darkened; there would have been no harm if we had held converse *then*. But we could not bring ourselves to utter a word; neither of us made even a formal inquiry after the other's health. Only we stood gazing at the darkness. At our feet swirled the dense, black, wild, roaring torrent of death.

Today, Surabala has come to *my* side, leaving the whole world. Today she has none besides *me*. In our far-off childhood this Surabala had come from some dark primeval realm of mystery, from a life in another orb, and stood by my side on this luminous peopled earth; and today, after a wide span of time, she has left that earth, so full of light and human beings, to stand alone by my side amidst this terrible desolate gloom of Nature's death-convulsion. The stream of birth had flung that tender bud before me, and the flood of death had wafted the same flower, now in full bloom, to *me* and to none else. One more wave and we shall be swept away from this extreme point of the earth, torn from the stalks on which we now sit apart, and made one in death.

May that wave never come! May Surabala live long and happily, girt round by husband and children, household and kinsfold! This one night, standing on the brink of Nature's destruction, I have tasted eternal bliss.

The night wore out, the tempest ceased, the flood abated; without a word spoken, Surabala went back to her house, and I, too, returned to my shed without having uttered a word.

I reflected: True, I have become no *Nazir* or Head Clerk, nor a Garibaldi; I am only the second master of a beggarly school. But one night had for its brief space beamed upon my whole life's course.

That one night, out of all the days and nights of my allotted span, has been the supreme glory of my humble existence.

# Raja and Rani

Bipin Kisore was born 'with a golden spoon in his mouth'; hence he knew how to squander money twice as well as how to earn it. The natural result was that he could not live long in the house where he was born.

He was a delicate young man of comely appearance, an adept in music, a fool in business, and unfit for life's handicap. He rolled along life's road like the wheel of Jagannath's car. He could not long command his wonted style of magnificent living.

Luckily, however, Raja Chittaranjan, having got back his property from the Court of Wards, was intent upon organising an Amateur Theatre Party. Captivated by the prepossessing looks of Bipin Kisore and his musical endowments, the Raja gladly 'admitted him into his crew.'

Chittaranjan was a B.A. He was not given to any excesses. Though the son of a rich man, he used to dine and sleep at appointed hours and even at appointed places. And, he suddenly became enamoured of Bipin like one unto drink. Often did meals cool and nights grow old while he listened to Bipin and discussed with him the merits of operatic compositions. The Dewan remarked that the only blemish in the otherwise perfect character of his master was his inordinate fondness for Bipin Kisore.

Rani Basanta Kumari raved at her husband, and said that he was wasting himself on a luckless baboon. The sooner she could do away with him, the easier she would feel.

The Raja was much pleased in his heart at this seeming jealousy of his youthful wife. He smiled, and thought that women-folk know only one man upon the earth—him whom they love; and never think of other men's deserts. That there may be many whose merits deserve regard, is not recorded in the scriptures of women. The only good man and the only object of a woman's favours is he who has blabbered into her ears the matrimonial incantations. A little moment behind the usual hour of her husband's meals is a world of anxiety to her, but she never cares a brass button if her husband's dependents have a mouthful or not. This inconsiderate partiality of the softer sex might be cavilled at, but to Chittaranjan it did not seem unpleasant. Thus, he would often indulge in hyperbolic laudations of Bipin in his wife's presence, just to provoke a display of her delightful fulminations.

But what was sport to the 'royal' couple, was death to poor Bipin. The servants of the house, as is their wont, took their cue from the Rani's apathetic and wilful neglect of the wretched hanger-on, and grew more apathetic and wilful still. They contrived to forget to look after his comforts, to Bipin's infinite chagrin and untold sufferings.

Once, the Rani rebuked the servant Puté, and said: 'You are always shirking work; what do you do all through the day?' 'Pray, madam, the whole day is taken up in serving Bipin Babu under the Maharaja's orders,' stammered the poor valet.

The Rani retorted: 'Your Bipin Babu is a great Nawab, eh?' This was enough for Puté. He took the hint. From the very next day he left Bipin Babu's comforts as they were, and at times forgot to cover the food for him. With unpractised hands Bipin often scoured his own dishes and not unfrequently went without meals. But it was not in him to whine and report to the Raja. It was not in him to lower himself by petty squabblings with menials. He did not mind it; he took everything in good part. And thus, while the Raja's favours grew, the Rani's disfavour intensified, and at last knew no bounds.

Now the opera of *Subhadraharan* was ready after due rehearsal. The stage was fitted up in the palace courtyard. The Raja acted the part of 'Krishna,' and Bipin that of 'Arjuna.' Oh, how sweetly he sang! How beautiful he looked! The audience applauded in transports of joy.

The play over, the Raja came to the Rani and asked her how she liked it. The Rani replied: 'Indeed, Bipin acted the part of "Arjuna" gloriously! He does look like the scion of a noble family. His voice is rare!' The Raja said jocosely: 'And, how do I look? Am I not fair? Have I not a sweet voice?' 'Oh, yours is a different case!' added the Rani, and again fell to dilating on the histrionic abilities of Bipin Kisore.

The tables were now turned. He who used to praise, now began to deprecate. The Raja, who was never weary of indulging in high-sounding panegyrics of Bipin before his consort, now suddenly fell reflecting that, after all, unthinking people made too much of Bipin's actual merits. What was extraordinary about his appearance of voice? A short while before he himself was one of those unthinking men, but in a sudden and mysterious way he developed symptoms of thoughtfulness!

From the day following, every good arrangement was made for Bipin's meals. The Rani told the Raja: 'It is undoubtedly wrong to lodge Bipin Babu with the petty officers of the Raj in the *Kachari*[1]; for all he now is, he was once a man of means.' The Raja ejaculated curtly: 'Ha!' and turned the subject. The Rani proposed that there might be another performance on the occasion of the first-rice ceremony of the 'royal' weanling. The Raja heard and heard her not.

Once, on being reprimanded by the Raja for not properly laying his cloth, the servant Puté replied: 'What can I do? According to the Rani's behests I have to look after Bipin Babu and wait on him the livelong day.' This angered the Raja, and he exclaimed, highly nettled. 'Pshaw! Bipin Babu is a veritable Nawab, I see! Can't he cleanse his own dishes himself?' The servant,

1. *Kachari*, generally anglicised as cuteberry: officers and courts.

as before, took his cue, and Bipin lapsed back into his former wretchedness.

The Rani liked Bipin's songs—they were sweet—there was no gainsaying it. What her husband sat with Bipin to the wonted discourses of sweet music of an evening, she would listen from behind the screen in an adjoining room. Not long afterwards, the Raja began again his old habit of dining and sleeping at regular hours. The music came to an end. Bipin's evening services were no more needed.

Raja Chittaranjan used to look after his *zemindari* affairs at noon. One day, he came earlier to the *zenana*, and found his consort reading something. On his asking her what she read, the Rani was a little taken aback, but promptly replied: 'I am conning over a few songs from Bipin Babu's song-book. We have not had any music since you tired abruptly of your musical hobby.' Poor woman! It was she who had herself made no end of efforts to eradicate the hobby from her husband's mind.

On the morrow the Raja dismissed Bipin—without a thought as to how and where the poor fellow would get a morsel henceforth!

Nor was this the only matter of regret to Bipin. He had been bound to the Raja by the dearest and most sincere tie of attachment. He served him more for affection than for pay. He was fonder of his friend than of the wages he received. Even after deep cogitation, Bipin could not ascertain the cause of the Raja's sudden estrangement. 'T'is Fate! All is Fate!' Bipin said to himself. And then, silently and bravely, he heaved a deep sigh, picked up his old guitar, put it up in the case, paid the last two coins in his pocket as a farewell *bakshish* to Puté, and walked out into the wide wide world where he had not a soul to call his friend.

# The Trust Property

## I

Brindaban Kundu came to his father in a rage and said: 'I am off this moment.'

'Ungrateful wretch!' sneered the father, Jagannath Kundu. 'When you have paid me back all that I have spent on your food and clothing, it will be time enough to give yourself these airs.'

Such food and clothing as was customary in Jagannath's household could not have cost very much. Our *rishis* of old managed to feed and clothe themselves on an incredibly small outlay. Jaganath's behaviour showed that his ideal in these respects was equally high. That he could not fully live up to it was due partly to the bad influence of the degenerate society around him, and partly to certain unreasonable demands of Nature in her attempt to keep body and soul together.

So long as Brindaban was single, things went smoothly enough, but after his marriage he began to depart from the high and rarefied standard cherished by his sire. It was clear that the son's ideas of comfort were moving away from the spiritual to the material, and imitating the ways of the world. He was unwilling to put up with the discomforts of heat and cold, thirst and hunger. His minimum of food and clothing rose apace.

Frequent were the quarrels between the father and the son. At last, Brindaban's wife became seriously ill and a *kabiraj*[1] was called in. But when the doctor prescribed a costly medicine for his patient, Jagannath took it as a proof of sheer incompetence, and turned him out immediately. At first, Brindaban besought his father to allow the treatment to continue; then he quarrelled with him about it, but to no purpose. When his wife died, he abused his father and called him a murderer.

'Nonsense!' said the father. 'Don't people die even after swallowing all kinds of drugs? If costly medicines could save life, how is it that kings and emperors are not immortal? You don't expect your wife to die with more pomp and ceremony than did your mother and your grandmother before her, do you?'

Brindaban might really have derived a great consolation from these words, had he not been overwhelmed with grief and incapable of proper thinking. Neither his mother nor his grandmother had taken any medicine before making their exit from this world, and this was the time-honoured custom of the family. But, alas! the younger generation was unwilling to die according to ancient custom. The English had newly come to the country at the time we speak of. Even in those remote days, the good old folks were horrified

1. Country doctor, unqualified by any medical training.

at the unorthodox ways of the new generation, and sat speechless, trying to draw comfort from their *hookas*.

Be that as it may, the modern Brindaban said to his old fogy of a father: 'I am off.'

The father instantly agreed, and wished publicly that, should he ever give his son one single pice in future, the gods might reckon his act as shedding the holy blood of cows. Brindaban in his turn similarly wished that, should he ever accept anything from his father, his act might be held as bad as matricide.

The people of the village looked upon this small revolution as a great relief after a long period of monotony. And, when Jagannath disinherited his only son, everyone did his best to console him. All were unanimous in the opinion that to quarrel with a father for the sake of a wife was possible only in these degenerate days. And, the reason they gave was sound, too. 'When your wife dies,' they said, 'you can find a second one without delay. But when your father dies, you can't get another to replace him for love or money.' Their logic no doubt was perfect, but we suspect that the utter hopelessness of getting another father did not trouble the misguided son very much. On the contrary, he looked upon it as a mercy.

Nor, did separation from Brindaban weigh heavily on the mind of his father. In the first place, his absence from home reduced the household expenses. Then, again, the father was freed from a great anxiety. The fear of being poisoned by his son and heir had always haunted him.

When he ate his scanty fare, he could never banish the thought of poison from his mind. This fear had abated somewhat after the death of his daughter-in-law, and, now that the son was gone, it disappeared altogether.

But there was one tender spot in the old man's heart. Brindaban had taken away with him his four-year-old son, Gokul Chándra. Now, the expense of keeping the child was comparatively small, and so Jagannath's affection for him was without a drawback. Still, when Brindaban took him away, his grief, sincere as it was, was mingled at first with calculation as to how much he would save a month by the absence of the two, how much the sum would come to in the year, and what would be the capital to bring it in as interest.

But the empty house, without Gokul Chandra in it to make mischief, became more and more difficult for the old man to live in. There was no one now to play tricks upon him when he was engaged in his *puja*,[2] no one to snatch away his food and eat it, no one to run away with his ink-pot, when he was writing up his accounts. His daily routine of life, now uninterrupted, became an intolerable burden to him. He bethought that this unworried peace was endurable only in the world to come. When he caught sight of the holes made in his quilt by his grandchild, and the pen-and-ink sketches executed by the same artist on his rush-mat, his heart was heavy with grief. Once upon a time he

2. A ceremonial worship.

had reproached the boy bitterly because he had torn his *dhoti* into pieces within the short space of two years; now tears stood in Jaganath's eyes as he gazed upon the dirty remnants lying in the bedroom. He carefully put them away in his safe, and registered a vow that, should Gokul ever come back again, he should not be reprimanded even if he destroyed one *dhoti* a year.

But Gokul did not return, and poor Jagannath aged rapidly. His empty home seemed emptier every day.

No longer could the old man stay peacefully at home. Even in the middle of the day, when all respectable folks in the village enjoyed their after-dinner siesta, Jagannath might be seen roaming over the village, *hooka*, in hand. The boys, at sight of him, would give up their play, and, retiring in a body to a safe distance, chant verses composed by a local poet, praising the old gentleman's economical habits. No one ventured to say his real name, lest he should have to go without his meal that day[3]—and so people gave him names after their own fancy. Elderly people called him Jagannash,[4] but the reason why the younger generation preferred to call him a vampire was hard to guess. It may be that the bloodless, dried-up skin of the old man had some physical resemblance to the vampire's.

---

3. It is a supersition current in Bengal that if a man pronounces the name of a very miserly individual, he has to go without his meal that day.
4. Jagannath is the Lord of Festivity, and *Jagannash* would mean the despoiler of it.

## II

One afternoon, when Jagannath was rambling as usual through the village lanes shaded by mango topes, he saw a boy, apparently a stranger, assuming the captaincy of the village boys and explaining to them the scheme of some new prank. Won by the force of his character and the startling novelty of his ideas, the boys had all sworn allegiance to him. Unlike the others, he did not run away from the old man as he approached, but came quite close to him and began to shake his own *chadar*. The result was that a live lizard sprang out of it on the old man's body, ran down his back and off towards the jungle. Sudden fright made the poor man shiver from head to foot, to the great amusement of the other boys, who shouted with glee. Before Jagannath had gone far, cursing and swearing, the *gamcha* on his shoulder suddenly disappeared, and the next moment it was seen on the head of the new boy, transformed into a turban.

The novel attentions of this manikin came as a great relief to Jagannath. It was long since any boy had taken such freedom with him. After a good deal of coaxing and many fair promises, he at last persuaded the boy to come to him, and this was the conversation which followed:

'What's your name, my boy?'

'Nitai Pal.'

'Where's your home?'

'Won't tell.'

'Who's your father?'

'Won't tell.'

'Why won't you?'

'Because I have run away from home.'

'What made you do it?'

'My father wanted to send me to school'.

It occurred to Jagannath that it would be useless extravagance to send such a boy to school, and his father must have been an unpractical fool not to have thought so.

'Well, well,' said Jagannath, 'how would you like to come and stay with me?'

'Don't mind,' said the boy, and forthwith he installed himself in Jagannath's house. He felt as little hesitation as though it were the shadow of a tree by the wayside. And, not only that. He began to proclaim his wishes as regards his food and clothing with such coolness that you would have thought he had paid his reckoning in full beforehand; and, when anything went wrong, he did not scruple to quarrel with the old man. It had been easy enough for Jagannath to get the better of his own child; but now, where another man's child was concerned, he had to acknowledge defeat.

## III

The people of the village marvelled when Nitai Pal was unexpectedly made so much of by Jagannath. They felt sure that the old man's end was near, and the prospect of his bequeathing all his property to this unknown brat made their hearts sore. Furious with envy, they determined to do the boy an injury, but the old man took care of him as though he was a rib in his breast.

At times, the boy threatened that he would go away, and the old man used to say to him temptingly: 'I will leave you all the property I possess.' Young as he was, the boy fully understood the grandeur of this promise.

The village people then began to make inquiries after the father of the boy. Their hearts melted with compassion for the agonised parents, and they declared that the son must be a rascal to cause them so much suffering. They heaped abuses on his head, but the heat with which they did it betrayed envy rather than a sense of justice.

One day, the old man learned from a wayfarer that one Damodar Pal was seeking his lost son, and was even now coming towards the village. Nitai, when he heard this, became very restless and was ready to run away, leaving his future wealth to take care of itself. Jagannath reassured him, saying: 'I mean to hide you where nobody can find you—not even the village people themselves.'

This whetted the curiosity of the boy and he said: 'Oh, where? Do show me.'

'People will know, if I show you now. Wait till it is night,' said Jagannath.

The hope of discovering the mysterious hiding-place delighted Nitai. He planned to himself how, as soon as his father had gone away without him, he would have a bet with his comrades, and play hide-and-seek. Nobody would be able to find him. Wouldn't it be fun? His father, too, would ransack the whole village, and not find him—that would be rare fun also.

At noon, Jagannath shut the boy up in his house, and disappeared for some time. When he came home again, Nitai worried him with questions.

No sooner was it dark than Nitai said: 'Grandfather, shall we go now?'

'It isn't night yet,' replied Jagannath.

A little while later the boy exclaimed: 'It is night now, grandfather; come let's go.'

'The village people haven't gone to bed yet,' whispered Jagannath.

Nitai waited but a moment, and said: 'They have gone to bed now, grandfather; I am sure they have. Let's start now.'

The night advanced. Sleep began to weigh heavily on the eyelids of the poor boy, and it was a hard struggle for him to keep awake. At midnight, Jagannath caught hold of the boy's arm, and left the house, groping through the dark lanes of the sleeping village. Not a sound disturbed the stillness, except the occasional howl of a dog, when all the other dogs far and near would join in chorus, or perhaps the flapping of a night-bird, scared by the sound of human footsteps at that unusual hour. Nitai trembled with fear, and held Jagannath fast by the arm.

Across many a field they went, and at last came to a jungle, where stood a dilapidated temple without a god in it. 'What, here!' exclaimed Nitai in a tone of disappointment. It was nothing like what he had imagined. There was not much mystery about it. Often, since running away from home, he had passed nights in deserted temples like this. It was not a bad place for playing hide-and-seek; still, it was quite possible that his comrades might track him there.

From the middle of the floor inside, Jagannath removed a slab of stone, and an underground room with a lamp burning in it was revealed to the astonished eyes of the boy. Fear and curiosity assailed his little heart. Jagannath descended by a ladder and Nitai followed him.

Looking around, the boy saw that there were brass *ghurras*[5] on all sides of him. In the middle lay spread an *assan*,[6] and in front of it were arranged vermilion, sandal paste, flowers, and other articles of *puja*. To satisfy his curiosity the boy dipped his hand into some of the *ghurras*, and drew out their contents. They were rupees and gold *mohurs*.

Jagannath, addressing the boy, said: 'I told you, Nitai, that I would give you all my money. I have not got much,—these *ghurras* are all that I possess. These I will make over to you today.'

The boy jumped with delight. 'All?' he exclaimed; 'you won't take back a rupee, will you?'

5. A water-pot holding about three gallons of water.
6. A prayer carpet.

'If I do,' said the old man in solemn tones, 'may my hand be attacked with leprosy. But there is one condition. If ever my grandson, Gokul Chandra, or his son, or his grandson, or his great-grandson or any of his progeny should happen to pass this way, then you must make over to him, or to them, every rupee and every *mohur* here.'

The boy thought that the old man was raving. 'Very well,' he replied.

'Then, sit on this *assan*,' said Jagannath.

'What for?'

'Because *puja* will be done to you.'

'But why?' said the boy, taken aback.

'This is the rule.'

The boy squatted on the *assan* as he was told. Jagannath smeared his forehead with sandal paste, put a mark of vermilion between his eyebrows, flung a garland of flowers round his neck, and began to recite *mantras*.[7]

To sit there like a god, and hear *mantras* recited, made poor Nitai feel very uneasy. 'Grandfather,' he whispered.

But Jagannath did not reply, and went on muttering his incantations.

Finally, with great difficulty he dragged each *ghurra* before the boy and made him repeat the following vow after him.

'I do solemnly promise that I will make over all this

---

7. Incantations.

treasure to Gokul Chandra Kundu, the son of Brindaban Kundu, the grandson of Jagannath Kundu, or to the son or to the grandson or to the great-grandson of the said Gokul Chandra Kundu, or to any other progeny of his who may be the rightful heir.'

The boy repeated this over and over again, until he felt stupefied, and his tongue began to grow stiff in his mouth. When the ceremony was over, the air of the cave was laden with the smoke of the earthern lamp and the breath-poison of the two. The boy felt that the roof of his mouth had become dry as dust, and his hands and feet were burning. He was nearly suffocated.

The lamp became dimmer and dimmer, and then went out altogether. In the total darkness that followed, Nitai could hear the old man climbing up the ladder. 'Grandfather, where are you going to?' said he, greatly distressed.

'I am going now,' replied Jagannath; 'you remain here. No one will be able to find you. Remember the name Gokul Chandra, the son of Brindaban, and the grandson of Jagannath.'

He then withdrew the ladder. In a stifled, agonised voice the boy implored: 'I want to go back to father.'

Jagannath replaced the slab. He then knelt down and placed his ear on the stone. Nitai's voice was heard once more–'Father'–and then came a sound of some heavy object falling with a bump—and then—everything was still.

Having thus placed his wealth in the hands of a *yak*,[8] Jagannath began to cover up the stone with earth. Then, he piled broken bricks and loose mortar over it. On the top of all he planted turfs of grass and jungle weeds. The night was almost spent, but he could not tear himself away from the spot. Now and again, he placed his ear to the ground, and tried to listen. It seemed to him that from far far below—from the abysmal depth of the earth's interior—came a wailing. It seemed to him that the night-sky was flooded with that one sound, that the sleeping humanity of all the world was awake, and was sitting on its beds, trying to listen.

The old man in his frenzy kept on heaping earth higher and higher. He wanted somehow to stifle that sound, but still he fancied he could hear 'Father.'

He struck the spot with all his might and said: 'Be quiet—people might hear you.' But still, he imagined he heard 'Father.'

The sun lighted up the eastern horizon. Jagannath then left the temple, and came into the open fields.

There, too, somebody called out 'Father.' Startled at the sound, he turned back and saw his son at his heels.

'Father,' said Brindaban, 'I hear my boy is hiding himself in your house. I must have him back.'

With eyes dilated and distorted mouth, the old man

8. *Yak or Yaksa* is a supernatural being described in Sanskrit mythology and poetry. In Bengal, *Yak* has come to mean a ghostly custodian of treasure, under such circumstances as in this story.

leaned forward and exclaimed: 'Your boy?'

'Yes, my boy Gokul. He is Nitai Pal now, and I myself go by the name of Damodar Pal. Your *fame* has spread so widely in the neighbourhood, that we were obliged to cover up our origin, lest people should have refused to pronounce our names.'

Slowly, the old man lifted both his arms above his head. His fingers began to twitch convulsively, as though he was trying to catch hold of some imaginary object in the air. He then fell on the ground.

When he came to his senses again, he dragged his son towards the ruined temple. When they were both inside it, he said: 'Do you hear any wailing sound?'

'No, I don't,' said Brindaban.

'Just listen very carefully. Do you hear anybody calling out "Father"?'

'No.'

This seemed to relieve him greatly.

From that day forward, he used to go about asking people: 'Do you hear any wailing sound?' They laughed at the raving dotard.

About four years later, Jagannath lay on his deathbed. When the light of this world was gradually fading away from his eyes, and his breathing became more and more difficult, he suddenly sat up in a state of delirium. Throwing both his hands in the air he seemed to grope about for something, muttering: 'Nitai, who has removed my ladder?'

Unable to find the ladder to climb out of his terrible

dungeon, where there was no light to see and no air to breathe, he fell on his bed once more, and disappeared into that region where no one has ever been found out in the world's eternal game of hide-and-seek.[9]

9. The incidents described in this story, now happily a thing of the past, were by no means rare in Bengal at one time. Our author, however, slightly departs from the current accounts. Such criminally superstitious practices were resorted to by miserly persons under the idea that they themselves would re-acquire the treasure in a future state of existence. 'When you see me in a future birth passing this way, you must make over all this treasure to me. Guard it till then and stir not,'—was the usual promise exacted from the victim before he became *yak*. Many were the 'true' stories we heard in childhood, of people becoming suddenly rich by coming across ghostly custodians of wealth belonging to them in a past birth.

# The Riddle Solved

## I

Krishna Gopal Sircar, *zemindar* of Jhikrakota, made over his estates to his eldest son, and retired to Kasi, as befits a good Hindu, to spend the evening of his life in religious devotion. All the poor and the destitute of the neighbourhood were in tears at the parting. Everyone declared that such piety and benevolence were rare in these degenerate days.

His son, Bipin Bihari, was a young man well educated after the modern fashion, and had taken the degree of Bachelor of Arts. He sported a pair of spectacles, wore a beard, and seldom mixed with others. His private life was unsullied. He did not smoke, and never touched cards. He was a man of stern disposition, though he looked soft and pliable. This trait of his character soon came home to his tenantry in diverse ways. Unlike his father, he would on no account allow the remission of one single pice out of the rents justly due to him. In no circumstances would he grant any tenant one single day's grace in paying up.

On taking over the management of the property, Bipin Bihari discovered that his father had allowed a large number of Brahmins to hold land entirely rent-free, and a larger number at rents much below the prevailing rates. His father was incapable of resisting the importunate solicitation of others—such was the weakness of his character.

Bipin Bihari said this could never be. He could not abandon the income of half his property—and he reasoned with himself thus: *Firstly*, the persons who were in actual enjoyment of the concessions and getting fat at his expense were a lot of worthless people, and wholly undeserving of charity. Charity bestowed on such objects only encouraged idleness. *Secondly*, living nowadays had become much costlier than in the days of his ancestors. Wants had increased apace. For a gentleman to keep up his position had become four times as expensive as in days past. So, he could not afford to scatter gifts right and left as his father had done. On the contrary, it was his bounden duty to call back as many of them as he possibly could.

So, Bipin Bihari lost no time in carrying into effect what he conceived to be his duty. He was a man of strict principles.

What had gone out of his grasp, returned to him little by little. Only a very small portion of his father's grants did he allow to remain undisturbed, and he took good care to arrange that even those should not be deemed permanent.

The wails of the tenants reached Krishna Gopal at Benares through the post. Some even made a journey to that place to represent their grievances to him in person. Krishna Gopal wrote to his son intimating his displeasure. Bipin Bihari replied, pointing out that the times had changed. In former days, he said, the *zemindar*, was compensated for the gifts he made by the many customary presents he received from his tenantry. Recent statutes had made all such impositions illegal. The *zemindar* had now to rest content with just the stipulated rent, and nothing more. 'Unless,' he continued, 'we keep a strict watch over the payment of our just dues, what will be left to us? Since the tenants won't give us anything extra now, how can we allow them concessions? Our relations must henceforth be strictly commercial. We shall be ruined if we go on making gifts and endowments, and the preservation of our property and the keeping up of our position will be rendered very difficult.

Krishna Gopal became uneasy at finding that times should have changed so much. 'Well, well,' he murmured to himself, the younger generation knows best, I suppose. Our old-fashioned methods won't do now. If I interfere, my son might refuse to manage the property, and insist on my going back. No, thank you—I would rather not. I prefer to devote the few days that are left me to the service of my God.'

## II

So, things went on. Bipin Bihari put his affairs in

order after much litigation in the Courts, and by less constitutional methods outside. Most of the tenants submitted to his will out of fear. Only a fellow called Asimuddin, son of Mirza Bibi, remained refractory.

Bipin's displeasure was keenest against this man. He could quite understand his father having granted rent-free lands to Brahmins, but why this Mohammedan should be holding so much land, some free and some at rents lower than the prevailing rates, was a riddle to him. And, what was he? The son of a low Mohammedan widow, giving himself air and defying the whole world, simply because he had learnt to read and write a little at the village school. To Bipin it was intolerable.

He made inquiries of his clerks about Asimuddin's holdings. All that they could tell him was that Babu Krishna Gopal himself had made these grants to the family many years ago, but they had no idea as to what his motive might have been. They imagined, however, that perhaps the widow won the compassion of the kind-hearted *zemindar*, by representing to him her woe and misery.

To Bipin these favours seemed to be utterly undeserved. He had not seen the pitiable condition of these people in days gone by. Their comparative ease at the present day and their arrogance drove him to the conclusion that they had impudently swindled his tender-hearted father out of a part of his lawful income.

Asimuddin was a stiff-necked sort of a fellow, too. He vowed that he would lay down his life sooner than give up an inch of his land. Then came open hostilities.

The poor old widow tried her best to pacify her son. 'It is no good fighting with the *zemindar*,' she would often say to him. 'His kindness has kept us alive so long; let us depend upon him still though he may curtail his favours. Surrender to him part of the lands as he desires.'

'Oh, mother!' protested Asimuddin. 'What do you know of these matters, pray?'

One by one, Asimuddin lost the cases instituted against him. The more he lost, the more his obstinacy increased. For the sake of his all, he staked all that was his.

One afternoon, Mirza Bibi collected some fruits and vegetables from her little garden, and unknown to her son went and sought an interview with Bipin Babu. She looked at him with a tenderness maternal in its intensity, and spoke: 'May Allah bless you, my son. Do not destroy Asim—it wouldn't be right of you. To your charge I commit him. Take him as though he were one whom it is your duty to support—as though he were a ne'er-do-well younger brother of yours. Vast is your wealth—don't grudge him a small particle of it, my son.'

This assumption of familiarity on the part of the garrulous old woman annoyed Bipin not a little. 'What do you know of these things, my good woman?' he condescended to say. 'If you have any representations to make, send your son to me.'

Being assured for the second time that she knew nothing about these affairs, Mirza Bibi returned home, wiping her eyes with her apron all the way, and offering her silent prayers to Allah.

## III

The litigation dragged its weary length from the Criminal to the Civil Courts, and thence to the High Court, where at last Asimuddin met with a partial success. Eighteen months passed in this way. But he was a ruined man now—plunged in debts up to his very ears. His creditors took this opportunity to execute the decrees they had obtained against him. A date was fixed for putting up to auction every stick and stone that he had left.

It was Monday. The village market had assembled by the side of a tiny river, now swollen by the rains. Buying and selling were going on, partly on the bank and partly in the boats moored there. The hubbub was great. Among the commodities for sale jack-fruits preponderated, it being the month of *Asadh*. *Hilsa* fish were seen in large quantities also. The sky was cloudy. Many of the stall-holders, apprehending a downpour, had stretched, a piece of cloth overhead, across bamboo poles put up for the purpose.

Asimuddin had come too—but he had not a copper with him. No shopkeepers allowed him credit nowadays. He therefore had brought a brass *thali*[1] and a

---

1. *Thali*: plate.

*dao*[2] with him. These he would pawn, and then buy what he needed.

Towards evening, Bipin Babu was out for a walk attended by two or three retainers armed with *lathis.*[3] Attracted by the noise, he directed his steps towards the market. On his arrival, he stopped awhile before the stall of Dwari, the oilman, and made kindly inquiries about his business. All on a sudden, Asimuddin raised his *dao* and ran towards Bipin Babu, roaring like a tiger. The market people caught hold of him half-way, and quickly disarmed him. He was forthwith given in custody to the police. Business in the market then went on as usual.

We cannot say that Bipin Babu was not inwardly pleased at this incident. It is intolerable that the creature we are hunting down should turn and show fight. 'The *badmash,*' Bipin chuckled; 'I have got him at last.'

The ladies of Bipin Babu's house, when they heard the news, exclaimed with horror: 'Oh, the ruffian! What a mercy they seized him in time!' They found consolation in the prospect of the man being punished as he richly deserved.

In another part of the village the same evening the widow's humble cottage, devoid of bread and bereft of her son, became darker than death. Others dismissed the incident of the afternoon from their minds, sat down to their meals, retired to bed and went to sleep, but to the

2. *Dao:* knife.
3. *Lathis:* sticks.

widow the event loomed larger than anything else in this wide world. But, alas, who was there to combat it? Only a bundle of wearied bones and a helpless mother's heart trembling with fear.

## IV

Three days have passed in the meanwhile. Tomorrow the case would come up for trial before a Deputy Magistrate. Bipin Babu would have to be examined as a witness. Never before this did a *zemindar* of Jhikrakota appear in the witness-box, but Bipin did not mind.

The next day at the appointed hour, Bipin Babu arrived at the Court in a palanquin in great state. He wore a turban on his head, and a watch-chain dangled on his breast. The Deputy Magistrate invited him to a seat on the daïs, beside his own. The Court-room was crowded to suffocation. So great a sensation had not been witnessed in this Court for many a year.

When the time for the case to be called drew near, a *chaprassi* came and whispered something in Bipin Babu's ear. He got up very agitated and walked out, begging the Deputy Magistrate to excuse him for a few minutes.

Outside he saw his old father a little way off, standing under a banian tree, barefooted and wrapped in a piece of *namabali*.[4] A string of beads was in his hand. His slender form shone with a gentle lustre, and tranquil compassion seemed to radiate from his forehead.

4. A garment with the name of Krishna printed over it.

Bipin, hampered by his close-fitting trousers and his flowing *chapkan*, touched his father's feet with his forehead. As he did this his turban came off and kissed his nose, and his watch, popping out of his pocket, swung to and fro in the air. Bipin hurriedly straightened his turban, and begged his father to come to his pleader's house close by.

'No, thank you,' Krishna Gopal replied, 'I will tell you here what I have got to say.'

A curious crowd had gathered by this time. Bipin's attendants pushed them back.

Then, Krishna Gopal said: 'You must do what you can to get Asim acquitted, and restore him the lands that you have taken away from him.'

'Is it for this, father,' said Bipin, very much surprised, 'that you have come all the way from Benares? Would you tell me why you have made these people the objects of your special favour?'

'What would you gain by knowing it, my boy?'

But Bipin persisted. 'It is only this, father,' he went on; 'I have revoked many a grant because I thought the tenants were not deserving. There were many Brahmins among them, but of them you never said a word. Why are you so keen about these Mohammedans now? After all that has happened, if I drop this case against Asim, and give him back his lands, what shall I say to people?'

Krishna Gopal kept silence for some moments. Then, passing the beads through his shaky fingers with rapidity, he spoke with a tremulous voice: 'Should it be necessary to explain your conduct to people, you may tell them that Asimuddin is my son—and your brother.'

'What?' exclaimed Bipin in painful surprise. 'From a Musalman's womb?'

'Even so, my son,' was the calm reply.

Bipin stood there for some time in mute astonishment. Then, he found words to say: 'Come home, father; we will talk about it afterwards.'

'No, my son,' replied the old man, 'having once relinquished the world to serve my God, I cannot go home again. I return hence. Now, I leave you to do what your sense of duty may suggest.' He then blessed his son, and, checking his tears with difficulty, walked off with tottering steps.

Bipin was dumbfounded, not knowing what to say nor what to do. 'So, such was the piety of the older generation,' he said to himself. He reflected with pride how much better he was than his father in point of education and morality. This was the result, he concluded, of not having a principle to guide one's actions.

Returning to the Court, he saw Asimuddin outside between two constables, awaiting his trial. He looked emaciated and worn out. His lips were pale and dry, and his eyes unnaturally bright. A dirty piece of cloth worn to shreds covered him. 'This my brother!' Bipin shuddered at the thought.

The Deputy Magistrate and Bipin were friends and the case ended in a fiasco. In a few days, Asimuddin was restored to his former condition. Why all this happened, he could not understand. The village people were greatly surprised also.

However, the news of Krishna Gopal's arrival just before the trial soon got abroad. People began to exchange meaningful glances. The pleaders in their shrewdness guessed the whole affair. One of them, Ram Taran Babu, was beholden to Krishna Gopal for his education and his start in life. Somehow or other he had always suspected that the virtue and piety of his benefactor were shams. Now, he was fully convinced that, if a searching inquiry were made, all 'pious' men might be found out. 'Let them tell their beads as much as they like,' he thought with glee, 'everybody in this world is just as bad as myself. The only difference between a good and a bad man is that the good practise dissimulation while the bad don't.' The revelation that Krishna Gopal's far-famed piety, benevolence, and magnanimity were nothing but a cloak of hypocrisy, settled a difficulty that had oppressed Ram Taran Babu for many years. By what process of reasoning, we do not know, the burden of gratitude was greatly lifted off his mind. It was a vast relief to him!

# The Elder Sister

## I

Having described at length the misdeeds of an unfortunate woman's wicked, tyrannical husband, Tara, the woman's neighbour in the village, very shortly declared her verdict: 'Fire be to such a husband's mouth.'

At this Joygopal Babu's wife felt much hurt; it did not become womankind to wish, in any circumstances whatever, a worse species of fire than that of a cigar in a husband's mouth.

When, therefore, she mildly disapproved the verdict, hard-hearted Tara cried with redoubled vehemence: ''Twere better to be a widow seven births over than the wife of such a husband,' and saying this she broke up the meeting and left.

Sasi said within herself: 'I can't imagine any offence in a husband that could so harden the heart against him.' Even as she turned the matter over in her mind, all the tenderness of her loving soul gushed forth towards her own husband now abroad. Throwing herself with outstretched arms on that part of the bed whereon her husband was wont to lie, she kissed the empty pillow, caught the smell of her husband's head, and, shutting the door, brought out from a wooden box an old and almost faded photograph with some letters in his handwriting, and sat gazing upon them. Thus, she passed the hushed noontide alone in her room, musing of old memories and shedding tears of sadness.

It was no new yoke this between Sasikala and Joygopal. They had been married at an early age and had children. Their long companionship had made the days go by in an easy, commonplacc sort of way. On neither side had there been any symptoms of excessive passion. They had lived together nearly sixteen years without a break, when her husband was suddenly called away from home on business, and then a great impulse of love awoke in Sasi's soul. As separation strained the tie, love's knot grew tighter, and the passion, whose existence Sasi had not felt, now made her throb with pain.

So, it happened that after so many long years, and at such an age, and being the mother of children, Sasi, on this spring noon, in her lonely chamber, lying on the bed of separation, began to dream the sweet dream of a bride in her budding youth. That love of which hitherto she had been unconscious suddenly aroused her with its murmuring music. She wandered a long way up the stream, and saw many a golden mansion and many a grove on either bank; but no foothold could she find now amid the vanished hopes of happiness. She began to say to herself that, when next she met her husband, life should not be insipid nor should the spring come in vain. How very often, in idle disputation or some petty quarrel, had she teased her husband! With all the singleness of a penitent heart she vowed that she would never show impatience again, never oppose her husband's wishes, bear all his commands, and with a tender heart submit to whatever he wished of good or ill; for the husband was all-in-all, the husband was the dearest object of love, the husband was divine.

Sasikala was the only and much-petted daughter of her parents. For this reason, though he had only a small property of his own, Joygopal had no anxieties about the future. His father-in-law had enough to support them in a village with royal state.

And then, in his old age a son was born untimely to Sasikala's father. To tell the truth, Sasi was very sore in her mind at this unlooked-for, improper, and unjust action of her parents; nor was Joygopal particularly pleased.

The parents' love centred in this son of their advanced years, and when the newly arrived, diminutive, sleepy brother-in-law seized with his two weak tiny fists all the hopes and expectations of Joygopal, Joygopal found a place in a tea-garden in Assam.

His friends urged him to look for employment nearby, but whether out of a general feeling of resentment, or knowing the chances of rapid rise in a tea-garden, Joygopal would not pay heed to anybody. He sent his wife and children to his father-in-law's, and left for Assam. It was the first separation between husband

and wife in their married life.

This incident made Sasikala very angry with her baby brother. The soreness which may not pass the lips is felt the more keenly within. When the little fellow sucked and slept at his ease, his big sister found a hundred reasons, such as the rice is cold, the boys are too late for school, to worry herself and others, day and night, with her petulant humours.

But in a short time the child's mother died. Before her death, she committed her infant son to her daughter's care.

Then did the motherless child easily conquer his sister's heart. With loud whoops he would fling himself upon her, and with right goodwill try to get her mouth, nose, eyes within his own tiny mouth; he would seize her hair within his little fists and refuse to give it up; awaking before the dawn, he would roll over to her side and thrill her with his soft touch, and babble like a noisy brook; later on, he would call her *jiji* and *jijima*, and in hours of work and rest, by doing forbidden things, eating forbidden food, going to forbidden places, would set up a regular tyranny over her; then Sasi could resist no longer. She surrendered herself completely to this wayward little tyrant. Since the child had no mother, his influence over her became the greater.

## II

The child was named Nilmani. When he was two years

old his father fell seriously ill. A letter reached Joygopal asking him to come as quickly as possible. When after much trouble he got leave and arrived, Kaliprasanna's last hour had come.

Before he died Kaliprasanna entrusted Joygopal with the charge of his son, and left a quarter of his estate to his daughter.

So, Joygopal gave up his appointment, and came home to look after his property.

After a long time husband and wife met again. When a material body breaks it may be put together again. But when two human beings are divided, after a long separation, they never re-unite at the same place, and to the same time; for the mind is a living thing, and moment by moment it grows and changes.

In Sasi reunion stirred a new emotion. The numbness of age-long habit in their old marriage was entirely removed by the longing born of separation, and she seemed to win her husband much more closely than before. Had she not vowed in her mind that whatever days might come, and how long so-ever they might be, she would never let the brightness of this glowing love for her husband be dimmed.

Of this reunion, however, Joygopal felt differently. When they were constantly together before he had been bound to his wife by his interests and idiosyncrasies. His wife was then a living truth in his life, and there would have been a great rent in the web of his daily habit if she were left out. Consequently, Joygopal found himself in deep waters at first when he went abroad. But in time, this breach in habit was patched up by a new habit.

And, this was not all. Formerly, his days went by in the most indolent and careless fashion. For the last two years, the stimulus of bettering his condition had stirred so powerfully in his breast that he had nothing else in his thoughts. As compared with the intensity of this new passion, his old life seemed like an unsubstantial shadow. The greatest changes in a woman's nature are wrought by love; in a man's, by ambition.

Joygopal, when he returned after two years, found his wife not quite the same as of old. To her life his infant brother-in-law had added a new breadth. This part of her life was wholly unfamiliar to him—here he had no communion with his wife. His wife tried hard to share her love for the child with him, but it cannot be said that she succeeded. Sasi would come with the child in her arms, and hold him before her husband with a smiling face—Nilmani would clasp Sasi's neck, and hide his face on her shoulder, and admit no obligation of kindred. Sasi wished that her little brother might show Joygopal all the arts he had learnt to capture a man's mind. But Joygopal was not very keen about it. How could the child show any enthusiasm? Joygopal could not at all understand what there was in the heavy-pated, grave-faced, dusky child that so much love should be wasted on him.

Women quickly understand the ways of love. Sasi at once understood that Joygopal did not care for Nilmani.

Henceforth, she used to screen her brother with the greatest care—to keep him away from the unloving, repelling look of her husband. Thus, the child came to be the treasure of her secret care, the object of her isolated love.

Joygopal was greatly annoyed when Nilmani cried; so Sasi would quickly press the child to her breast, and with her whole heart and soul try to soothe him. And, when Nilmani's cry happened to disturb Joygopal's sleep at night, and Joygopal with an expression of displeasure, and in a tortured spirit, growled at the child, Sasi felt humbled and fluttered like a guilty thing. Then, she would take up the child in her lap, retire to a distance, and in a voice of pleading love, with such endearments as 'my gold, my treasure, my jewel,' lull him to sleep.

Children will fall out for a hundred things. Formerly, in such cases, Sasi would punish her children, and side with her brother, for he was motherless. Now, the law changed with the judge. Nilmani had often to bear heavy punishment without fault and without inquiry. This wrong went like a dagger to Sasi's heart; so she would take her punished brother into her room, and with sweets and toys, and by caressing and kissing him, solace as much as she could his stricken heart.

Thus, the more Sasi loved Nilmani, the more Joygopal was annoyed with him. On the other hand, the more Joygopal showed his contempt for Nilmani, the more would Sasi bathe the child with the nectar of her love.

And, when Joygopal behaved harshly to his wife, Sasi would minister to him silently, meekly, and with loving kindness. But inwardly they hurt each other, moment by moment, about Nilmani.

The hidden clash of a silent conflict like this is far harder to bear than an open quarrel.

## III

Nilmani's head was the largest part of him. It seemed as if the Creator had blown through a slender stick a big bubble at its top. The doctors feared sometimes that the child might be as frail and as quickly evanescent as a bubble. For a long time he could neither speak nor walk. Looking at his sad grave face, you might think that his parents had unburdened all the sad weight of their advanced years upon the head of this little child.

With his sister's care and nursing, Nilmani passed the period of danger, and arrived at his sixth year.

In the month of Kartik, on the *bhaiphoto*[1] day, Sasi had dressed Nilmani up as a little Babu, in coat and *chadar* and red-bordered *dhoti*, and was giving him the 'brother's mark,' when her outspoken neighbour Tara

---

1. Lit. the 'brother's mark.' A beautiful and touching ceremony in which a Hindu sister makes a mark of sandalwood paste on the forehead of her brother and utters a formula, 'putting the barrier in Yama's doorway' (figurative for wishing long life). On these occasions, the sisters entertain their brothers and make them presents of clothes, etc.

came in and, for one reason or another, began a quarrel.

''Tis no use,' cried she, 'giving the "brother's mark" with so much show and ruining the brother in secret.'

At this, Sasi was thunderstruck with astonishment, rage, and pain. Tara repeated the rumour that Sasi and her husband had conspired together to put the minor Nilmani's property up for sale for arrears of rent, and to purchase it in the name of her husband's cousin. When Sasi heard this, she uttered a curse that those who could spread such a foul lie might be stricken with leprosy in the mouth. And then, she went weeping to her husband, and told him of the gossip. Joygopal said: 'Nobody can be trusted in these days. Upen is my aunt's son, and I felt quite safe in leaving him in charge of the property. He could not have allowed the *taluk* Hasilpur to fall into arrears and purchase it himself in secret, if I had had the least inkling about it.'

'Won't you sue then?' asked Sasi in astonishment.

'Sue one's cousin!' said Joygopal. 'Besides, it would be useless, a simple waste of money.'

It was Sasi's supreme duty to trust her husband's word, but Sasi could not. At last her happy home, the domesticity of her love seemed hateful to her. That home life which had once seemed her supreme refuge was nothing more than a cruel snare of self-interest, which had surrounded them, brother and sister, on all sides. She was a woman, single-handed, and she knew not how she could save the helpless Nilmani. The more she thought, the more her heart filled with terror, loathing, and an infinite love for her imperilled little brother. She thought that, if she only knew how, she would appear before the Lat *Saheb*,[2] nay, write to the Maharani herself, to save her brother's property. The Maharani would surely not allow Nilmani's *taluk*[3] of Hasilpur, with an income of seven hundred and fifty-eight rupees a year, to be sold.

When Sasi was thus thinking of bringing her husband's cousin to book by appealing to the Maharani herself, Nilmani was suddenly seized with fever and convulsions.

Joygopal called in the village doctor. When Sasi asked for a better doctor, Joygopal said: 'Why, Matilal isn't a bad sort.'

Sasi fell at his feet, and charged him with an oath on her own head; whereupon Joygopal said: 'Well, I shall send for the doctor from town.'

Sasi lay with Nilmani in her lap, nor would Nilmani let her out of his sight for a minute; he clung to her lest by some pretence she should escape; even while he slept he would not loosen his hold of her dress.

Thus, the whole day passed, and Joygopal came after nightfall to say that the doctor was not at home; he had gone to see a patient at a distance. He added that he himself had to leave that very day on account of a lawsuit, and that he had told Matilal, who would

---

2. The Viceroy.
3. Land.

regularly call to see the patient.

At night Nilmani wandered in his sleep. As soon as the morning dawned, Sasi, without the least scruple, took a boat with her sick brother, and went straight to the doctor's house. The doctor was at home—he had not left the town. He quickly found lodgings for her, and having installed her under the care of an elderly widow, undertook the treatment of the boy.

The next day Joygopal arrived. Blazing with fury, he ordered his wife to return home with him at once.

'Even if you cut me to pieces, I won't return,' replied his wife. 'You all want to kill my Nilmani, who has no father, no mother, none other than me, but I will save him.'

'Then you remain here, and don't come back to my house,' cried Joygopal indignantly.

Sasi at length fired up. '*Your* house! Why, 'tis my brother's!'

'Alright, we'll see,' said Joygopal. The neighbours made a great stir over this incident. 'If you want to quarrel with your husband,' said Tara, 'do so at home. What is the good of leaving your house? After all, Joygopal is your husband.'

By spending all the money she had with her, and selling her ornaments, Sasi saved her brother from the jaws of death. Then, she heard that the big property which they had in Dwarigram, where their dwelling-house stood, the income of which was more than Rs 1500 a year, had been transferred by Joygopal into his own name with the help of the *zemindar*. And now, the whole property belonged to them, not to her brother.

When he had recovered from his illness, Nilmani would cry plaintively: 'Let us go home, sister.' His heart was pining for his nephews and nieces, his companions. So, he repeatedly said: 'Let us go home, sister, to that old house of ours.' At this Sasi wept. Where was their home?

But it was no good crying. Her brother had no one else besides herself in the world. Sasi thought of this, wiped her tears, and, entering the *zenana* of the Deputy Magistrate, Tarini Babu, appealed to his wife. The Deputy Magistrate knew Joygopal. That a woman should foresake her home, and engage in a dispute with her husband regarding matters of property, greatly incensed him against Sasi. However, Tarini Babu kept Sasi diverted, and instantly wrote to Joygopal. Joygopal put his wife and brother-in-law into a boat by force, and brought them home.

Husband and wife, after a second separation, met again for the second time! The decree of Prajapati![4]

Having got back his old companions after a long absence, Nilmani was perfectly happy. Seeing his unsuspecting joy, Sasi felt as if her heart would break.

## IV

The Magistrate was touring in the Mofussil during the

4. The Hindu god of marriage.

cold weather and pitched his tent within the village to shoot. The Saheb met Nilmani on the village *maidan*. The other boys gave him a wide berth, varying Chanakya's couplet a little, and adding the Saheb to the list of 'the clawed, the toothed, and the horned beasts.' But grave-natured Nilmani in imperturbable curiosity serenely gazed at the Saheb.

The Saheb was amused and came up and asked in Bengali: 'You read at the *pathasala*?'

The boy silently nodded. 'What *pustaks*[5] do you read?' asked the Saheb.

As Nilmani did not understand the word *pustak*, he silently fixed his gaze on the Magistrate's face. Nilmani told his sister the story of his meeting the Magistrate with great enthusiasm.

At noon, Joygopal, dressed in trousers, *chapkan*,[6] and *pagri*,[7] went to pay his salams to the Saheb. A cro vd of suitors, *chaprassis*,[8] and constables stood about him. Fearing the heat, the Saheb had seated himself at a court-table outside the tent, in the open shade, and placing Joygopal in a chair, questioned him about the state of the village. Having taken the seat of honour in open view of the community, Joygopal swelled inwardly, and thought it would be a good thing if any of the Chakrabartis or Nandis came and saw him there.

---

5. A literary word for books. The colloquial will be boi.
6. A *chapkan* is a long coat.
7. Turban.
8. Servants.

At this moment, a woman, closely veiled, and accompanied by Nilmani, came straight up to the Magistrate. She said: 'Saheb, into your hands I resign my helpless brother. Save him.' The Saheb, seeing the large-headed, solemn boy, whose acquaintance he had already made, and thinking that the woman must be of a respectable family, at once stood up and said: 'Please, enter the tent.'

The woman said: 'What I have to say I will say here.'

Joygopal writhed and turned pale. The curious villagers thought it capital fun, and pressed closer. But the moment the Saheb lifted his cane they scampered off.

Holding her brother by the hand, Sasi narrated the history of the orphan from the beginning. As Joygopal tried to interrupt now and then, the Magistrate thundered with a flushed face, '*Chup rao*,' and with the tip of his cane motioned to Joygopal to leave the chair and stand up.

Joygopal, inwardly raging against Sasi, stood speechless. Nilmani nestled up close to his sister, and listened awe-struck.

When Sasi had finished her story, the Magistrate put a few questions to Joygopal, and on hearing his answers, kept silence for a long while, and then addressed Sasi thus: 'My good woman, though this matter may not come up before me, still rest assured I will do all that is needful about it. You can return home with your brother without the least misgiving.'

Sasi said: 'Saheb, so long as he does not get back his own home, I dare not take him there. Unless you keep Nilmani with you none else will be able to save him.'

'And, what would you do?' queried the Saheb.

'I will retire to my husband's house,' said Sasi; 'there is nothing to fear for me.'

The Saheb smiled a little, and, as there was nothing else to do, agreed to take charge of this lean, dusty, grave, sedate, gentle Bengali boy whose neck was ringed with amulets.

When Sasi was about to take her leave, the boy clutched her dress. 'Don't be frightened, *baba*,—come,' said the Saheb. With tears streaming behind her veil, Sasi said: 'Do go, my brother, my darling brother—you will meet your sister again!'

Saying this she embraced him and stroked his head and back, and releasing her dress, hastily withdrew; and just then the Saheb put his left arm round him. The child wailed out: 'Sister, oh, my sister!' Sasi turned round at once, and with outstretched arm made a sign of speechless solace, and with a bursting heart withdrew.

Again, in that old, ever-familiar house husband and wife met. The decree of Prajapati!

But this union did not last long. For, soon after the villagers learnt one morning that Sasi had died of cholera in the night, and had been instantly cremated.

None uttered a word about it. Only neighbour Tara would sometimes be on the point of bursting out, but people would shut up her mouth, saying, 'Hush!'

At parting, Sasi gave her word to her brother they would meet again. Where that word was kept none can tell.

# Subha

When the girl was given the name of Subhashini,[1] who could have guessed that she would prove dumb? Her two elder sisters were Sukeshini[2] and Suhasini,[3] and for the sake of uniformity her father named his youngest girl Subhashini. She was called Subha for short.

Her two elder sisters had been married with the usual cost and difficulty, and now the youngest daughter lay like a silent weight upon the heart of her parents. All the world seemed to think that, because she did not speak, therefore she did not feel; it discussed her future and its own anxiety freely in her presence. She had understood from her, earliest childhood that God had sent her like a curse to her father's house, so she withdrew herself from ordinary people, and tried to live apart. If only they would all forget her she felt she could endure it. But who can forget pain? Night and day her parents' minds were aching on her account. Especially

---

1. Sweetly speaking.
2. Lovely-locked.
3. Sweetly smiling.

her mother looked upon her as a deformity in herself. To a mother a daughter is a more closely intimate part of herself than a son can be; and a fault in her is a source of personal shame. Banikantha, Subha's father, loved her rather better than his other daughters; her mother regarded her with aversion as a stain upon her own body.

If Subha lacked speech, she did not lack a pair of large dark eyes, shaded with long lashes; and her lips trembled like a leaf in response to any thought that rose in her mind.

When we express our thought in words, the medium is not found easily. There must be a process of translation, which is often inexact, and then we fall into error. But black eyes need no translating; the mind itself throws a shadow upon them. In them thought opens or shuts, shines forth, or goes out in darkness, hangs steadfast like the setting moon, or, like the swift and restless lightning, illumines all quarters of the sky. They who from birth have had no other speech than the trembling of their lips learn a language of the eyes, endless in expression, deep as the sea, clear as the heavens, wherein play dawn and sunset, light and shadow. The dumb have a lonely grandeur like Nature's own. Wherefore the other children almost dreaded Subha, and never played with her. She was silent and companionless as noontide.

The hamlet where she lived was Chandipur. Its river, small for a river of Bengal, kept to its narrow bounds like a daughter of the middle class. This busy streak of water never overflowed its banks, but went about its duties as though it were a member of every family in the villages beside it. On either side were houses and banks shaded with trees. So. stepping from her queenly throne, the river-goddess became a garden deity of each home; and forgetful of herself, performed her task of endless benediction with swift and cheerful foot.

Banikantha's house looked upon the stream. Every hut and stack in the place could be seen by the passing boatmen. I know not if amid these signs of worldly wealth any, one noticed the little girl who, when her work was done, stole away to the waterside, and sat there. But here Nature fulfilled her want of speech, and spoke for her. The murmur of the brook, the voice of the village-folk, the songs of the boatmen, the crying of the birds and rustle of trees mingled, and were one with the trembling of her heart. They became one vast wave of sound, which beat upon her restless soul. This murmur and movement of Nature were the dumb girl's language; that speech of the dark eyes, which the long lashes shaded, was the language of the world about her. From the trees, where the cicalas chirped, to the quiet stars there was nothing but signs and gestures, weeping and sighing. And, in the deep mid-noon, when the boatmen and fisherfolk had gone to their dinner, when the villagers slept, and birds were still, when the ferry-boats were idle, when the great busy world paused in its toil, and became suddenly a lonely, awful giant, then beneath the vast impressive heavens there were only dumb Nature and a dumb girl, sitting very silent—one under the spreading sunlight, the other where a small tree cast its shadow.

But Subha was not altogether without friends. In the stall were two cows, Sarbbashi and Panguli. They had never heard their names from her lips, but they knew her footfall. Though she had no words, she murmured lovingly and they understood her gentle murmuring better than all speech. When she fondled them or scolded or coaxed them, they understood her better than men could do. Subha would come to the shed, and throw her arms round Sarbbashi's neck; she would rub her cheek against her friend's, and Panguli would turn her great kind eyes and lick her face. The girl paid them three regular visits every day, and others that were irregular. Whenever she heard any words that hurt her, she would come to these dumb friends out of due time. It was as though they guessed her anguish of spirit from her quiet look of sadness. Coming close to her, they would rub their horns softly against her arms, and in dumb, puzzled fashion try to comfort her. Besides these two, there were goats and a kitten; but Subha had not the same equality of friendship with them, though they showed the same attachment. Every time it got a chance, night or day, the kitten would jump into her lap, and settle down to slumber, and show its appreciation of an aid to sleep as Subha drew her soft fingers over its neck and back.

Subha had a comrade also among the higher animals, and it is hard to say what were the girl's relations with him, for he could speak, and his gift of speech left them without any common language. He was the youngest boy of the Gosains, Pratap by name, an idle fellow. After long effort, his parents had abandoned the hope that he would ever make his living. Now, losers have this advantage, that, though their own folk disapprove of them, they are generally popular with everyone else. Having no work to chain them, they become public property. Just as every town needs an open space where all may breathe, so a village needs two or three gentlemen of leisure, who can give time to all; so that, if we are lazy and want a companion, one is to hand.

Pratap's chief ambition was to catch fish. He managed to waste a lot of time this way, and might be seen almost any afternoon so employed. It was thus most often that he met Subha. Whatever he was about, he liked a companion; and, when one is catching fish, a silent companion is best of all. Pratap respected Subha for her taciturnity, and, as everyone called her Subha, he showed his affection by calling her Su. Subha used to sit beneath a tamarind, and Pratap, a little distance off, would cast his line. Pratap took with him a small allowance of betel, and Subha prepared it for him. And, I think that, sitting and gazing a long while, she desired ardently to bring some great help to Pratap, to be of real aid, to prove by any means that she was not a useless burden to the world. But there was nothing to do. Then, she turned to the Creator in prayer for some rare power, that by an astonishing miracle she might startle Pratap into exclaiming: 'My! I never dreamt our Su could have done this!'

Only think! if Subha had been a water nymph, she might have risen slowly from the river, bringing the gem of a snake's crown to the landing place. Then Pratap, leaving his paltry fishing, might dive into the lower world, and see there, on a golden bed in a palace of silver, who else but dumb little Su, Banikantha's child? Yes, our Su, the only daughter of the king of that shining city of jewels! But that might not be, it was impossible. Not that anything is really impossible, but Su had been born, not into the royal house of Patalpur,[4] but into Banikantha's family, and she knew no means of astonishing the Gosains' boy.

Gradually she grew up. Gradually she began to find herself. A new inexpressible consciousness like a tide from the central places of the sea, when the moon is full, swept through her. She saw herself, questioned herself, but no answer came that she could understand.

Once upon a time, late on a night of full moon, she slowly opened her door, and peeped out timidly. Nature, herself at full moon, like lonely Subha, was looking down on the sleeping earth. Her strong young life beat within her; joy and sadness filled her being to its brim; she reached the limits even of her own illimitable, loneliness, nay, passed beyond them. Her heart was heavy, and she could not speak! At the skirts of this silent, troubled Mother there stood a silent troubled girl.

---

4. The Lower World.

The thought of her marriage filled her parents with an anxious care. People blamed them, and even talked of making them outcasts. Banikantha was well off; they had fish-curry twice daily; and consequently he did not lack enemies. Then, the women interfered, and Bani went away for a few days. Presently he returned, and said: 'We must go to Calcutta.'

They got ready to go to this strange country. Subha's heart was heavy with tears, like a mistwrapt dawn. With a vague fear that had been gathering for days, she dogged her father and mother like a dumb animal. With her large eyes wide open, she scanned their faces as though she wished to learn something. But not a word did they vouchsafe. One afternoon in the midst of all this, as Pratap was fishing, he laughed: 'So then, Su, they have caught your bridegroom, and you are going to be married! Mind you don't forget me altogether!' Then, he turned his mind again to his fish. As a stricken doe looks in the hunter's face, asking in silent agony: 'What have I done to you?' so Subha looked at Pratap. That day she sat no longer beneath her tree. Banikantha, having finished his nap, was smoking in his bedroom when Subha dropped down at his feet and burst out weeping as she gazed towards him. Banikantha tried to comfort her, and his cheek grew wet with tears.

It was settled that on the morrow they should go to Calcutta. Subha went to the cow-shed to bid farewell to her childhood's comrades. She fed them with her hand; she clasped their necks; she looked into their faces, and tears fell fast from the eyes which spoke for her. That night was the tenth of the moon. Subha left her room, and flung herself down on her grassy couch beside her dear river. It was as if she threw her arms about Earth, her strong, silent mother, and tried to say: 'Do not let me leave you, mother. Put your arms about me, as I have put mine about you, and hold me fast.'

One day in a house in Calcutta, Subha's mother dressed her up with great care. She imprisoned her hair, knotting it up in laces, she hung her about with ornaments, and did her best to kill her natural beauty. Subha's eyes filled with tears. Her mother, fearing they would grow swollen with weeping, scolded her harshly, but the tears disregarded the scolding. The bridegroom came with a friend to inspect the bride. Her parents were dizzy with anxiety and fear when they saw the god arrive to select the beast for his sacrifice. Behind the stage, the mother called her instructions aloud, and increased her daughter's weeping twofold, before she sent her into the examiner's presence. The great man, after scanning her a long time, observed: 'Not so bad.'

He took special note of her tears, and thought she must have a tender heart. He put it to her credit in the account, arguing that the heart, which today was distressed at leaving her parents, would presently prove a useful possession. Like the oyster's pearls, the child's tears only increased her value, and he made no other comment.

The almanac was consulted, and the marriage took

place on an auspicious day. Having delivered over their dumb girl into another's hands, Subha's parents returned home. Thank God! Their caste in this and their safety in the next world were assured! The bridegroom's work lay in the west, and shortly after the marriage he took his wife thither.

In less than ten days everyone knew that the bride was dumb! At least, if anyone did not, it was not her fault, for she deceived no one. Her eyes told them everything, though no one understood her. She looked on every hand; she found no speech: she missed the faces, familiar from birth, of those who had understood a dumb girl's language. In her silent heart there sounded an endless, voiceless weeping, which only the Searcher of Hearts could hear.

Using both eyes and ears *this* time, her lord made another careful examination, and married a second wife who could speak.

# The Postmaster

The postmaster first took up his duties in the village of Ulapur. Though the village was a small one, there was an indigo factory nearby, and the proprietor, an Englishman, had managed to get a post office established.

Our postmaster belonged to Calcutta. He felt like a fish out of water in this remote village. His office and living-room were in a dark thatched shed, not far from a green, slimy pond, surrounded on all sides by a dense growth.

The men employed in the indigo factory had no leisure; moreover, they were hardly desirable companions for decent folk. Nor, is a Calcutta boy an adept in the art of associating with others. Among strangers he appears either proud or ill at ease. At any rate, the postmaster had but little company; nor had he much to do.

At times, he tried his hand at writing a verse or two. That the movement of the leaves and the clouds of the sky were enough to fill life with joy—such were the sentiments to which he sought to give expression. But God knows that the poor fellow would have felt it as the gift of a new life if some genie of the *Arabian Nights* had in one night swept away the trees, leaves and all, and replaced them with a macadamised road, hiding the clouds from view with rows of tall houses.

The postmaster's salary was small. He had to cook his own meals, which he used to share with Ratan, an orphan girl of the village, who did odd jobs for him.

When in the evening the smoke began to curl up from the village cow-sheds,[1] and the cicalas chirped in every bush; when the *faquirs* of the Baül sect sang their shrill songs in their daily meeting-place, when any poet, who had attempted to watch the movement of the leaves in the dense bamboo thickets, would have felt a ghostly shiver run down his back, the postmaster would light his little lamp, and call out 'Ratan.'

Ratan would sit outside waiting for this call, and, instead of coming in at once, would reply: 'Did you call me, sir?'

'What are you doing?' the postmaster would ask.

'I must be going to light the kitchen fire,' would be the answer.

And, the postmaster would say: 'Oh, let the kitchen fire be for awhile; light me my pipe first.'

At last, Ratan would enter, with puffed-out cheeks, vigorously blowing into a flame a live coal to light the tobacco. This would give the postmaster an opportunity of conversing. 'Well, Ratan,' perhaps he would begin 'do you remember anything of your mother?' That was a fertile subject. Ratan partly remembered, and partly

1. Smoky fires are lit in the cow-sheds to drive off mosquitoes.

didn't. Her father had been fonder of her than her mother; him she recollected more vividly. He used to come home in the evening after his work, and one or two evenings stood out more clearly than others, like pictures in her memory. Ratan would squat on the floor near the postmaster's feet, as memories crowded in upon her. She called to mind a little brother that she had—and how on some bygone cloudy day she had played at fishing with him on the edge of the pond, with a twig for a make-believe fishing-rod. Such little incidents would drive out greater events from her mind. Thus, as they talked, it would often get very late, and the postmaster would feel too lazy to do any cooking at all. Ratan would then hastily light the fire, and toast some unleavened bread, which, with the cold remnants of the morning meal, was enough for their supper.

On some evenings, seated at his desk in the corner of the big empty shed, the postmaster too would call up memories of his own home, of his mother and his sister, of those for whom in his exile his heart was sad,—memories which were always haunting him, but which he could not talk about with the men of the factory, though he found himself naturally recalling them aloud in the presence of the simple little girl. And so, it came about that the girl would allude to his people as mother, brother, and sister,[2] as if she had known them all her life.

---

2. Family servants call the master and mistress father and mother and the children, elder brothers and sisters.

In fact, she had a complete picture of each one of them painted in her little heart.

One noon, during a break in the rains, there was a cool soft breeze blowing; the smell of the damp grass and leaves in the hot sun felt like the warm breathing of the tired earth on one's body. A persistent bird went on all the afternoon repeating the burden of its one complaint in Nature's audience chamber.

The postmaster had nothing to do. The shimmer of the freshly washed leaves, and the banked-up remnants of the retreating rain-clouds were sights to see; and the postmaster was watching them, and thinking to himself: 'Oh, if only some kindred soul were near—just one loving human being whom I could hold near my heart!' This was exactly, he went on to think, what that bird was trying to say, and it was the same feeling which the murmuring leaves were striving to express. But no one knows, or would believe, that such an idea might also take possession of an ill-paid village postmaster in the deep, silent midday interval of his work.

The postmaster sighed, and called out, 'Ratan.' Ratan was then sprawling beneath the *guava*-tree, busily engaged in eating unripe *guavas*. At the voice of her master, she ran up breathlessly, saying: 'Were you calling me, Dada?'[3]

'I was thinking,' said the postmaster, 'of teaching you to read,' and then for the rest of the afternoon he taught her the alphabet.

---

3. Dada = elder brother.

Thus, in a very short time, Ratan had got as far as the double consonants.

It seemed as though the showers of the season would never end. Canals, ditches, and hollows were all overflowing with water. Day and night, the patter of rain was heard, and the croaking of frogs. The village roads became impassable, and marketing had to be done in punts.

One heavily clouded morning, the postmaster's little pupil had been long waiting outside the door for her call, but, not hearing it as usual, she took up her dog-eared book, and slowly entered the room. She found her master stretched out on his pallet, and, thinking he was resting, she was about to retire on tip-toe, when she suddenly heard her name—'Ratan!' She turned at once and asked: 'Were you sleeping, Dada?' The postmaster in a plaintive voice said: 'I am not well. Feel my hand; is it very hot?'

In the loneliness of his exile, and in the gloom of the rains, his ailing body needed a little tender nursing. He longed to remember the touch on the forehead of soft hands with tinkling bracelets, to imagine the presence of loving womanhood, the nearness of mother and sister. And, the exile was not disappointed. Ratan ceased to be a little girl. She at once stepped into the post of mother, called in the village doctor, gave the patient his pills at the proper intervals, sat up all night by his pillow, cooked his gruel for him, and every now and then asked: 'Are you feeling a little better, Dada?'

It was some time before the postmaster, with weakened body, was able to leave his sick-bed. 'No more of this,' said he with decision. 'I must get a transfer.' He at once wrote off to Calcutta an application for a transfer, on the ground of the unhealthiness of the place.

Relieved from her duties as nurse, Ratan again took up her old place outside the door. But she no longer heard the same old call. She would sometimes peep inside furtively to find the postmaster sitting on his chair, or stretched on his pallet, and staring absent-mindedly into the air. While Ratan was awaiting her call, the postmaster was awaiting a reply to his application. The girl read her old lessons over and over again—her great fear was lest, when the call came, she might be found wanting in the double consonants. At last, after a week, the call did come one evening. With an overflowing heart Ratan rushed into the room with her—'Were you calling me, Dada?'

The postmaster said: 'I am going away tomorrow, Ratan.'

'Where are you going, Dada?'

'I am going home.'

'When will you come back?'

'I am not coming back.'

Ratan asked no other question. The postmaster, of his own accord, went on to tell her that his application for a transfer had been rejected, so he had resigned his post, and was going home.

For a long time neither of them spoke another word.

The lamp went on dimly burning, and from a leak in one corner of the thatch water dripped steadily into an earthen vessel on the floor beneath it.

After a while Ratan rose, and went off to the kitchen to prepare the meal; but she was not so quick about it as on other days. Many new things to think of had entered her little brain. When the postmaster had finished his supper, the girl suddenly asked him: 'Dada, will you take me to your home?'

The postmaster laughed. 'What an idea!' said he; but he did not think it necessary to explain to the girl wherein lay the absurdity.

That whole night, in her waking and in her dreams, the postmaster's laughing reply haunted her—'What an idea!'

On getting up in the morning, the postmaster found his bath ready. He had stuck to his Calcutta habit of bathing in water drawn and kept in pitchers, instead of taking a plunge in the river as was the custom of the village. For some reason or other, the girl could not ask him about the time of his departure, so she had fetched the water from the river long before sunrise, that it should be ready as early as he might want it. After the bath came a call for Ratan. She entered noiselessly, and looked silently into her master's face for orders. The master said: 'You need not be anxious about my going away, Ratan; I shall tell my successor to look after you.' These words were kindly meant, no doubt: but inscrutable are the ways of a woman's heart!

Ratan had borne many a scolding from her master without complaint, but these kind words she could not bear. She burst out weeping, and said: 'No, no, you need not tell anybody anything at all about me; I don't want to stay on here.'

The postmaster was dumbfounded. He had never seen Ratan like this before.

The new incumbent duly arrived, and the postmaster, having given over charge, prepared to depart. Just before starting he called Ratan, and said: 'Here is something for you; I hope it will keep you for some little time.' He brought out from his pocket the whole of his months' salary, retaining only a trifle for his travelling expenses. Then, Ratan fell at his feet and cried: 'Oh, Dada, I pray you, don't give me anything, don't in any way trouble about me,' and then she ran away out of sight.

The postmaster heaved a sigh, took up his carpet bag, put his umbrella over his shoulder, and, accompanied by a man carrying his many-coloured tin trunk, he slowly made for the boat.

When he got in and the boat was under way, and the rain-swollen river, like a stream of tears welling up from the earth, swirled and sobbed at her bows, then he felt a sort of pain at heart; the grief-stricken face of a village girl seemed to represent for him the great unspoken pervading grief of Mother Earth herself. At one time he had an impulse to go back, and bring away along with him that lonesome waif, forsaken of the world. But the wind had just filled the sails, the boat had got well into the middle of the turbulent current, and already the village was left behind, and its outlying burning-ground came in sight.

S,o the traveller, borne on the breast of the swift-flowing river, consoled himself with philosophical reflections on the numberless meetings and partings going on in the world—on death, the great parting, from which none returns.

But Ratan had no philosophy. She was wandering about the post office in a flood of tears. It may be that she had still a lurking hope in some corner of her heart that her Dada would return, and that is why she could not tear herself away. Alas! for the foolish human heart!

# The River Stairs

If you wish to hear of days gone by, sit on this step of mine, and lend your ears to the murmur of the rippling water.

The month of *Ashwin* (September) was about to begin. The river was in full flood. Only four of my steps peeped above the surface. The water had crept up to the low-lying parts of the bank, where the *kachu* plant grew dense beneath the branches of the mango grove. At that bend of the river, three old brick-heaps towered above the water around them. The fishing-boats, moored to the trunks of the *ba¯bla* trees on the bank, rocked on the heaving flow-tide at dawn. The path of tall grasses on the sandbank had caught the newly risen sun; they had just begun to flower, and were not yet in full bloom.

The little boats puffed out their tiny sails on the sunlit river. The Brahmin priest had come to bathe with his ritual vessels. The women arrived in twos and threes to draw water. I knew this was the time of Kusum's coming to the bathing-stairs.

But that morning I missed her. Bhuban and Swarno

mourned at the *ghāt*.[1] They said that their friend had been led away to her husband's house, which was a place far away from the river, with strange people, strange houses, and strange roads.

In time she almost faded out of my mind. A year passed. The women at the *ghāt* now rarely talked of Kusum. But one evening I was startled by the touch of the long familiar feet. Ah, yes, but those feet were now without anklets, they had lost their old music.

Kusum had become a widow. They said that her husband had worked in some far-off place, and that she had met him only once or twice. A letter brought her the news of his death. A widow at eight years old, she had rubbed out the wife's red mark from her forehead, stripped off her bangles, and come back to her old home by the Ganges. But she found a few of her old playmates there. Of them, Bhuban, Swarno, and Amala were married, and gone away; only Sarat remained, and she too, they said, would be wed in December next.

As the Ganges rapidly grows to fulness with the coming of the rains, even so did Kusum day by day grow to the fulness of beauty and youth. But her dull-coloured robe, her pensive face, and quiet manners drew a veil over her youth, and hid it from men's eyes as in a mist. Ten years slipped away, and none seemed to have noticed that Kusum had grown up.

One morning such as this, at the end of a far-off

---

1. Bathing-place.

September, a tall, young, fair-skinned Sanyasi, coming I know not whence, took shelter in the Shiva temple in front of me. His arrival was noised abroad in the village. The women left their pitchers behind, and crowded into the temple to bow to the holy man.

The crowd increased day by day. The Sanyasi's fame rapidly spread among the women kind. One day he would recite the *Bhágbat*, another day he would expound the *Gita*, or hold forth upon a holy book in the temple. Some sought him for counsel, some for spells, some for medicines.

So, months passed away. In April, at the time of the solar eclipse, vast crowds came here to bathe in the Ganges. A fair was held under the *bābla* tree. Many of the pilgrims went to visit the Sanyasi, and among them were a party of women from the village where Kusum had been married.

It was morning. The Sanyasi was counting his beads on my steps, when all of a sudden one of the women pilgrims nudged another, and said: 'Why! He is our Kusum's husband!' Another parted her veil a little in the middle with two fingers and cried out: 'Oh, dear me! So it is! He is the younger son of the Chatterji family of our village!' Said a third, who made little parade of her veil: 'Ah! he has got exactly the same brow, nose, and eyes!' Yet another woman, without turning to the Sanyasi, stirred the water with her pitcher, and sighed: 'Alas! That young man is no more; he will not come back. Bad luck to Kusum!'

But, objected one, 'He had not such a big beard'; and another, 'He was not so thin'; or 'He was most probably not so tall.' That settled the question for the time, and the matter spread no further.

One evening, as the full moon arose, Kusum came and sat upon my last step above the water, and cast her shadow upon me.

There was no other at the *ghāt* just then. The crickets were chirping about me. The din of brass gongs and bells had ceased in the temple—the last wave of sound grew fainter and fainter, until it merged like the shade of a sound in the dim groves of the farther bank. On the dark water of the Ganges lay a line of glistening moonlight. On the bank above, in bush and hedge, under the porch of the temple, in the base of ruined houses, by the side of the tank, in the palm grove, gathered shadows of fantastic shapes. The bats swung from the *chhatim* boughs. Near the houses the loud clamour of the jackals rose and sank into silence.

Slowly, the Sanyasi came out of the temple. Descending a few steps of the *ghāt* he saw a woman sitting alone, and was about to go back, when suddenly Kusum raised her head, and looked behind her. The veil slipped away from her. The moonlight fell upon her face, as she looked up.

The owl flew away hooting over their heads. Starting at the sound, Kusum came to herself and put the veil back on her head. Then, she bowed low at the Sanyasi's feet.

He gave her blessing and asked: 'Who are you?' She replied: 'I am called Kusum.'

No other word was spoken that night. Kusum went slowly back to her house which was nearby. But the Sanyasi remained sitting on my steps for long hours that night. At last, when the moon passed from the east to the west, and the Sanyasi's shadow, shifting from behind, fell in front of him, he rose up and entered the temple.

Henceforth, I saw Kusum come daily to bow at his feet. When he expounded the holy books, she stood in a corner listening to him. After finishing his morning service, he used to call her to himself and speak on religion. She could not have understood it all; but, listening attentively in silence, she tried to understand it. As he directed her, so she acted implicitly. She daily served at the temple—ever alert in the god's worship—gathering flowers for the *puja*, and drawing water from the Ganges to wash the temple floor.

The winter was drawing to its close. We had cold winds. But now and then in the evening the warm spring breeze would blow unexpectedly from the south; the sky would lose its chilly aspect; pipes would sound, and music be heard in the village after a long silence. The boatmen would set their boats drifting down the current, stop rowing, and begin to sing the songs of Krishna. This was the season.

Just then I began to miss Kusum. For some time she had given up visiting the temple, the *ghāt*, or the Sanyasi.

What happened next I do not know, but after a

while the two met together on my steps one evening.

With downcast looks, Kusum asked: 'Master, did you send for me?'

'Yes, why do I not see you? Why have you grown neglectful of late in serving the gods?'

She kept silent.

'Tell me your thoughts without reserve.'

Half, averting her face, she replied: 'I am a sinner, Master, and hence I have failed in the worship.'

The Sanyasi said: 'Kusum, I know there is unrest in your heart.'

She gave a slight start, and, drawing the end of her saari over her face, she sat down on the step at the Sanyasi's feet, and wept.

He moved a little away, and said: 'Tell me what you have in your heart, and I shall show you the way to peace.'

She replied in a tone of unshaken faith, stopping now and then for words: 'If you bid me, I must speak out. But then, I cannot explain it clearly. You, Master, must have guessed it all. I adored one as a god, I worshipped him, and the bliss of that devotion filled my heart to fulness. But one night, I dreamt that the lord of my heart was sitting in a garden somewhere, clasping my right hand in his left, and whispering to me of love. The whole scene did not appear to me at all strange. The dream vanished, but its hold on me remained. Next day, when I beheld him he appeared in another light than before. That dream-picture continued to haunt my mind. I fled far from him in fear, and the picture clung to me. Thenceforth, my heart has known no peace,—all has grown dark within me!'

While she was wiping her tears and telling this tale, I felt that the Sanyasi was firmly pressing my stone surface with his right foot.

Her speech done, the Sanyasi said:

'You must tell me whom you saw in your dream.'

With folded hands, she entreated: 'I cannot.'

He insisted: 'You must tell me who he was.'

Wringing her hands she asked: 'Must I tell it?'

He replied: 'Yes, you must.'

Then crying, 'You are he, Master!' she fell on her face on my stony bosom, and sobbed.

When she came to herself, and sat up, the Sanyasi said slowly: 'I am leaving this place tonight that you may not see me again. Know that I am a Sanyasi, not belonging to this world. *You* must forget me.'

Kusum replied in a low voice: 'It will be so, Master.'

The Sanyasi said: 'I take my leave.'

Without a word more Kusum bowed to him, and placed the dust of his feet on her head. He left the place.

The moon set; the night grew dark. I heard a splash in the water. The wind raved in the darkness, as if it wanted to blow out all the stars of the sky.

# The Castaway

Towards evening the storm was at its height. From the terrific downpour of rain, the crash of thunder, and the repeated flashes of lightning, you might think that a battle of the gods and demons was raging in the skies. Black clouds waved like the Flags of Doom. The Ganges was lashed into a fury, and the trees of the gardens on either bank swayed from side to side with sighs and groans.

In a closed room of one of the riverside houses at Chandernagore, a husband and his wife were seated on a bed-spread on the floor, intently discussing. An earthen lamp burned beside them.

The husband, Sharat, was saying: 'I wish you would stay on a few days more; you would then be able to return home quite strong again.'

The wife, Kiran, was saying: 'I have quite recovered already. It will not, cannot possibly, do me any harm to go home now.'

Every married person will at once understand that the conversation was not quite so brief as I have reported it. The matter was not difficult, but the arguments for and against did not advance it towards a solution. Like a rudderless boat, the discussion kept turning round and round the same point; and at last, it threatened to be overwhelmed in a flood of tears.

Sharat said: 'The doctor thinks you should stop here a few days longer.'

Kiran replied: 'Your doctor knows everything!'

'Well,' said Sharat, 'you know that just now all sorts of illness are abroad. You would do well to stop here a month or two more.

'And, at this moment I suppose everyone in this place is perfectly well!'

What had happened was this: Kiran was a universal favourite with her family,and neighbours, so that, when she fell seriously ill, they were all anxious. The village wiseacres thought it shameless for her husband to make so much fuss about a mere wife and even to suggest a change of air, and asked if Sharat supposed that no woman had ever been ill before, or whether he had found out that the folk of the place to which he meant to take her were immortal. Did he imagine that the writ of Fate did not run there? But Sharat and his mother turned a deaf ear to them, thinking that the little life of their darling was of greater importance than the united wisdom of a village. People are wont to reason thus when danger threatens their loved ones. So, Sharat went to Chandernagore, and Kiran recovered, though she was still very weak. There was a pinched look on her face which filled the beholder with pity, and made his heart tremble, as he thought how narrowly she had escaped death.

Kiran was fond of society and amusement; the loneliness of her riverside villa did not suit her at all. There was nothing to do, there were no interesting neighbours, and she hated to be busy all day with medicine and dieting. There was no fun in measuring doses and making fomentations. Such was the subject discussed in their closed room on this stormy evening.

So long as Kiran deigned to argue, there was a chance of a fair fight. When she ceased to reply, and with a toss of her head disconsolately looked the other way, the poor man was disarmed. He was on the point of surrendering unconditionally when a servant shouted a message through the shut door.

Sharat got up, and, opening the door, learnt that a boat had been upset in the storm, and that one of the occupants, a young Brahmin boy, had succeeded in swimming ashore in their garden.

Kiran was at once her own sweet self, and set to work to get out some dry clothes for the boy. She then warmed a cup of milk, and invited him to her room.

The boy had long curly hair, big expressive eyes, and no sign yet of hair on the face. Kiran, after getting him to drink some milk, asked him all about himself.

He told her that his name was Nilkanta, and that he belonged to a theatrical troupe. They were coming to play in a neighbouring villa when the boat had suddenly foundered in the storm. He had no idea what had become of his companions. He was a good swimmer, and had just managed to reach the shore.

The boy stayed with them. His narrow escape from a terrible death made Kiran take a warm interest in him. Sharat thought the boy's appearance at this moment rather a good thing, as his wife would now have something to amuse her, and might be persuaded to stay on for some time longer. Her mother-in-law, too, was pleased at the prospect of profiting their Brahmin guest by her kindness. And, Nilkanta himself was delighted at his double escape from his master and from the other world, as well as at finding a home in this wealthy family.

But in a short while, Sharat and his mother changed their opinion, and longed for his departure. The boy found a secret pleasure in smoking Sharat's hookas; he would calmly go off in pouring rain with Sharat's best silk umbrella for a stroll through the village, and make friends with all whom he met. Moreover, he had got hold of a mongrel village dog which he petted so recklessly that it came indoors with muddy paws, and left tokens of its visit on Sharat's spotless bed. Then, he gathered about him a devoted band of boys of all sorts and sizes, and the result was that not a solitary mango in the neighbourhood had a chance of ripening that season.

There is no doubt that Kiran had a hand in spoiling the boy. Sharat often warned her about it, but she would not listen to him. She made a dandy of him with Sharat's cast-off clothes, and gave him new ones, too. And, because she felt drawn towards him, and also had a curiosity to know more about him, she was constantly calling him to her own room. After her bath and midday meal Kiran would be seated on the bedstead with her betel-leaf box by her side; and while her maid combed and dried her hair, Nilkanta would stand in front and recite pieces out of his repertory with appropriate gesture and song, his elf-locks waving wildly. Thus, the long afternoon hours passed merrily away. Kiran would often try to persuade Sharat to sit with her as one of the audience, but Sharat, who had taken a cordial dislike to the boy, refused, nor could Nilkanta do his part half so well when Sharat was there. His mother would sometimes be lured by the hope of hearing sacred names in the recitation; but love of her mid-day sleep speedily overcame devotion, and she lay lapped in dreams.

The boy often got his ears boxed and pulled by Sharat, but as this was nothing to what he had been used to as a member of the troupe, he did not mind it in the least. In his short experience of the world he had come to the conclusion that, as the earth consisted of land and water, so human life was made up of eatings and beatings, and that the beatings largely predominated.

It was hard to tell Nilkanta's age. If it was about fourteen or fifteen, then his face was too old for his years; if seventeen or eighteen, then it was too young. He was either a man too early or a boy too late. The fact was that, joining the theatrical band when very young, he had played the parts of Radhika, Damayanti, Sita and Bidya's companion. A thoughtful Providence so arranged things that he grew to the exact stature that his manager required, and then growth ceased. Since everyone saw how small he was, and he himself felt small, he did not receive due respect for his years. These causes, natural and artificial, combined to make him sometimes seem immature for seventeen years, and at other times a lad of fourteen but far too knowing for seventeen. And, as no sign of hair appeared on his face, the confusion became greater. Either because he smoked or because he used language beyond his years, his lips puckered into lines that showed him to be old and hard; but innocence and youth shone in his large eyes. I fancy that his heart remained young, but the hot glare of publicity had been a forcing-house that ripened untimely his outward aspect.

In the quiet shelter of Sharat's house and garden at Chandernagore, Nature had leisure to work her way unimpeded. He had lingered in a kind of unnatural youth, but now he silently and swiftly overpassed that stage. His seventeen or eighteen years came to adequate revelation. No one observed the change, and its first sign was this, that when Kiran treated him like a boy, he felt ashamed. When the gay Kiran one day proposed that he should play the part of a lady's companion, the idea of a woman's dress hurt him, though he could not say why. So now, when she called for him to act over again his old characters he disappeared. It never occurred to him that he was even now not much more than a lad-of-all-work in a strolling company. He even made up his mind to pick up a little education from Sharat's factor. But, because Nilkanta was the pet of his master's wife, the factor could not endure the sight of him. Also, his restless training made it impossible for him to keep his mind long engaged; presently, the alphabet did a misty dance before his eyes. He would sit long enough with an open book on his lap, leaning against a *champak* bush beside the Ganges. The waves sighed below, boats floated past, birds flitted and twittered restlessly above. What thoughts passed through his mind as he looked down on that book he alone knew, if indeed he did know. He never advanced from one word to another, but the glorious thought that he was actually reading a book filled his soul with exultation. Whenever a boat went by, he lifted his book, and pretended to be reading hard, shouting at the top of his voice. But his energy dropped as soon as the audience was gone.

Formerly, he sang his songs automatically, but now their tunes stirred in his mind. Their words were of little import, and full of trifling alliteration. Even the little meaning they had was beyond his comprehension; yet when he sang—

*Twice-born[1] bird, ah! wherefore stirred*
*To wrong our royal lady?*
*Goose, ah! say why wilt thou slay*
*Her in forest shady?*

---

1. Once in the egg, and again once out of the egg.

then he felt as if transported to another world, and to far other folk. This familiar earth and his own poor life became music, and he was transformed. That tale of goose and king's daughter flung upon the mirror of his mind a picture of surpassing beauty. It is impossible to say what he imagined he himself was, but the destitute little slave of the theatrical troupe faded from his memory.

When with evening the child of want lies down, dirty and hungry, in his squalid home, and hears of prince and princess and fabled gold, then in the dark hovel with its dim flickering candle, his mind springs free from her bonds of poverty and misery, and walks in fresh beauty and glowing raiment, strong beyond all fear of hindrance, through that fairy realm where all is possible.

Even so, this drudge of wandering players fashioned himself and his world anew, as he moved in spirit amid his songs. The lapping water, rustling leaves, and calling birds; the goddess who had given shelter to him, the helpless, the Godforsaken; her gracious, lovely face, her exquisite arms with their shining bangles, her rosy feet as soft as flower-petals; all these by some magic became one with the music of his song. When the singing ended, the mirage faded, and Nilkanta of the stage appeared again, with his wild elf-locks. Fresh from the complaints of his neighbour, the owner of the despoiled mango-orchard, Sharat would come and box his ears, and cuff him. The boy Nilkanta, the misleader of adoring youths, went forth once more, to make ever new mischief by land and water and in the branches that are above the earth.

Shortly after the advent of Nilkanta, Sharat's younger brother, Satish, came to spend his college vacation with them. Kiran was hugely pleased at finding a fresh occupation. She and Satish were of the same age, and the time passed pleasantly in games and quarrels and makings-up and laughter and even tears. Suddenly, she would clasp him over the eyes, from behind, with vermilion-stained hands, she would write 'monkey' on his back, and sometimes bolt the door on him from outside amidst peals of laughter. Satish in his turn did not take things lying down; he would take her keys and rings, he would put pepper among her betel; he would tie her to the bed when she was not looking.

Meanwhile, heaven only knows what possessed poor Nilkanta. He was suddenly filled with a bitterness which he must avenge on somebody or something. He thrashed his devoted boy-followers for no fault, and sent them away crying. He would kick his pet mongrel till it made the skies resound with its whinings. When he went out for a walk, he would litter his path with twigs and leaves beaten from the roadside shrubs with his cane.

Kiran liked to see people enjoying good fare. Nilkanta had an immense capacity for eating, and never refused a good thing, however often it was offered. So, Kiran liked to send for him to have his meals in her presence, and ply him with delicacies, happy in the bliss of seeing this Brahmin boy eat to satiety. After Satish's arrival she had much less spare time on her hands, and was seldom present when Nilkanta's meals were served. Before her absence made no difference to the boy's appetite, and he would not rise till he had drained his cup of milk, and rinsed it thoroughly with water.[2]

But now, if Kiran was not present to ask him to try this and that, he was miserable, and nothing tasted right. He would get up without eating much, and say to the serving-maid in a choking voice: 'I am not hungry.' He thought in imagination that the news of his repeated refusal, 'I am not hungry,' would reach Kiran, he pictured her concern, and hoped that she would send for him, and press him to eat. But nothing of the sort happened. Kiran never knew, and never sent for him; and the maid finished whatever he left. He would then put out the lamp in his room and throw himself on his bed in the darkness, burying his head in the pillow in a paroxysm of sobs. What was his grievance? Against whom? And, from whom did he expect redress? At last, when none else came, Mother Sleep soothed with her soft caresses the wounded heart of the motherless lad.

Nilkanta came to the unshakable conviction that Satish was poisoning Kiran's mind against him. If Kiran was absent-minded, and had not her usual smile, he would jump to the conclusion that some trick of Satish had made her angry with him. He took to praying to the gods, with all the fervour of his hate, to make him at the

---

2. A habit which was relic from his days of poverty, when milk was too rare, a luxury to allow of even its stains in the cup being wasted.

next rebirth Satish, and Satish him. He had an idea that a Brahmin's wrath could never be in vain; and the more he tried to consume Satish with the fire of his curses, the more did his own heart burn within him. And, upstairs he would hear Satish laughing and joking with his sister-in-law.

Nilkanta never dared openly to show his enmity to Satish. But he would contrive a hundred petty ways of causing him annoyance. When Satish went for a swim in the river, and left his soap on the steps of the bathing-place, on coming back for it he would find that it had disappeared. Once he found his favourite striped tunic floating past him on the water, and thought it had been blown away by the wind.

One day Kiran, desiring to entertain Satish, sent for Nilkanta to recite as usual, but he stood there in gloomy silence. Quite surprised, Kiran asked him what was the matter. But he remained silent. And, when again pressed by her to repeat some particular favourite piece of hers he answered: 'I don't remember,' and walked away.

At last, the time came for their return home. Everybody was busy packing up. Satish was going with them. But to Nilkanta nobody said a word. The question whether he was to go or not seemed not to have occurred to anybody.

The question, as a matter of fact, had been raised by Kiran, who had proposed to take him along with them. But her husband and his mother and brother had all objected so strenuously that she let the matter drop. A couple of days before they were to start, she sent for the boy, and with kind words advised him to go back to his own home.

So many days had he felt neglected that this touch of kindness was too much for him; he burst into tears. Kiran's eyes were also brimming over. She was filled with remorse at the thought that she had created a tie of affection, which could not be permanent.

But Satish was much annoyed at the blubbering of this overgrown boy. 'Why does the fool stand there howling instead of speaking?' said he. When Kiran scolded him for an unfeeling creature, he replied: 'Sister mine, you do not understand. You are too good and trustful. This fellow turns up from the Lord knows where, and is treated like a king. Naturally, the tiger has no wish to become a mouse again.[3] And, he has evidently discovered that there is nothing like a tear or two to soften your heart.'

Nilkanta hurriedly left the spot. He felt he would like to be a knife to cut Satish to pieces: a needle to pierce him through and through; a fire to burn him to ashes. But Satish was not even scarred. It was only his own heart that bled and bled.

Satish had brought with him from Calcutta a grand inkstand. The inkpot was set in a mother-of-pearl boat drawn by a German-silver goose supporting a penholder.

---

3. A reference to a folk-story of a saint who turned a pet mouse into a tiger.

It was a great favourite of his, and he cleaned it carefully every day with an old silk handkerchief. Kiran would laugh and, tapping the silver bird's beak, would say—

*Twice-born bird, ah! wherefore stirred*
*To wrong our royal lady?*

and the usual war of words would break out between her and her brother-in-law.

The day before they were to start, the inkstand was missing, and could nowhere be found. Kiran smiled, and said: 'Brother-in-law, your goose has flown off to look for your Damayanti.'[4]

But Satish was in a great rage. He was certain that Nilkanta had stolen it—for several people said they had seen him prowling about the room the night before. He had the accused brought before him. Kiran also was there. 'You have stolen my inkstand, you thief!' he blurted out. 'Bring it back at once.' Nilkanta had always taken punishment from Sharat, deserved or undeserved, with perfect equanimity. But, when he was called a thief in Kiran's presence, his eyes blazed with a fierce anger, his breast swelled, and his throat choked. If Satish had said another word he would have flown at him like a wild cat, and used his nails like claws.

Kiran was greatly distressed at the scene, and taking the boy into another room said in her sweet, kind way: 'Nilu, if you really have taken that inkstand give it to me quietly, and I shall see that no one says another word to

4. To find Satish a wife.

you about it.' Big tears coursed down the boy's cheeks, till at last he hid his face in his hands, and wept bitterly. Kiran came back from the room, and said: 'I am sure Nilkanta has not taken the inkstand.' Sharat and Satish were equally positive that no other than Nilkanta could have done it.

But Kiran said determinedly: 'Never.'

Sharat wanted to cross-examine the boy, but his wife refused to allow it.

Then, Satish suggested that his room and box should be searched. And, Kiran said; 'If you dare do such a thing I will never, never forgive you. You shall not spy on the poor innocent boy.' And as she spoke, her wonderful eyes filled with tears. That settled the matter, and effectually prevented any further molestation of Nilkanta!

Kiran's heart overflowed with pity at this attempted outrage on a homeless lad. She got two new suits of clothes and a pair of shoes, and with these and a banknote in her hand she quietly went into Nilkanta's room in the evening. She intended to put these parting presents into his box as a surprise. The box itself had been her gift.

From her bunch of keys she selected one that fitted, and noiselessly opened the box. It was so jumbled up with odds and ends that the new clothes would not go in. So, she thought she had better take everything out and pack the box for him. At first, knives, tops, kite-flying reels, bamboo twigs, polished shells for peeling green mangoes, bottoms of broken tumblers and such like things dear to a boy's heart were discovered. Then, there came a layer of linen, clean and otherwise. And, from under the linen there emerged the missing inkstand, goose and all!

Kiran, with flushed face, sat down helplessly with the inkstand in her hand, puzzled and wondering.

In the meantime, Nilkanta had come into the room from behind without Kiran knowing it. He had seen the whole thing, and thought that Kiran had come like a thief to catch him in his thieving,—and that his deed was out. How could he ever hope to convince her that he was not a thief, and that only revenge had prompted him to take the inkstand, which he meant to throw into the river at the first chance? In a weak moment he had put it in his box instead. 'He was not a thief,' his heart cried out, 'not a thief!' Then, what was he? What could he say? He had stolen, and yet he was not a thief! He could never explain to Kiran how grievously wrong she was in taking him for a thief; how could he bear the thought that she had tried to spy on him?

At last, Kiran with a deep sigh replaced the inkstand in the box, and, as if she were the thief herself, covered it up with the linen and the trinkets as they were before; and at the top she placed the presents together with the banknote which she had brought for him.

The next day, the boy was nowhere to be found. The villagers had not seen him; the police could discover no trace of him. Said Sharat: 'Now, as a matter of curiosity, let us have a look at his box.' But Kiran was obstinate in her refusal to allow that to be done.

She had the box brought up to her own room; and taking out the inkstand alone, threw it into the river.

The whole family went home. In a day the garden became desolate. And, only that starving mongrel of Nilkanta's remained prowling along the river-bank, whining and whining as if its heart would break.

# Saved

Gouri was the beautiful, delicately nurtured child of an old and wealthy family. Her husband, Paresh, had recently by his own efforts improved his straitened circumstances. So long as he was poor, Gouri's parents had kept their daughter at home, unwilling to surrender her to privation; so she was no longer young when at last she went to her husband's house. And, Paresh never felt quite that she belonged to him. He was an advocate in a small western town, and had no close kinsman with him. All his thought was about his wife, so much so that sometimes he would come home before the rising of the Court. At first, Gouri was at a loss to understand why he came back suddenly. Sometimes, too, he would dismiss one of the servants without reason; none of them ever suited him long. Especially if Gouri desired to keep any particular servant because he was useful, that man was sure to be got rid of forthwith. The high-spirited Gouri greatly resented this, but her resentment only made her husband's behaviour still stranger.

At last, when Paresh, unable to contain himself any longer, began in secret to cross-question the maid about her, the whole thing reached his wife's ears. She was a woman of few words; but her pride raged within like a wounded lioness at these insults, and this mad suspicion swept like a destroyer's sword between them. Paresh, as soon as he saw that his wife understood his motive felt no more delicacy about taxing Gouri to her face; and the more his wife treated it with silent contempt, the more did the fire of his jealousy consume him.

Deprived of wedded happiness, the childless Gouri betook herself to the consolations of religion. She sent for Paramananda Swami, the young preacher of the Prayer-House nearby, and, formally acknowledging him as her spiritual preceptor, asked him to expound the *Gita* to her. All the wasted love and affection of her woman's heart was poured out in reverence at the feet of her Guru.

No one had any doubts about the purity of Paramananda's character. All worshiped him. And, because Paresh did not dare to hint at any suspicion against him, his jealousy ate its way into his heart like a hidden cancer.

One day, some trifling circumstance made the poison overflow. Paresh reviled Paramananda to his wife as a hypocrite, and said: 'Can you swear that you are not in love with this crane that plays the ascetic?'

Gouri sprang up like a snake that has been trodden on, and, maddened by his suspicion, said with bitter irony: 'And what if I am?' At this, Paresh forthwith went off to the Court-house, and locked the door on her.

In a white heat of passion at this last outrage, Gouri

got the door open somehow, and left the house.

Paramananda was poring over the scriptures in his lonely room in the silence of noon. All at once, like a flash of lightning out of a cloudless sky, Gouri broke in upon his reading.

'You here?' questioned her Guru in surprise.

'Rescue me, O my lord Guru,' said she, 'from the insults of my home life, and allow me to dedicate myself to the service of your feet.'

With a stern rebuke, Paramananda sent Gouri back home. But I wonder whether he ever again took up the snapped thread of his reading.

Paresh, finding the door open, on his return home, asked: 'Who has been here?'

'No one!' his wife replied. 'I have been to the house of my Guru.'

'Why?' asked Paresh, pale and red by turns.

'Because I wanted to.'

From that day, Paresh had a guard kept over the house, and behaved so absurdly that the tale of his jealousy was told all over the town.

The news of the shameful insults that were daily heaped on his disciple disturbed the religious meditations of Paramananda. He felt he ought to leave the place at once; at the same time he could not make up his mind to forsake the tortured woman. Who can say how the poor ascetic got through those terrible days and nights?

At last, one day, the imprisoned Gouri got a letter.

'My child,' it ran, 'it is true that many holy women have left the world to devote themselves to God. Should it happen that the trials of this world are driving your thoughts away from God, I will with God's help rescue his handmaid for the holy service of his feet. If you desire, you may meet me by the tank in your garden at two o'clock tomorrow afternoon.'

Gouri hid the letter in the loops of her hair. At noon next day when she was undoing her hair before her bath she found that the letter was not there. Could it have fallen on to the bed and got into her husband's hands, she wondered. At first, she felt a kind of fierce pleasure in thinking that it would enrage him; and then she could not bear to think that this letter, worn as a halo of deliverance on her head, might be defiled by the touch of insolent hands.

With swift steps she hurried to her husband's room. He lay groaning on the floor, with eyes rolled back and foaming mouth. She detached the letter from his clenched fist, and sent quickly for a doctor.

The doctor said it was a case of apoplexy. The patient had died before his arrival.

That very day, as it happened, Paresh had an important appointment away from home. Paramananda had found this out, and accordingly had made his appointment with Gouri. To such a depth had he fallen!

When the widowed Gouri caught sight from the window of her Guru stealing like a thief to the side of the pool, she lowered her eyes as at a lightning flash.

And, in that flash she saw clearly what a fall his had been.

The Guru called: 'Gouri.'

'I am coming,' she replied.

When Paresh's friends heard of his death and came to assist in the last rites, they found the dead body of Gouri lying beside that of her husband. She had poisoned herself. All were lost in admiration of the wifely loyalty she had shown in her *sati*, a loyalty, rare indeed, in these degenerate days.

# My Fair Neighbour

My feelings towards the young widow who lived in the next house to mine were feelings of worship, at least, that is what I told to my friends and myself. Even my nearest intimate, Nabin, knew nothing of the real state of my mind. And, I had a sort of pride that I could keep my passion pure by thus concealing it in the inmost recesses of my heart. She was like a dew-drenched *sephali*-blossom, untimely fallen to earth. Too radiant and holy for the flower-decked marriage-bed, she had been dedicated to Heaven.

But passion is like the mountain stream, and refuses to be enclosed in the place of its birth; it must seek an outlet. That is why I tried to give expression to my emotions in poems; but my unwilling pen refused to desecrate the object of my worship.

It happened curiously that just at this time my friend Nabin was afflicted with a madness of verse. It came upon him like an earthquake. It was the poor fellows' first attack, and he was equally unprepared for rhyme and rhythm. Nevertheless, he could not refrain, for he succumbed to the fascination, as a widower to his second wife.

So, Nabin sought help from me. The subject of his poems was the old, old one, which is ever new: his poems were all addressed to the beloved one. I slapped his back in jest, and asked him: 'Well, old chap, who is she?'

Nabin laughed, as he replied: 'That I have not yet discovered!'

I confess that I found considerable comfort in bringing help to my friend. Like a hen brooding on a duck's egg, I lavished all the warmth of my pent-up passion on Nabin's effusions. So vigorously did I revise and improve his crude productions, that the larger part of each poem became my own.

Then, Nabin would say in surprise: 'That is just what I wanted to say, but could not. How on earth do you manage to get hold of all these fine sentiments?'

Poet-like, I would reply: 'They come from my imagination; for, as you know, truth is silent, and it is imagination only which waxes eloquent. Reality represses the flow of feeling like a rock; imagination cuts out a path for itself.'

And, the poor puzzled Nabin would say: 'Y-e-s, I see, of course'; and then after some thought would murmur again: 'Yes, yes, you are right!'

As I have already said, in my own love there was a feeling of reverential delicacy which prevented me from putting it into words. But with Nabin as a screen, there was nothing to hinder the flow of my pen; and a true warmth of feeling gushed out into these vicarious poems.

Nabin in his lucid moments would say: 'But these

are yours! Let me publish them over your name.'

'Nonsense!' I would reply. 'They are yours, my dear fellow; I have only added a touch or two here and there.'

And, Nabin gradually came to believe it.

I will not deny that, with a feeling akin to that of the astronomer gazing into the starry heavens, I did sometimes turn my eyes towards the window of the house next door. It is also true that now and again my furtive glances would be rewarded with a vision. And, the least glimpse of the pure light of that countenance would at once still and clarify all that was turbulent and unworthy in my emotions.

But one day I was startled. Could I believe my eyes? It was a hot summer afternoon. One of the fierce and fitful nor'-westers was threatening. Black clouds were masses in the north-west corner of the sky; and against the strange and fearful light of that background my fair neighbour stood, gazing out into empty space. And, what a world of forlorn longing did I discover in the far-away look of those lustrous black eyes! Was there then, perchance, still some living volcano within the serene radiance of that moon of mine? Alas! that look of limitless yearning, which was winging its way through the clouds like an eager bird, surely sought—not heaven—but the nest of some human heart!

At the sight of the unutterable passion of that look I could hardly contain myself. I was no longer satisfied with correcting crude poems. My whole being longed to express itself in some worthy action. At last, I thought

I would devote myself to making widow-remarriage popular in my country. I was prepared not only to speak and write on the subject, but also to spend money on its cause.

Nabin began to argue with me. 'Permanent widowhood,' said he, 'has in it a sense of immense purity and peace; a calm beauty like that of the silent places of the dead shimmering in the wan light of the eleventh moon.[1] Would not the mere possibility of remarriage destroy its divine beauty?'

Now, this sort of sentimentality always makes me furious. In time of famine, if a well-fed man speaks scornfully of food, and advises a starving man at point of death to glut his hunger on the fragrance of flowers and the song of birds, what are we to think of him? I said with some heat: 'Look here, Nabin, to the artist a ruin may be a beautiful object; but houses are built not only for the contemplations of artists, but that people may live therein; so, they have to be kept in repair in spite of artistic susceptibilities. It is all very well for you to idealise widowhood from your safe distance, but you should remember that within widowhood there is a sensitive human heart, throbbing with pain and desire.'

I had an impression that the conversion of Nabin would be a difficult matter, so perhaps, I was more impassioned than I need have been. I was somewhat surprised to find at the conclusion of my little speech

---

1. The eleventh day of the moon is a day of fasting and penance.

that Nabin after a single thoughtful sigh completely agreed with me. The even more convincing peroration which I felt I might have delivered was not needed!

After about a week Nabin came to me, and said that if I would help him he was prepared to lead the way by marrying a widow himself.

I was overjoyed. I embraced him effusively, and promised him any money that might be required for the purpose. Then, Nabin told me his story.

I learned that Nabin's loved one was not an imaginary being. It appeared that Nabin, too, had for some time adored a widow from a distance, but had not spoken of his feelings to any living soul. Then, the magazines in which Nabin's poems, or rather my poems, used to appear had reached the fair one's hands; and the poems had not been ineffective.

Not that Nabin had deliberately intended, as he was careful to explain, to conduct love-making in that way. In fact, said he, he had no idea that the widow knew how to read. He used to post the magazine, without disclosing the sender's name addressed to the widow's brother. It was only a sort of fancy of his, a concession to his, hopeless passion. It was flinging garlands before a deity; it is not the worshipper's affair whether the god knows or not, whether he accepts or ignores the offering.

And, Nabin particularly wanted me to understand that he had no definite end in view when on diverse pretexts he sought and made the acquaintance of the widow's brother. Any near relation of the loved one needs must have a special interest for the lover.

Then followed a long story about how an illness of the brother at last brought them together. The presence of the poet himself naturally led to much discussion of the poems; nor was the discussion necessarily restricted to the subject out of which it arose.

After his recent defeat in argument at my hands, Nabin had mustered up courage to propose marriage to the widow. At first, he could not gain her consent. But when he had made full use of my eloquent words, supplemented by a tear or two of his own, the fair one capitulated unconditionally. Some money was now wanted by her guardian to make arrangements.

'Take it at once,' said I.

'But,' Nabin went on, 'you know it will be some months before I can appease my father sufficiently for him to continue my allowance. How are we to live in the meantime?' I wrote out the necessary cheque without a word, and then I said: 'Now, tell me who she is. You need not look on me as a possible rival, for I swear I will not write poems to her; and even if I do I will not send them to her brother, but to you!'

'Don't be absurd,' said Nabin; 'I have not kept back her name because I feared your rivalry! The fact is, she was very much perturbed at taking this unusual step, and had asked me not to talk about the matter to my friends. But it no longer matters, now that everything has been satisfactorily settled. She lived at No. 19, the house next to yours.'

If my heart had been an iron boiler it would have burst. 'So, she has no objection to remarriage?' I simply asked.

'Not at the present moment,' replied Nabin with a smile.

'And, was it the poems alone which wrought the magic change?'

'Well, my poems were not so bad, you know,' said Nabin, 'were they?'

I swore mentally.

But at whom was I to swear? At him? At myself. At Providence? All the same, I swore.